MEETING THE BLUES

MEETING THE BLUES

ALAN GOVENAR

Taylor Publishing Company
Dallas, Texas

Copyright 1988 by Alan Govenar

Published by Taylor Publishing Company
          1550 West Mockingbird Lane
          Dallas, Texas 75235

Library of Congress Cataloging-in-Publication Data
Govenar, Alan B., 1952—
   Meeting the blues / Alan Govenar.
     p. cm.
   Includes index.
   ISBN 0-87833-623-0 : $24.95
   1. Blues musicians—United States—Interviews. 2. Afro-Ameri-
cans—United States—Interviews. 3. Blues (Music)—History and
criticism. I. Title.
   ML3521.G68 1988
   784.5′3′00922—dc19   88-13980
                                            CIP

Printed in the United States of America

10 9 8 7 6 5 4 3 2

BOOK DESIGN BY GEORGE TOOMER

CONTENTS

STARTING OUT

With the coming of spring the Texas landscape greens quickly. On Highway 75, in Freestone County south of Dallas, the morning sun lifts the haze from the horizon and the cotton fields of East Texas come into view. Depression-era shotgun houses scattered along the road appear deserted. Then an old black woman crosses the road, two children slam a screen door, and it becomes clear that people still live inside.

Quincy Cox, an eighty-three-year-old black cemetery caretaker in Wortham, Texas, points to the grave of Blind Lemon Jefferson that lies across the highway in the Negro burying ground. He recalls with sudden clarity Blind Lemon's funeral, his body brought back from Chicago, where he had died lost in the snow after a Paramount recording session in 1929. "Anyone over the age of sixty," he says in a hoarse voice, "remembers that day well. Two or three hundred people came, black and white, to watch his coffin lowered in the ground, but not too many people come through these days talking about Blind Lemon."

To find Blind Lemon Jefferson's grave you have to ask someone for directions. The marker, at the far end of the Wortham cemetery on Highway 14, is easy to miss. There are no road signs leading the way. The cemetery itself is on an unmarked dirt road and the gravestone is an unmarked concrete slab, occupying roughly one square foot of ground. Someone has left a wreath of plastic flowers; a plaque placed by the Texas State Historical Association in 1967 identifies the grave.

The history surrounding the short but influential recording career of Blind Lemon Jefferson has been well-established. However, the details of his personal life remain obscured by legend and a lack of solid documentation. There is only one known photograph of Blind Lemon, a publicity still that was reproduced as a graphic in ads for his records.

I had hoped to find out more information in Wortham, but the cemetery caretaker didn't remember much more than the funeral. He did suggest, however, that I talk to Bertha and Mamie Williams, who lived in the country near where Blind Lemon was born and knew him as a young boy. I listened to the directions carefully, and found the house without any problem, but when I knocked on the door there was no answer. I heard a television and knocked again. As I turned to leave, a stoop-shouldered woman came to the door with a cane. I tried to explain that Quincy Cox told me about her, but she had difficulty hearing me.

"What?!" she called out in frustration and I repeated, "Do you remember Blind Lemon Jefferson?"

"Who?" she replied, still confused, but then a smile came to her face. With a deep voice she said, "Why, he's been dead for nearly fifty years," and closed the door in front of me, saying, "Thank you."

As I drove off I realized the absurdity of what I was doing. Looking for new stories about Blind Lemon was in part motivated by my interest in the Swedish blues magazine, *Jefferson*, named for the legendary singer. In *Jefferson* magazine, a caricature of Blind Lemon, modeled after his publicity still, appears on the inside back cover with a blurb that changes each month. In the cartoon, editor Tommy Löfgren puts words in Blind Lemon's mouth, which are at times amusing: "Can I change my shirt now? Is the world ready for me yet?"

The paradox of Blind Lemon Jefferson's local obscurity and the international interest in his career is nowhere more evident than in these cartoons. Despite the neglect he suffered in Texas, Blind Lemon Jefferson is celebrated abroad as a seminal figure in the history of blues music. Texas blues itself continued to suffer the same paradox until recently. It too had been largely neglected in its own back yard and, consequently, had not been well-documented as a regional style.

The earliest reference to what might be considered blues in Texas was made in 1890 by collector Gates Thomas, who transcribed a song titled "Nobody There" with the following single stanza:

That you Nigger man, knockin' at my door?
Here me tell you, Nigger man, nobody there.

Thomas doesn't indicate whether the singing was accompanied by an instrument, but as folklorist David Evans points out, Thomas shows a pentatonic tune containing tonic, minor, third, fourth, fifth, and seventh chords, all of which combine together in a manner similar to a blues tune. Later Thomas published other song texts that he had collected from blacks in South Texas. Some of these included verses that had been noted by other writers in different areas of the South. The song, "Baby, Take a Look at Me," for example, was transcribed both by Thomas and Charles Peabody in Mississippi. And "Alabama Bound" and "C.C. Rider" are variants of blues songs that Jelly Roll Morton sang in New Orleans.

Geographically diffuse sources suggest that blues musicians were itinerent and that blues was part of an oral tradition that developed in different areas of the South. By all accounts, the blues was widespread in the early 1900s. Thousands of blacks during this period were migratory, looking for work and escape from all too prevalent racism. Blues singers were often migrant

Shotgun house
Dallas, circa 1920s
Courtesy Texas/Dallas History and
Archives Division, Dallas Public Library

Cotton pickers weigh in
Archives Division
Texas State Library, Austin

Dallas County, circa 1920s
Courtesy Texas/Dallas History and Archives Division
Dallas Public Library

Baptism in the river
Source: unknown
Courtesy Institute of Texan Cultures

workers, following the crop harvests, lumber camps, and boom towns. Some settled down and labored as sharecroppers, leasing small tracts of land controlled by white landowners. Others continued roving from town to town, working odd jobs in the growing urban centers — Dallas, Houston, Shreveport, and Atlanta — cities whose black immigrant populations were crowded into neighborhoods of shotgun shacks and pasteboard houses.

Blues music expresses the hardships of newly freed black Americans. The freedoms offered by Reconstruction were hard-won — racism, Jim Crow laws, and the Ku Klux Klan were major obstacles to their economic independence and self-determination. Still, leisure, even under the most desolate circumstances, was vitally new and served as a catalyst in the development of the blues. Early blues answered the need for a release from everyday life.

The blues is an intensely personal music; it identifies itself with the feelings of the audience — suffering and hope, economic failure, the break-up of the family, the desire to escape reality through wandering, love, and sex. In this way, blues is somewhat different from African songs, which usually concern the lives and works of gods, the social unit (tribe and community), and nature. With its emphasis on the experience of the individual and his/her trials and successes on earth, blues reflects a Western concept of life. Yet, as a musical form it shows little Western influence. The traditional three-line, twelve-bar, AAB verse form of the blues arises from no apparent Western source, although some blues does incorporate Anglo-American ballad forms that have six-, ten-, or sixteen-bar structures. Early blues drew from the music of

its time: field hollers and shouts, which it most closely resembles melodically; songster ballads, from which it borrows imagery and guitar patterns; spirituals and gospel, which trained the voices and ears of black children. These, with exception of the ballad, were the descendents of African percussive rhythms and call-and-response singing.

Although blues drew from the religious music of both African and Western cultures, it was often considered sinful by the church. Blues singers were stereotyped as "backsliders" in their own communities. In many areas blues was known as the devil's music.

As historian Larry Levine points out, blues blended the sacred and the secular. Like the spirituals and folktales of the nineteenth century, blues was a plea for release, a mix of despair, hope, and humor that had a cathartic effect upon the listener. The blues singer had an expressive role that mirrored the power of the preacher, and because of this power, blues was both embraced and rejected by the black community and the church.

In Texas, blues musician Lil Son Jackson explained to British blues aficionado Paul Oliver that it was, in effect, the spiritual power of the blues that made the music sinful.

"If a man hurt within and he sing a church song then he's askin' God for help...if a man sing the blues it's more or less out of himself...He's not askin' no one for help. And he's really not really clingin' to no one. But he's expressin' how he feel. He's expressin' to someone and that fact makes it a sin, you know... you're tryin' to get your feelin's over to the next person through the blues, and that's what make it a sin."

Given the lack of centralized bureaucracy in the black American church, however, community opposition to the blues varied from place to place. Rarely were blues singers completely ostracized. They lived on the margins of what was acceptable and derived their livelihood from itinerent work at house parties and dances.

With the growth of the recording industry during the 1920s the audience for blues expanded within black communities nation-

Bandwagon
Bonham, Texas, 1910-1915
Photograph by Erwin E. Smith
Courtesy Library of Congress

Lightnin' and his group singing
Darrington State Prison Farm
Sandy Point, Texas, 1934
Photograph by John A. Lomax
Courtesy Library of Congress

T-Bone Walker
Circa 1940s
Courtesy Institute of Jazz Studies

wide. For example, demographic studies indicate that Blind Lemon Jefferson's records sold thousands of copies to blacks in the urban ghettos of the North, but in Dallas Blind Lemon Jefferson was known primarily as a street singer who performed daily with a tin cup at the corner of Elm Street and Central Tracks.

Despite his limited commercial success in Dallas, Blind Lemon Jefferson did have a great influence on the development of Texas blues. (Leadbelly credited him as an inspiration, as did T-Bone Walker.) What distinguishes Blind Lemon Jefferson from the other blues performers of his generation was his singular approach to the guitar, which established the basis of what is today known as the Texas style. Blind Lemon Jefferson strummed or "hammered" the strings with repetitive bass figures and produced a succession of open and fretted notes, using a quick release and picking single-string, arpeggio runs. T-Bone Walker later applied this technique to the electric guitar and, combined with the influences of the jump and swing blues of the regional or "Territory" jazz bands of the 1920s and 1930s, created the modern sound.

In the Territory jazz bands of the Southwest, the guitar was used as a rhythm instrument to underlie the voice and horn sections. The introduction of the electric guitar occurred first in these bands and was pioneered by Eddie Durham of San Marcos, Texas, and Charlie Christian of Fort Worth. By using electric amplification jazz guitarists were able to increase the resonance and volume of their sound. Charlie Christian is credited with teaching T-Bone Walker about the electric guitar and its potential as a solo instrument.

In the rhythm and blues of T-Bone Walker the electric guitar assumed a role that superseded the saxophone, which had until then been the prominent solo instrument in jazz. The interplay between the saxophone and the guitar remained important in rhythm and blues, but the relationship between the instruments was transformed. The rhythm and blues band sound became tighter and depended more on the interplay of the electric guitar with the horn section, piano, and drums.

In Texas, blues has developed a unique character that results not only from the introduction of the electric guitar, but also from the cross-pollination of musical styles — itself a result of the migratory patterns of blacks — as well as the impact of the recording industry and mass media commercialization. Not only is the black population of Texas less concentrated than that of other states in the South, but blues music in Texas also evolved in proximity to other important musical traditions: the rural Anglo, the Cajun and Creole, the Hispanic, and the Eastern and Central European.

The white crossover to blues in Texas began in the nineteenth century when black fiddlers and guitar songsters played at white country dances. Eddie Durham recalled in interviews that his father was a fiddler who played jigs and reels as well as blues. Mance Lipscomb's and Gatemouth Brown's fathers were songsters who played fiddle and guitar.

White musicians were exposed to blues at country dances and minstrel shows, and among black workers in the fields, road gangs, turpentine camps, and railroad yards. Country singer Bill Neely says that he first heard blues when he picked cotton in Collin County north of Dallas in the 1920s, but he learned to play blues by listening to Jimmie Rodgers.

"Jimmie Rodgers was a bluesman," Bill Neely maintains. "A lot of those songs Jimmie Rodgers didn't write. He got them from the blacks he heard when he was growing up in Mississippi and when he worked as a brakeman on the railroad."

Jimmie Rodgers
Circa 1929

Prison road gang
Texas, 1934
Photograph by Alan Lomax
Courtesy Library of Congress

Lionel Hampton and his band
Longhorn Ranch House
Dallas, March 1953
Photograph by R.C. Hickman
Courtesy Barker Texas History Center

The influence of blues and jazz is also apparent in the early western swing bands of Bob Wills and Milton Brown, where the horn sections of the Territory jazz bands were imitated and developed through different instrumentation. In addition, blues and jazz influenced Hispanic as well as Anglo-European popular music.

The emphasis in this book is upon living performers and, consequently, the text primarily concerns itself with rhythm and blues. The term "rhythm and blues" was introduced in 1949 by *Billboard* magazine as a substitute for the word "race" in a chart that had been headed until then "Top 15 Best Selling Race Records." The phrase "race records" had been in use since 1920 when the success of an Okeh record, "Crazy Blues" by Mamie Smith, motivated other record labels to record black female vocalists, many of whom would later be regarded as the classic blues singers. In time the term "race" became a catchall for any type of black recording — jazz, folk, pop, big band. After World War II the connotations of "race" seemed offensive and "rhythm and blues" came into use.

Rhythm and blues is different musically from the blues that had preceded it. As musicologist Arnold Shaw points out, "If the blues was trouble music and urban blues adjustment song, then rhythm and blues was good-time dance music. If the blues was loneliness and self-expression song, and urban blues nostalgia and growing music, then rhythm and blues was group and joy music. If the country bluesman wailed and the urban bluesman sang, the rhythm and bluesman shouted."

Rhythm and blues was a response to a new environment, to the realities of inner-city ghettos and urban migration. The most important source of rhythm and blues was gospel music, which gave it a vital repertoire, form, and style. In rhythm and blues the twelve-bar patterning of country blues is replaced with the eight-bar form of gospel and pop songs. It was rhythm and blues that gave rise to what disc jockey Alan Freed called rock 'n' roll, and rock 'n' roll spelled the demise of rhythm and blues until the mid-1960s, when the Rolling Stones, the Beatles, and other English groups appeared in America and acknowledged their musical mentors. British rock 'n' roll musicians refocused popular attention to the great black rhythm and bluesmen by recording their songs and by promoting their performances.

In the 1970s rhythm and blues was again eclipsed by popular music in America, but this time foreign interest grew. With the rise of European record labels and the international festival circuit, black Americans gained a new and vital forum for preserving and developing their music. The audience abroad has saved rhythm and blues from extinction and continues today to provide an arena where older musicians are revered and younger musicians, both black and white, are able to launch their careers. Stevie Ray Vaughan, for example, began to attract international attention after a 1982 performance at the Montreux International Jazz Festival in Switzerland. Among European audiences, rhythm and blues, like jazz, is appreciated intellectually as well as musically.

In the 1980s there has been a resurgence of enthusiasm for blues in America. The Chicago Blues Festival, now in its fifth year, draws as many as 500,000 people over the course of three days. Blues festivals are held throughout the United States and blues performers are recognized through Grammy and W.C. Handy awards. Within this environment, Texas blues musicians have achieved new prominence and have, consequently, become more introspective with regard to their respective roles in the the development of Texas blues.

My intent has been to take the accounts of these musicians and with the help of a wide selection of documentary photographs, examine the development and diversity of Texas blues. I interviewed more than a hundred people between 1981 and 1987, and traveled throughout Texas, to Chicago, New Orleans, Oakland, San Francisco, New York, London, Copenhagen, Helsinki, Stockholm, The Hague, Amsterdam, Paris, Nice, and Montreux. I went to neighborhood clubs, international festivals and concerts, to libraries and to the streets themselves in search of insights into Texas blues.

During each interview session the questions were essentially the same. I asked each musician to talk about his or her early years, training, influences, key recordings, anecdotes, instruments and instrumentation, performance style, audience response, and the meaning of the blues on a personal level and in its context within American culture. In assembling this book, I transcribed my interviews and also drew on the work of researchers and collectors, such as Glen Myers, Tary Owens, Chuck Nevitt, Tim Schuller, Tom Mazzolini, Dick Shurman, Ray

Topping, Bruce Bastin, Marcel Vos, and Tommy Lofgren.

The result lies between history and personal chronicle. The sense of time within the interviews is more associative than linear and the point of view varies with the different perspectives of the speakers. Each of the musicians has a separate story, and there are many instances where contradictory accounts are told by and about the same musicians.

In presenting a variety of perspectives the lack of a single style that distinguishes Texas blues from that found elsewhere in the South becomes apparent. However, even if the attempt does more to underscore rather than clarify its complexity as a regional, or more accurately multi-regional, music, the definitive history of Texas blues can only be established through the consideration of different oral accounts, discography, and photographic documentation.

The photography in this book is taken from a variety of sources, including historical collections and the work of contemporary photographers. My own work over the last decade, which has focused on black musicians and community life in Austin, San Antonio, Houston, and Dallas, comprises the majority of these photographs. To supplement my work I have selected from archival photographs and the portfolios of current photographers, including Benny Joseph (Houston), Calvin Littlejohn (Fort Worth), R.C. Hickman (Dallas), Susan Antone (Austin), Tracy Hart (Houston), Valerie Wilmer (London), Michael Smith (New Orleans), Patricia Monaco (San Francisco), Hans Ekestang and Erik Lindahl (Stockholm). The interplay between oral accounts and photography creates a series of portraits wherein the musicians emerge as individuals and performers. These portraits articulate the emotive and visual power of the blues experience.

DALLAS
& FORT WORTH

n the 1890s the boll weevil ravaged the East Texas cotton fields, displacing thousands of field hands and sharecroppers, forcing them to migrate to the cities. By the turn of the century Dallas and Fort Worth had rapidly expanding black populations, which increased from 9,000 in 1899 to 50,000 in 1930.

Deep Ellum was the area of Elm Street in Dallas, north and east of downtown, where immigrants to the city flocked. At Elm Street and Central Avenue was a railroad stop, a place where day laborers were picked up and dropped off, taken to the cotton fields of Collin County or to other jobs. Central Avenue connected Elm Street with Freedmen's Town, the black neighborhood that grew up after the Civil War and branched off from the corner of Thomas and Hall streets.

Deep Ellum was a mix of cultures; small businesses — pawnshops, tailors, secondhand clothing stores, shoeshine stands, cafes, juke joints, and sporting houses — were clustered together. J.H. Owens summed up the ambiance in a July 1937 article in the black weekly *Gazette*.

"Down on Deep Ellum in Dallas, where Central Avenue empties into Elm Street is where Ethiopia stretches forth her hands. It is the one spot in the city that needs no daylight savings time because there is no bedtime, and working hours have no limits. The only place recorded on earth where business, religion, hoodooism and gambling and stealing go on without friction...last Saturday a prophet held the best audience in this 'Madison Square Garden' in announcing that Jesus Christ would come to Dallas in person in 1939. At the same time a pickpocket was lifting a week's wages from another guy's pocket, who stood open-mouthed to hear the prophesy."

By all accounts Deep Ellum was a rough place, though in the 1920s and 1930s the black music performed there was legendary. Living in the black communities of Dallas and playing the steamy joints of Deep Ellum were some of the greatest musicians of the day.

Probably the most well known and widely imitated of the Deep Ellum blues singers was Blind Lemon Jefferson, who followed Central Tracks to Elm Street with a walking stick and a guitar slung over his shoulder. The area of Dallas known as Central Tracks was a stretch of railroad near the Texas and Pacific depot and crossed by the H&TC line. Lying east of the downtown business district and north of Deep Ellum, Central Tracks was the heart of the black community. Located in the area were Ella B. Moore's Park Theater with vaudeville and minstrel shows, the Tip

Top (on the second floor of the Hart Furniture warehouse), Hattie Burleson's dance hall, the Green Parrot, and the Pythian Temple, designed by black architect William Sidney Pittman.

In 1912 Huddie Ledbetter, better known as Leadbelly, met Blind Lemon Jefferson in Deep Ellum and together they played on the streets and in the nightspots, such as the Big Four, where Leadbelly remembered, "The women would come running, Lawd have mercy! They'd hug and kiss us so much we could hardly play."

In the mid-1920s, on the basis of reports sent by boogie-woogie piano player Sam Price to his employer, R.T. Ashford, who owned a local record store, a Paramount record company executive found Blind Lemon Jefferson on a Deep Ellum sidewalk and invited him to Chicago to make "race" records. Blind Lemon's first recording, "Black Snake Moan," was a huge success and he returned to Chicago often. Between 1926 and his untimely death in 1929, Blind Lemon was the biggest selling black blues singer in the United States.

In addition to Blind Lemon Jefferson and Leadbelly, there were other important blues guitar stylists in Deep Ellum, such as Lonnie Johnson, Little Hat Jones, Texas Alexander, and Funny Papa Smith, as well as jazz guitarists Eddie Durham and Charlie Christian and the horn players Hot Lips Page, Buster Smith, Budd and Keg Johnson, Herschel Evans, Buddy Tate, and countless others. There were classic blues singers, such as Jewell Nelson, Bobby Cadillac, Emma Wright, Lillian Glinn, and Bessie Tucker and numerous barrelhouse piano players, including Jesse Crump, Alex Moore, Sam Price, and Doug Finnell. The major blues and jazz performers of the day, from Bessie Smith and Ma Rainey to Alphonso Trent and Benny Moten, always stopped in Dallas on the black T.O.B.A. (Theater Owners Booking Association) tours, and played in the Central Tracks area.

In the 1920s Dallas became a recording center. Ironically, Blind Lemon Jefferson never recorded there; he always went to Paramount's studios in Chicago. However, other race labels, still catering to blacks, held regular sessions in Dallas. Okeh, Vocalion, Brunswick, Columbia, and RCA Victor sent scouts and engineers to record local artists once or twice a year. Engineers came into the city, set up their equipment in a hotel room, put the word out, and itinerant musicians found their way to Dallas, among them the legendary Delta bluesman Robert Johnson, who recorded there in 1937.

With the Great Depression of the 1930s, race recording declined, but the Dallas and Fort Worth area remained a center of

Elm Street theaters at night
Dallas, 1925
Courtesy Texas/Dallas History and Archives Division
Dallas Public Library

Richmond, Texas
Circa 1960s
Photograph by Chris Strachwitz
Courtesy Arhoolie Records

Deep Ellum
Circa late 1940s
Courtesy Dallas/Texas History and Archives Division
Dallas Public Library

Deep Ellum
Dallas, 1922
Courtesy Texas/Dallas History and Archives Division
Dallas Public Library

music activity: blues, jazz, country, and western swing. One of the most well-known black groups of this period was Coley Jones and the Dallas String Band, which had varying personnel configurations that sometimes included one or two violins, two guitars, mandolin, string bass, clarinet, and trumpet. The Dallas String Band performed at dances, picnics, and shows for white and black audiences, and often serenaded on the streets or outside Ella B. Moore's Park Theater.

The bass player for Coley Jones was Marco Washington, who had himself run a string band that included his stepson, Aaron "T-Bone" Walker, as a child guitarist. Walker was born in Linden, Texas, in 1910. He moved with his mother to Dallas at age two and lived there and in Fort Worth until 1933, when he moved to California. His first recordings were made in Dallas in 1929 for the Columbia label under the name Oak Cliff T-Bone, but he did not achieve widespread success until after he settled in California.

In the 1940s the railroad tracks on Central Avenue in Dallas were torn up to make room for Central Expressway, which was built in the 1950s, and for R.L. Thornton Freeway in the 1960s. These changes choked Deep Ellum off from downtown and what street life was left died. Deep Ellum became a warehouse district with industrial suppliers and repair shops mixed in.

Nonetheless, blues and jazz continued to flourish in the Dallas black communities. The Rose Ballroom, opened by T.H. Smith in March 1942 and re-opened as the Rose Room in April 1943, became a showplace for the best of the local and nationally known blues artists. T-Bone Walker, on his frequent returns to Dallas, performed at the Rose Room, as did Big Joe Turner, Pee Wee Crayton, Lowell Fulson, King Kolax, Red Calhoun, Buster Smith, Eddie Vinson, and Jimmy Nelson. The Rose Room was renamed the Empire Room in 1951 and continued to feature the most popular rhythm and blues of the day: ZuZu Bollin, Lil Son Jackson, Clarence "Nappy Chin" Evans, Mercy Baby, Frankie Lee Sims, and Smokey Hogg. Both Sims and Hogg performed often in Dallas and were recorded at Sellers studio on Commerce Street for the Blue Bonnet label in the late 1940s. (Hogg had actually recorded his first session in Dallas for Decca in 1937.) In "Goin' Back Home" Hogg sings about Deep Ellum and refers to Frankie Lee Sims' "Lucy Mae Blues," which Sims himself had cut for Blue Bonnet.

From the late 1940s to the early 1960s some of the most important blues recordings in North Texas were made at Sellers studio in Dallas and at Big Jim Beck's studio in Fort Worth. These studios were used by a variety of small independent labels, including Blue Bonnet, Star Talent, and Atco, and featured performers such as Rattlesnake Cooper, Willie Lane, Sonny Boy Davis, ZuZu Bollin,

Segregated bus terminal
Dallas, February 1953
Photograph by R.C. Hickman
Courtesy Barker Texas History Center

Royal Earl and the Swingin' Kools, Ray Sharpe and the Blue Whalers, Finney-Mo, and Louis Howard and the Red Hearts.

During this time white musicians developed a growing interest in blues. According to singer and blues aficionado Delbert McClinton, the musical environment in the Dallas–Fort Worth area was unique. Not only did it have a long history of western swing, but it was possible to hear Ray Price, Ornette Coleman, Cornell Dupree, Jimmy Reed, T-Bone Walker, Roger Miller, Bob Wills, and Doc Severinsen, all "comfortably co-existing within the same musical setting." There were weekly shows at the White Sands Supper Club and the Skyliner Ballroom in Fort Worth, and at the Empire Room (renamed the Ascot in the 1960s) and the Longhorn Ranch in Dallas. In addition, black bands often played at white fraternity parties and dances. This diversity, combined with the influences of rock 'n' roll, western swing, rockabilly, and soul, which were heard live and on the radio, yielded a cultural context in which the crossing of musical styles occurred.

By the late 1960s and early 1970s numerous white musicians were experimenting with blues, including Steve Miller, Boz Scaggs, Jimmie Vaughan, Denny Freeman, and Stevie Ray Vaughan. Moreover, there was a wide array of black groups. Freddie King and Al Braggs were active, as were Cal Valentine, Big Bo and His Twisting Arrows, Z.Z. Hill, R.L. Griffin, and Johnny Taylor. Many of these musicians were eventually forced to leave the Dallas–Fort Worth area to launch their careers. With the growing popularity of disco and rock, there were fewer opportunities for live performances, radio air play, and recording.

The 1980s resurgent interest in the blues has benefited local musicians. Anson Funderburgh and the Rockets in Dallas and the Juke Jumpers in Fort Worth are steadily gaining a regional and national reputation. In the black community, R.L. Griffin operates an after-hours club, Blues Alley, near Fair Park in Dallas and has featured performers such as Ernie Johnson, Al Braggs, Little Joe Blue, James Braggs, and Charlie Roberson. In Fort Worth the Bluebird, operated by Robert Ealey, showcases some of the best of the local rhythm and blues bands.

The enthusiasm for blues grows in post-boom Dallas and Fort Worth, and older musicians are coming out of retirement. In 1987 Alex Moore became the first blues performer from Texas to win a National Heritage Fellowship from the National Endowment for the Arts. At eighty-eight, he is still looking for work, performing his rollicking barrelhouse piano as often as he can. Band leader Buster Smith, drummer Herbie Cowens, saxophone stylists Al Dupree, Aldophus Sneed, and Duke Huddleston, and guitarists ZuZu Bollin and U.P. Wilson have all begun performing again. The Harambee Festival (since the 1970s), and the Dallas Folk Festival (started in 1981), along with the newly formed Dallas Blues Society are helping to insure a context in which the musical history of Dallas–Fort Worth can be preserved and supported.

Melba Theater protest
Dallas, March 1955
Photograph by R.C. Hickman
Courtesy Barker Texas History Center

14

ON BLIND LEMON JEFFERSON
(1897-1929)

" In Deep Ellum there was an alley called "death row" where someone would get killed every Saturday. And there was a stool pigeon for the police and his name was "Yellow Britches." If someone came into town that he didn't know he'd put some chalk on the back of [the stranger's] pants so that the police could identify him and arrest him. The area near Deep Ellum where there were black folks was a community that engulfed maybe five or six blocks on Central Avenue, and extended for about two blocks on Elm Street. Deep Ellum was the crossing point, where they'd come and take you to pick cotton. Blind Lemon Jefferson stood on that corner. Black folks would gather around him. And there was no comingling with

Blind Lemon Jefferson
Circa 1927

the white folks that went about their business on Elm Street. There were Jewish shopkeepers, secondhand clothing stores, pawnshops on the other side of the same block. The railroad tracks ran up Central Avenue and the street was lined with dance halls, Fat Jack's Theater, the Tip Top Club, shoeshine parlors, and beer joints.

Blind Lemon Jefferson would start out from South Dallas about eleven o'clock in the morning and follow the railroad tracks to Deep Ellum, and he'd get to the corner where Central Tracks crossed Elm about one or two in the afternoon and he'd play guitar and sing until about ten o'clock at night. Then he'd start back home. He was a little chunky fellow who wasn't only a singer. He was a bootlegger and when he'd get back home he had such a sensitive ear. He didn't want his wife to drink. Well, when he'd go away she'd take two or three drinks out of the bottle and she'd think he wouldn't know it. But he'd take the bottle when he came home and say, "Hey, how you doin' baby? How'd we do today?"

"Nobody bought no whiskey."

Well, he'd take the bottle and shake it, and he could hear that there were two or three drinks missing. And what he'd do, he'd beat the hell out of her for that. **"**

Sam Price
Harlem, 1986

" I was fourteen or fifteen when I heard those blues records, heard them on my cousin's record player. Ben William had one. They played them and I'd hear them. Blind Lemon Jefferson, Bessie Smith. She was a woman's blues singer. She sang "Back water risin', Comin' in my windows and doors, And my house fell down, I can't live there no more."

I haven't stopped listening to the blues. I still hear them on these programs on television. Well, some of those blues tell things real true.

My grandmother and mother told me, "Don't sing the blues," and I never sang any around. Tradition, I guess, old people thought it was wrong to sing songs that wasn't allowed in the church. And they call them blues, and you don't call the church songs blues. Old people in the old days thought the blues was just terrible, but some truth was in those songs. They said, "That's the devil's work. Just leave it alone. That's the devil's work. I don't want to hear you sing those songs." And I couldn't sing them. I grew out where I just didn't. I believed it was the devil's work.

I loved to hear Blind Lemon Jefferson. One song he sang I remember.

"I was standin' on the courthouse square
One day, one dime was all I have.
Everybody gets in hard luck some time.
Say I'm broke and ain't got a dime,
But everybody gets in hard luck some time.
Do you want your friend to be bad like Jesse James?
Take two six-shooters and rob some passenger train?
Oh, one dime was all I had.
One dime was all I had.
The woman I love is five feet from the ground.
She's a tailor made woman.
She ain't no hand-me-down.
One dime was all I had.

Ain't but one thing that give a woman the blues—
When she don't have no bottom on her last pair of shoes.

The blues ain't nothing but a good man feeling bad.
Blues is the worst thing that a good man ever had. **"**

Osceola Mays
Dallas, 1987

Race ads, Blind Lemon Jefferson
Rambling Thomas
Henry Thomas
Texas Alexander

Huddie Ledbetter
at Rutgers University
Newark, 1944
Courtesy Institute of Jazz Studies

Huddie Ledbetter (Leadbelly)
and his wife Martha Promise
New York, 1935
*Photograph by Alan Lomax
Courtesy Library of Congress*

LEADBELLY

By the time Huddie Ledbetter (1889-1949), also known as Leadbelly, reached Dallas in the early 1900s, he had already earned a reputation as a hard-working farm hand and cotton picker, a ladies' man, a gambler and a singer playing accordion, guitar, mandolin, harmonica, and piano.

Leadbelly had come to Dallas from Shreveport, where he had rollicked in the black night life of Fannin Street. By then he had developed a highly rhythmical guitar style, influenced by the bass figures of barrelhouse blues piano. In Dallas, Leadbelly found his way to Deep Ellum, much like Fannin Street in Shreveport. It was the place where hobos invariably landed, and where black, Hispanic, and white cotton pickers were picked up for transport to the cotton fields of Collin County.

On the crowded sidewalks of Deep Ellum and Central Avenue in 1912 Leadbelly met Blind Lemon Jefferson. They played together on the street and at house parties, and Jefferson taught Leadbelly to play new single-string arpeggio runs on the guitar, although in his later recordings he seemed to prefer the heavy strumming he learned from the bass figures of barrelhouse pianists and from the Mexicans who sold him a twelve-string guitar. In 1917 Leadbelly and Blind Lemon Jefferson parted ways; Leadbelly killed a man over a woman, and was sentenced to thirty years at Huntsville Prison Farm. There Leadbelly worked six years of hard labor and then tried to escape. Leadbelly's ability to improvise songs eventually won him his release in 1925 when he was officially pardoned by Gov. Pat Neff. Neff issued the pardon because of a song Leadbelly composed at a chance meeting while the Governor was inspecting the prison.

Nineteen hundred and twenty-three
The judge took my liberty away from me,
Left my wife wringin' her hands and cryin'
Lawd have mercy on the man of mine.
I am your servant to compose this song,
Please Governor Neff, lemme go back home.
I know my wife will jump and shout,
Train rolls up, I come stepping out.
Please Honorable Governor, be good and kind.
If I don't get a pardon will you cut my time?
Had you, Governor Neff, like you got me
Wake up in the morning and I'd set you free.

After his release from Huntsville, Leadbelly went back to the Caddo Lake area of Louisiana, where he resumed his life as a bluesman. In 1930 he was arrested again, convicted of assault, and sentenced to ten years in the Louisiana State Prison in Angola. In 1934, he met John Lomax. Lomax was doing field work at the prison collecting work songs, shouts, ballads, spirituals, and blues. Among the songs Lomax collected was another plea for a pardon, which he delivered personally to Louisiana Gov. O.K. Allen, who, in turn, set Leadbelly free that year.

For a brief period after his release from Angola Prison, Leadbelly worked as Lomax's chauffeur, and Lomax became Leadbelly's manager. Lomax arranged an extensive tour of white colleges and concert halls, and together Lomax and Leadbelly traveled in the Northeast. While performing on a concert tour, Leadbelly met and later married Martha Promise and decided not to return to Texas or Louisiana. Instead, Leadbelly and Martha settled in New York City, where Leadbelly sang at political rallies and at folk music revivals and concerts. He appeared on programs with Josh White, Sonny Terry, Brownie McGhee, as well as with Woody Guthrie, Burl Ives, and the Almanac Singers.

Herbert Cowens
Buck and Bubbles Show
New York, circa 1930s
Courtesy Herbert Cowens

Herbert Cowens
Dallas, 1926
Courtesy Herbert Cowens

HERBERT COWENS

Herbert Cowens
Rehearsing with Buster Smith
The Heat Waves of Swing
Dallas Folk Festival, 1986
Photograph by Alan Govenar

Herbert Cowens (b. 1905, Dallas) was from a musical family. Two brothers played drums, one sister was a dancer, and the other sister was a singer. Cowens started as a shoeshine boy, and with the money he earned street dancing, he bought his first set of drums. Until 1926, Cowens played with the Satisfied Five and other local jazz and vaudeville show bands. In 1927 he left Dallas with Cleo Mitchell's Shake Your Feet Company. From 1927 to 1980 Cowens lived in New York and worked in vaudeville, Broadway shows, musicals, and for several band leaders, including Eubie Blake, Fats Waller, Stuff Smith, and Fletcher Henderson. In addition, Cowens led his own band, The Kat and His Kittens, and made annual overseas U.S.O. tours to the Far East, Japan, Europe, and the Mediterranean. He retired from touring in 1980 and moved to Dallas with his wife, Rubye.

Mance Lipscomb
Navasota, 1960
Photograph by Chris Strachwitz
Courtesy Arhoolie Records

MANCE LIPSCOMB
(1895–1976)

In the mid-1930s Bill Neely (b. 1916) hitchhiked to the Deep Ellum area of Dallas from his home in McKinney to perform at Ma's Place, a tavern that was frequented by gangsters and gamblers like Raymond Hamilton, Baby Face Nelson, and Bonnie and Clyde.

Neely says Deep Ellum was "the roughest place in town. It was skid row...It was were the hobos landed; it was where the drunkards and winos and people tryin' to roll and rob one another hung out. There was all kinds of people: cowboys, coloreds, Mexicans, and down and out farmers." What attracted Neely to Deep Ellum was the legendary music. Neely had met Jimmie Rogers outside a tent show in Dallas when he was fourteen and was profoundly influenced by the way Rogers combined country songs with guitar blues.

Neely has written dozens of songs about traveling ("Lonesome Freight Train" and "Hills of Tennessee"), about heartbreak ("Don't Waste Your Tears on Me", and "Crying the Blues Over You") and about his Texas homeland ("Big Yellow Moon Over Texas" and "I Dreamed Last Night of Texas"). In addition, he had written instrumentals that show the influence of ragtime and piano blues. Overall, Neely's songs bring together the diverse regional traditions in Texas. In his guitar playing he maintains a steady alternating bass with a thumb pick to counterpoint his picking of the melody, and he integrates the chord strumming style of cowboy singers with the single-string runs of blues that he heard as a child. He learned the blues technique from Mance Lipscomb in Austin in the early 1970s.

Mance Lipscomb (1895-1976) was part of a songster tradition that began in the nineteenth century and involved a variety of styles common to both blacks and whites in the South. Lipscomb's repertoire included country blues as well as ballads, rags, dance pieces (breakdowns, waltzes, two-steps, reels) and popular sacred and secular songs.

As a young boy Mance Lipscomb played guitar accompaniment for his father, Charles, who was a fiddler at country dances in Navasota and elsewhere in Grimes County, Texas. One night when Mance was eleven his father disappeared and never returned home.

At sixteen Mance Lipscomb began working as a sharecropper on a twenty-acre plot of Brazos bottom land, which he farmed for the next forty-two years to support his family. In 1954 he was put in charge of a 200-acre farm, but he refused to work for a salary instead of a crop, and he quit. He took a job as a truck driver and later worked as a lawn mowing contractor until August 1960 when he was discovered by researchers Mack McCormick and Chris Strachwitz. They heard about Lipscomb from a local man named

Peg Leg. On the basis of their first meeting, Strachwitz decided to start his own label and record Lipscomb. He named his label Arhoolie, which means field song or call. Strachwitz released the first Mance Lipscomb album later that year and with its success he launched an extensive series of Texas blues recordings, featuring new material and reissue albums of Lightnin' Hopkins, Juke Boy Bonner, Black Ace, Son Jackson, Alex Moore, Bill Neely, Mercy Dee, Big Mama Thornton, and others.

66 We knew we were on the route to Dallas, but we didn't let other people know where we was going. It's anywhere we thought; first thing, we'd put them off, so they wouldn't follow us, you know. And that was our alibi.

When we got to Dallas, we hung around where we could hear Blind Lemon sing and play. Not only me and Son, there were hundreds of people up and down that [Central] Track. They went for that, country people, a lot of town people. So, that's where I got acquainted with him, 1917.

He hung out, 'round the track. Deep Ellum, the street called Deep Elm. You cross Deep Ellum and turn, go down the track. Central Track run right through Ellum.

They moved Blind Lemon out of town, forbid him right in town, but the law would let him stay out of town. He was a big, loud songster, and he'd have all that gang of people gathering around him so fast and wouldn't cluster in town. A certain distance away and they would allow him to play and sing. That way he wouldn't bother anybody. Some of them went for it, some of them didn't like it.

(Above): Bill Neely; Austin, 1984; *Photograph by Alan Govenar*

Mance Lipscomb
Austin, 1974
Photograph by Alan Pogue

They gave him privilege to play in a certain district in Dallas, and they call that "on the track." Right beside the place where he stood 'round there under a big old shade tree, call it a standpoint, right off the railroad track. And people started coming in there, from nine thirty until six o'clock that evening, then he would go home because it was getting dark and somebody carried him home.

It made his living. I don't know how much money he made, but he made his living that way. He was a big stout fella, husky fella, loud voice. And he played dance songs and never did much church song. I ain't never known him to play a church song. He's a blues man.

He had a tin cup, wired on the neck of his guitar. And when you pass to give him something, why he'd thank you. But he would never take no pennies. You could drop a penny in there and he'd know the sound. He'd take and throw it away.

Well, I like Blind Lemon Jefferson's playing and his kind of blues. He had double notes in his music.

"Oh, oh, I don't got no mama now."
Deedle deedle deedle dee du du Break time.
"Oh, oh, I don't like no mama now."
Deedle deedle deedle dee dee du

Well, that's not no time there. That's just like you in the field, ain't got no instrument at all. You just in the field workin', and if you ain't got no time at all, you just got your mind made up, you singin' to pass time. Just like you think if you sing, the sun go down quicker or the days go shorter. But when you get out to sing something in a mood with time, one, two, three, that's what music is made out of.

I never did go and interview with him. He was a big, husky fella. I was a country guy, you know. And I stood my ground with him, but I could hear all he was doing, and see what he's doing. I didn't want to approach him, that I was paying attention to him just because I was going to try learn how to play. I know he wouldn't have liked it. That's the reason I was staying my distance from him. Now, he didn't care

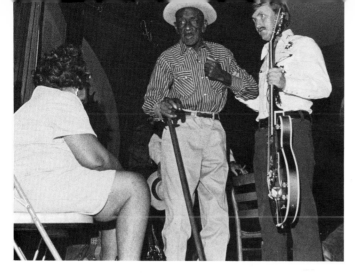

Mance Lipscomb with his wife and Larry Kirbo
Austin, 1974
Photograph by Alan Pogue

about how many people come near him who wasn't playing guitar, but somebody who was standing around there listening and trying to figure out what he's doing and how to play maybe like him or something, you know that didn't go so well with him. A lot of people would ask him, "How do you play so-and-so?" But I would never ask him nothin'. I just stayed quiet and listened to him. And when I got ready to leave I didn't say, "Hello" or "Goodbye."

We'd see him when we come to Dallas. We got through our crops, somewhere, long about September or August. And October and November, up until the next year, we'd have cotton to pick in Dallas. And we wouldn't be up there the whole season, just went out there for emergency, pick up a little Christmas money, maybe come a flood or drought or something at home. We get fifteen or twenty-five, thirty dollars, well, we rich, you know. Then we come back home to Navasota.

There [in Navasota] what you call a club now, we called them Saturday night dances, dance all night, all night long. I had three crews to interpretate with. The first crew was at eight o'clock. I played a hour for them. They had everything in full bloom. 'Long about twelve o'clock, here another crew come in there. Fresh crew! I fan them out, play all night 'til four o'clock in the morning, sometimes 'til eleven o'clock on Sunday, setting right in one chair.

Now when I get to playin' I go out of the bounds of reason because when I start, I don't like to stop. As long as it look like they payin' attention to me, I can play all night for them.

See, I play straight time. Straight, straight strictly time. I will play that there split time, well, I ain't gettin' nowhere because that's the way I learnt. Once you learnt, son, and been at it as long as me, you can't veer from it. You feel it, and you how you learnt, and then when you start, gonna start right. Gonna start, with a certain speed and different chords.

See, I know every chord that I wanta make and puttin' in music. I play, oh, about three-fifty say, and when I play those three-fifty songs, listen to me, it's a lot of different sounds coming out of that guitar. But I

never break my time, what you call rhythm. Three or four things you can call it. Rhythm, time, and the beat. All of it's the same thing.

Say, for instance, you say, "Well I can beat you from here to the highway." Well, you got a certain — you ain't got no gait. You got a certain limit of time. You could beat me here to the highway. You gonna run fast and try to beat me there. If you run slow, you can't beat me there. But that's what you call time, and then break your time, well you can keep up and do something with that time. But if you start off slow and then run fast, well that's not no time. You done broke time.

Well, [if] you go out there, say, "I'm goin' try to run from here to the road in ten minutes," you know it [got] a ten minute limit. So, you say I'm gonna run here, out to the road in three minutes, you speedin' up. You got to speed up because you done took some of them minutes away from there. See, that's what you call time.

You done heard me play over in Austin. Whenever I start a song, I keep it a real beat where I can tap my foot and you can pat your foot. Now you find music, it's not got no rhythm, that's time; ain't got no beat, that's time, and all things like that. If it ain't got the right rhythm or right time and right beat, it's some bad music coming up there.

You can get in the mood pattin' your foot or shakin' yourself or just settin' down you can get in the motion. You're shakin' yourself because you got that time and motion. But that's the same thing, that motion, that you just learned yourself thisaway. You're motionin'. And then if you ain't motionin', you can take your foot and tap there. That's what you call rhythm, and time, all right, comin' out of your foot. Then in the motion of your body. That's rhythm and time. It comes out that way.

It matches up a whole lot of ways, but it ain't but one thing. You got straight time, beat, rhythm and motion, all four of them things is the same thing, and gait right in there alongside of them. But once you go too fast, then jump over and go too slow, you broke down your time. [There] is no regular time there. Good music is time. It's not no good music if it's untimely.

You change music when you playing different songs. You can play a hundred songs in E sound, but they the same song. Lightnin' Hopkins' a E man, E and little A, only type he try to play. He can play E chord good as he want to. And everything he going to play that have any kind of sense to it, he going to play in E. And maybe some time in A.

That rascal can sing, though. He can play them, songs that me mix them up so bad you'll think he singing five thousand songs. But you know how many songs he singin'? Don't y'all tell him because I might see him and he'd kill me. He's singin' two songs out of five thousand. But see here, I'll show what key he's in. If you get him out of this key here, he ain't no good at all. That's E.

Say, "Play a C chord," that's a change in a song. He don't know how to mix his fingers up there. "Play a D chord." That's changin' song. You just as good as him in that. Anybody can make a D chord as good as him. But he going to run you crazy with E stuff, and A.

I can play five hundred songs in E, but I ain't playing nothing but one song. But if I change and put the song from E to C, G, F, B, sharps and sevenths, I'm playing different songs. You get the song by sounds of the ear, you can listen to them.

I first met Lightnin' in 1938, I believe. In Galveston. My sister and brother, who is a twin to my baby sister, they live in Galveston for thirty-five or forty years. I call them Coon and Pie, Willy and Little are their real names. And Pie got some kids, my nieces and nephews. So, I go to Galveston very often when I feel like it to see them.

My brother, he run around and he loved to drink, says, "Let's go out and hear Lightnin' Hopkins."

I said, "He's here?"

He said, "Yeah, he's here."

I said, "I wonder what you have to pay to go in and hear him."

He say, "Oh, it's a dollar. I'll pay your way in."

See, I didn't have much money in them days. I said, "Well, if you'll pay my way, I'll go out and hear him."

So, I went out. He [Lightnin'] had heard of me, but he didn't know me. I went to the place where he was playing, I believe it was on Thirty-third Street in Galveston. They had the house loaded up.

I sat down right by him. I didn't say nothing to him and he didn't say nothing to me because there were too many people for us to get to talking and knowing one another. And I didn't want him to know me no how. So I sat, catched on to what he was doing.

He had an electric guitar, you know, that plug in. He had his boots on, had one of his legs down in his boot, the other one was down here, had nice clothes on. He made a lot of money. They were paying him somewhere long about one hundred dollars a night. That was real good money in them times.

Well, his sister was there. He had a sister standing there and looking at what he was doing. She's a tall woman. And she looked there at me and I'm setting beside him. Somebody told her who I was, and she told her brother, Lightnin'. She says, "Brother? You got to play this guitar. You settin' beside a famous man."

He looked around at me, said, "Who's, what famous man? I ain't scared of nobody."

She says, "You liable to be scared of this man? Do you know who he is?"

He said, "No, I don't know who he is and damn if I care."

And she said, "Well, you gonna know him."

He says, "How am I gonna know him?"

She says, "'Cause people are going to want him to play a song."

Lightnin' says, "Who the hell is this man you talkin' about?"

She says, "That's Mance Lipscomb."

He jumped up out of his chair and shook hands with me. Said, "I'm sorry I said that about you. I'm gonna let you play a number."

I said, "No, I don't want to play. You gettin' paid."

He says, "Yeah, but the people gonna want you to play."

So, I refused to play for him, and a boy from my home town here in Navasota, raised up with me, he said, "Lightnin', I'll give you a dollar to let Mance play his 'Bumblebee.'"

And Lightnin' couldn't play it. He got mad when they asked him to let me play "Bumblebee," because he knew he couldn't play it. So, he said, "You oughta be walkin' while you're talkin'. I ain't gonna loan Mance my guitar."

The man says, "Well, I know you ain't gonna loan it to him, but I'll rent it."

"I ain't gonna rent it to him. Now when I get through playing here tonight, if Mance wants to go home and stay all night with me, I'll let him go home with me."

I said, "No, I'm right across the street here with my sister." So, that's the first time I seen him. We remained good friends from then on.

Lightnin' comes from Centerville, he stayed out from Centerville, and drifted in over to Conroe. From Conroe he went in the direction of Houston, and in Houston he got a big name because he was a good songster.

I'm glad the young people are catching up about what the music is. They know music now, but, but six or seven years ago they didn't know nothin'. Say, "Aww, play me some rock 'n' roll." Half the majority is going with rock 'n' roll now. You know who's doing it. The teenagers. But people get above teenagers, eighteen, nineteen, twenty on up, they want to hear that solid music, something you can remember. The best rock 'n' roll is related to the blues, got blues in it.

I don't try to criticize nobody's music because everybody doing their own thing. Now, understand what I'm talking about. There's plenty of people who can play something I cannot play. Why? They're doing their number. They doing their thing. But I can do some things a whole lot more than other fellas can do because I'm playing all kind of [chords] in music. Ever since I been here I been playing different sounds and music. 99

Interview by Glen Myers
Courtesy Barker Texas History Center

Lightnin' Hopkins
Circa 1960s
Photograph by Les Blank
Courtesy Flower Films

Lightnin' Hopkins
New Orleans Jazz and Heritage Festival, 1974
Photograph by Michael P. Smith

Lightnin' Hopkins
Sweden, 1972
Photograph by Erik Lindahl
Courtesy Tommy Löfgren

LIGHTNIN' HOPKINS

(available on two reissue albums on Arhoolie). In these recordings Lightnin' established his mastery as a down-home guitar stylist and singer, who was able to improvise his lyrics as he sang. According to Chris Strachwitz, "Can't Be Successful" was composed on the spot when Lightnin' discovered that his wife had collected his payment from Bill Quinn, and it wasn't enough.

The success of these recordings launched Lightnin' Hopkins' career and led to numerous opportunities for recording in the 1950s under Gold Star, Jax/Sittin' In With, and Herald. Although most of his recording were made with an acoustic guitar, he demonstrates his creative dexterity on the electric guitar in his 1954 Herald sessions, which resulted in twenty-six superb sides (re-issued in two albums on the Diving Duck label in the Netherlands).

By 1959, when Chris Strachwitz met him in a juke joint in Houston, Lightnin' Hopkins' commercial recording career had started to wane. This was the meeting that initially inspired Strachwitz, a Silesian immigrant teaching German in a California high school, to form Arhoolie and record Lightnin' Hopkins. Hopkins was at that time attracting the attention of other collectors, such as Mack McCormick, Sam Charters, and Paul Oliver. Over the next twenty years, until Lightnin' Hopkins death in 1982, dozens of his recordings were issued on folk revival labels, such as Folkways, Society, Bluesville, Candid, and later Sonet, Tomato, and Home Cooking. Of these, the Arhoolie releases are the most consistent. Many of the other recordings have uneven qualities and are often marred by low-end production and the inescapable fact that Lightnin' Hopkins had lost the raw vitality of his earlier years.

The music of Sam Lightnin' Hopkins (1901-1982) is firmly rooted in the Texas blues tradition. He grew up hearing the blues in Centerville, Texas, and in the surrounding areas, and learned to play the guitar from his brother John Henry. But in 1920, he heard Blind Lemon Jefferson at a Baptist church social. He went up to the stage and tried to play along, but Jefferson was displeased and shouted, "Boy, you got to play it right!"

From that day on Hopkins devoted himself to the blues and eventually developed a distinctive guitar style, which, though influenced by Blind Lemon Jefferson, was also influenced by Lonnie Johnson and his cousin, Alger "Texas" Alexander, as well as by other musicians whose styles he adapted. The best of Lightnin' Hopkins' recordings usually just feature him and his guitar, although over the years he used a variety of instruments for accompaniment, including piano, harmonica, additional guitar, trombone, bass, and percussion.

Lightnin' Hopkins did not begin recording until 1946, when Lola Cullen of Aladdin Records, talent-hunting in Houston, picked him up along with Thunder Smith and brought them to Los Angeles to record together, leaving behind the aging Texas Alexander. There Hopkins recorded his first solo sides (reissued by Pathe Maconi in France).

A year later, in 1947, Lightnin' Hopkins began recording for Bill Quinn's Houston-based Gold Star label and over the next two years produced his finest work

Alex Moore and Chris Strachwitz
Dallas, 1986
Photograph by Alan Govenar

Alex Moore at the piano
Dallas, 1984
Photograph by Alan Govenar

ALEX MOORE

(1899–   )

Alex Moore (b. 1899, Dallas) plays a distinctive style of blues piano that brings together elements of boogie-woogie with ragtime and stride. Characteristic of boogie-woogie is the use of recurring bass patterns that lay the foundation rhythmically and harmonically for the sometimes short melodic passages. Similarly, ragtime and stride piano depend on repetitive bass patterns, though the rhythms are often broken, incorporating more complex harmonies, shorter melodic passages, and chromatic figures. Together, these styles encourage spontaneity and improvisation in performance, and also retain African characteristics through the use of slurring up and down to a note, vibrato, call-and-response patterning and syncopation.

In Texas, the recordings of Alex Moore, Robert Shaw, Lavada Durst, L.T. Williams (Grey Ghost), and Walter Price all exhibit stylistic similarities (recurring bass pattern and broken complex harmonies), but the rhythm and articulation of their songs vary greatly.

❝ When I was first listening to blues music, a lot of colored cats played the piano. There were more piano players in North Dallas than anywhere in the United States. I could call them all — they'd be glad to have their name called off — Joe Curtis, Fred Curtis, Frank Ridge, Lovey Bookman, and see, the first washboard playin' I ever heard was a boy named Ben Nofsinger. That was around 1919, 1920.

I was deliverin' groceries in white folks houses, well, they had pianos, too. I'd always hit one note, and then sometime when I was in my teens, fifteen, sixteen, seventeen, eighteen, that's when I would try to play. Some of them people didn't care if I fooled around on that piano.

At that time people would herd cattle on foot from North Dallas through Hall Street and go clear out to Lamar. Cattle, cows, sheep, I don't know what they did with them horses, but I remember the cattle, the Armstrong Packing Company. One day they brought a herd of horses through North Dallas and my boss bought me a horse to deliver groceries, and a wagon. Then my job extended out further, clear out to Greenville. I got to see more pianos, trying to learn the piano. Around in 1920, '21, I got to hittin' on them pretty good and come back to North Dallas and fool around up and down them alleys and streets and chock [bootleg liquor] joints and such as that.

There were some kind of piano players. They played blues and boogie, that's all. Course, you take Jeff Garden, he was up in that little more classier playing, ragtime. That's what they played — blues and ragtime. Blind Bennie was ragtime. Bobby Bryant was a good ragtime player. K.D. Johnson, we called him "Forty-nine." He recorded with Bessie Tucker. He went up Nashville, Tennessee, and they recorded him there.

The blues songs I heard didn't have no name. I had a cousin that played piano, while I was playin' marbles. They danced and sang, doin' the belly rub, while she just played the piano. Dave Buckner, that was one of the first ones I heard after her. He was playin' a bass drum and one of those bazoos and a piano all at the same time. You take Luther Smith, Leroy Maloney, Jess Maloney, he could hit those keys and play like mad.

Chris [Strachwitz] and Paul Oliver named the songs they recorded, all but one, "Blue Bloomer Blues." They'd ask, "What was that?" and I'd say, "You name them." All of them but "Blue Bloomer Blues." That's what they call flowers in Germany. Women wear bloomers. [Sings, playing his distinctive rolling ragtime, boogie piano blues.]

Women winkin' and twinkin' at me,
Some of them in that key.
Women winkin' and wigglin' at me,
Some other men I see
Find out and sit beside of one
And scratch her on her knee.
Said, she couldn't go home with me, daddy.
I got to stay by myself.
Said, she couldn't go home with me, daddy.
I got to stay by myself.
I ask if she give me cab fare
And she say, "Yeah, and anything else."
I said, "Baby, baby, baby,"
Will you give me what mama did
When I was three months old.
Will you give me what mama did
When I was three months old.
I'll have to make you some sugar, dear;
I can't stay at the same household.
Hey, she pulled off them blue bloomers
And begin to whine and frown.
She pulled off them blue bloomers
And begin to whine and frown.
Yes, she pulled off her blue bloomers
And begin to whine and frown.
I says, "Sorry, sorry, Judge."
She let her milk come down.

My style of playing has changed a lot over the years. That's why they want to send me out of the country. They say, "Alex, you don't play piano like the rest of them." Most of my songs I make up when I sit down to go play. I never do practice. I go play dominoes every day. That's all I do. I don't ever play piano at this house, maybe once or twice a month. I love to play dominoes. Sometimes, it seems like I'd rather play dominoes than play piano. That's because I play dominoes more than I play piano. The music is always here when I get ready. I just go and sit down at that piano and play it. [Begins playing a hard driving rhythm.]

That piano kind of plays itself [Shifts the rhythm of his hands and hums a fast blues]. That's what I'm talking about. That's why nobody can play with me. They can't write that stuff, blues, boogie, ragtime, that's me. I've always said that if I don't improve every night, then you don't owe me nothing. But they always paid me.

Good lookin' baby,
Be my sweet little wife.
Come live with me,
Be my sweet little wife.
You can drink and smoke pretty mama,
If you like that kind of life.
My house is warm,
Why, my gas is on,
My rent is paid,
I'll get you a maid,
Come live with me, baby.

When I was a little boy
I used to run out in the back yard
And chase rainbows.
When I was a little boy
I used to run out in the back yard
And chase rainbows.
Now that I got to be a man
You see me standin' on the corner
Chasin' panty hose.

Love you, baby,
Want you for myself.
Love you, pretty baby,
Want you for myself.
Goin' to buy me an automobile
With lights on it for you
And nobody else.

You see I'm crazy [Stops playing]. Nobody else does that but Alex.

White man get the blues,
Take it to the river
And jump in and drown.
Black man get the blues,
Take a rockin' chair
To the river and set down. 🗣

Street corner
Waco, 1939
Photograph by Russell Lee
Courtesy Library of Congress

Looking for Eddie Durham
Small's Paradise
Harlem, 1985
Photograph by Alan Govenar

Eddie Durham
Circa 1940s
Courtesy Eddie Durham

Big band blues at Small's Paradise
Featuring Eddie Durham
Harlem, 1985
Photograph by Alan Govenar

David Fathead Newman and Leroy Cooper
London, 1975
Photograph by Val Wilmer/Format

Henry Buster Smith
Dallas, 1981
Photograph by Alan Govenar

HENRY "BUSTER" SMITH

(1904–   )

66 I met Charlie Parker after I got to Kansas City. He was a slow reader and he hung around me all the time. He liked my playing, said I was the king. And I'd tell him he was the king. So I hired him to play with me at Lucille's Paradise, and he followed me everywhere I go. He got that name "Bird" because when he'd go home at night, he'd say, "I'm goin' to get my wife to cook me one of them yard birds." And someone said, "What do you mean yard birds?" He'd say, "One of them fowls, chickens." So they called him "Yard Bird," then shortened it to "Bird."

They called me "Prof" because I was writin' some music. I'd write music every day. So, Charlie Parker hung around me, stayed in my band. He wanted to do everything I did. I was like his daddy and he was like my son.

Jobs got a little scarce in Kansas City, and I cut my band down to eight pieces. I did that for about a year and then I said, "I'm going to New York." I told Charlie Parker to take care of the job until I sent for him. And I went to New York and stayed there seven months. So while I was there Charlie Parker hoboed to New York to see what I was doing. He come there and didn't have no money, nothin'. He come to my house, where I was stayin', and my wife and me let him stay in the bed in the daytime and we stay in it at night. I'd be writin' music during the day and my wife would be workin' at a restaurant. But she made him move because he never would pull his clothes off. So he got with Dizzy Gillespie and went over to Philadelphia. Then Jay McShann sent for him, had him come back to Kansas City and make some records. Next thing I know he's with Earl Hines and came back to New York by himself, gigged around. I was with Don Redman, but Charlie couldn't work with me. He wasn't particular about readin' no how, liked to play a lot of solo horn. So he just stayed to himself all the time.

Charlie Parker
New York, circa late 1940s
Courtesy Sumter Bruton

Henry Buster Smith
with David Fathead Newman
Dallas, 1986
Photograph by Alan Govenar

I wrote my biggest song, "One O'Clock Jump," in 1934. We were playin' at the old Reno Club and Basie started things on the piano and say, "Take it, Prof, take it." He'd change keys. He started playin' the blues in F kind of fast. He said, "I'm gonna modulate the D flat and Prof, you set somethin'." So, I set them riffs and went to playin' and they liked it so much we had to play it three or four times a night. The name of it [at that time] was "Blue Ball."

So, finally we went down to Little Rock and played a big colored club. They wanted us to play on the radio one night at the station there. We had thirty minutes to go, and the announcer says, "That number you play with all that jazz is that 'Blue Ball.' Well, I can't say that on the air with the kids and everybody listening. What name can you give it?"

I said, "I don't know."

So, we set around there for ten or fifteen minutes, and said, "I tell you when to hit it, and we'll just call it 'One O'Clock Jump' since we're goin' to hit it at one."

I said, "That's all right with me." And that's the way it started.

Then when I got to New York in 1938 Basie was usin' the song as his theme song. I thought he kind of done me a dirty deal. I didn't know anything about copyrightin' it. I'll never forget, "Jus' don't sue me, Prof, and I'll record anything you write."

Then I wrote "Blues I Like to Hear," but I put it in D natural so he wouldn't be runnin' all over the piano because he couldn't play too much then in D natural. It was an uptown blues. I had someone offer me a hundred dollars for that score sheet, but my wife got a hold of it and it got destroyed somewhere. I can't find it. Basie said, God bless the dead, that "Blues I Like to Hear" was the greatest blues he ever had in his band.

Uptown blues has a little more power to it, plenty of reed chorus and the brass fill in. I had the brass way up in the air and really did a good send-off.

I left New York in 1943. I seen what it was comin' to. I had my time and I was ready to go home where a little time for hunting and fishing wasn't so hard to find. Back in Dallas, I had lots of bands [and influenced a lot of the young ones, like David Newman and others]. I did some writing, still do, arranging.

Jazz has more tricky stuff in it. Blues is a little more straight, making seventh chords all the time. That gives it that blues feel. That slow blues is what we call that cotton patch blues.

The blues was all around, growin' up, pickin' cotton up in Collin County. That's where I was born, 1904. I heard them work songs, church hymns. I tried that blues on my uncle's pump organ in Ennis, but my mother disapproved. I didn't get my first instrument until I was seventeen, a clarinet for three dollars and fifty cents, bought in a pawnshop with money I earned in the cotton fields [seventy-five cents for every hundred pounds]. In the 1920s I got my first saxophone and was playin' around Deep Ellum, Central Track. Then the [Oklahoma City] Blue Devils came through and I left with them [Walter Page, Lester Young, Oran Page, Eddie Durham, Bill Basie and Jimmy Rushing]. The Blue Devils went broke in 1932 and I joined the Benny Moten Band in Kansas City. We playin' that jump blues, which was a cleaner sound [than the cotton patch blues]. I used to write to a lot of blues built around that alto [saxophone]. I never did sing, always kept me a vocalist, either a woman or a man. I had four or five different boys that were with me in Kansas City.

Jump blues was more like jazz, but not as many notes. It's played with more of an up tempo than slow blues. Slow blues was what you heard in the chock house. They'd be sellin' pig ankles, pig feet, pig ears and they have a big tub full of chock with a dipper in it sittin' up on top of the piano. People drink as much as they want to. That's what you call a "good time house," home-made liquor, bootleg liquor. You hear that slow blues and there'd be fightin'.

I like that big band sound. I had to stop playin' alto when I lost my chops in 1959, but I'm still playin' some piano, took up that electric bass. In a way, it sums up the way my life has gone. It's one more thing I haven't done. **99**

Henry Buster Smith
The Heat Waves of Swing
Featuring T-Bone Walker
Louisiana, 1949
Courtesy Henry Smith and Sumter Bruton

HENRY HAYES

(1924–   )

(left to right): L.A. Hill, Henry Hayes, V. Wiser Turner
Houston, circa 1940s
Courtesy Henry Hayes

66 My daddy bought me a clarinet when I was about fourteen years old, and I played in the Lincoln High School band in Dallas. I was brought up in Dallas. I'm sixty-four now, but I've lived in Houston for about forty years. In Dallas I studied private lessons under E.S. Jackson, who had big bands up around Chicago and New York, and was at that time teaching in the school system. I studied the basics, and then I started to experiment with a little jazz, classical music. There used to be a fellow around named Shorty Clemmons and he used to help the younger musicians. Then there was Buster Smith, who had left for Kansas City, and he came home from New York when he was in his thirties. He was the man who taught Charlie Parker. I had a chance to listen to Buster after he came back to Dallas and I ended up playing trumpet in his band. He was one of the greatest alto players that I ever heard, and he inspired me to take up saxophone.

I moved to Houston because I wanted to make it on my own. I landed with three dollars in my pocket, and I went over to see my friend, Eddie Taylor, who had all the white clubs. I called him and asked him if he needed a sax player. He said, "No, but if you meet me on Main Street tonight and go out with me, I'll make it worth your while." And he liked my playing so well that he hired me. I started playing with him in the white clubs and I was able to enroll in Texas Southern to finish my degree in music. So I became a music teacher, thirty-two years in Dickinson, Texas, between here and Galveston.

I was a music instructor and played white clubs six nights a week, and played the matinee at the Tropicana, a black club, on Sunday. I met Albert Collins through Joe Hughes. He said, "Man, you got to hear Albert." So I made it over to see him and he was great.

I had a friend that had a small record label [Kangaroo] and Joe brought him out. I said, "Albert, you got to cut that number 'The Freeze.' " And first or second time we tried, that was it. Albert got his guitar, and I picked up a tenor and together the band played what we felt.

In no time, everybody around the country started to imitate Albert. They even came out with a dance on Dick Clark called "The Freeze." To me, "The Freeze" was a blues, but it was structured differently, with a kind of an African beat.

My style of saxophone added something to it. If you listen to my playing, it's different, comes from gospel, a lot of feeling. There's the right amount of repetition, so that people can feel what they're hearing. It's simplified, not too complicated.

Honking is what I call gut playing, getting on one note and squealing. It's a gimmick, growls, riding, it

Grand opening of the Rose Room
Red Calhoun and His Royal Swing Kings
April 1, 1943
Dallas Express advertisement
Courtesy Dallas Blues Society

was popular for a while, but I could put something more into my playing. The saxophone was the most popular solo instrument before the war, but then the guitar took over.

I used to record with a lot of the blues musicians around Houston, [like] Joe Hughes. We tried Joe's "Ants In My Pants," "We Can't Go On This Way." And I wrote some of my own numbers, "All Alone Blues" and "Hayes' Boogie," which I recorded for the Mesner brothers on Aladdin in the early 1950s. They were looking for that Three Blazers sound.

I started Elmore Nixon off when I wrote "Alabama Blues." We went out to Don Robey and put it on his label. After the number came out, it became a Southern hit. But Robey didn't want to use me too often because I knew too much about the business. He wanted those younger players, more inexperienced. So I only did one session with Robey.

I told Elmore, "Go ahead and try without me," but he didn't make it, because he needed me to help him with the styling of his voice, his ideas. They put Roy Milton behind him and nothing happened. So I got Elmore off Peacock and I wrote to New York, and they sent someone to Houston and put us on Savoy records.

Elmore was a piano player and singer, started when he was sixteen years old, hanging around with me. We traveled around after "Alabama Blues." We followed Lester Williams, who had a hit with "Wintertime Blues." We went to all the little towns in Louisiana and Texas. But then he decided he didn't need me, and that's when I started teaching school.

I always had to depend on someone else singing, but they seemed to always let me down. I'm doing a little singing now. Since retiring, I'm finally getting a chance to do what I always wanted to do, writing, trying to get an album out. I've written probably 150 to 200 numbers, but I've lost more than I can remember. 99

Exciting New Guitar Wizard Looms On Dallas Musical Horizon

By Staff Writer

DALLAS —For many years Dallas has been known as the "proving ground" for musicians from all over the nation. If a musician came to Dallas and failed to make a hit overnight, brother, he was a dead duck. However, few "dead ducks" have ever had the misfortune to leave Dallas (musically speaking) without feathering their nest with a choice assortment of Uncle Sam's green backs.

To get to the point, another musician is in Dallas for the purpose of making a name for himself, and take it from me, he is doing just that. I am speaking of none other than ZU ZU BOLLIN, the Frisco (Texas) born lad who battled LITTLE SON JACKSON to a stand still at Bob Wills Ranch

House last Thursday night, January 10.

ZU ZU started playing the guitar just three short years ago, but has won fame in Louisiana and Texas and leading cities.

ZU ZU started his career after being discharged from the Navy; came to Dallas and started working with Milton Thomas (Brother Bear), worked on the road four months with PERCY MAYFIELD

and then organized his own band. The gifted guitar player has made recordings for Torch Records Company, such as, "Why Don't You Eat Where You Slept Last Night" and "Midnight Blues." New recordings will be released in the near future.

The popular aggregation consists of Adolphus Sneed, tenor sax; Willie Taylor, piano; Bobby Davis, drum and Willie McNeil, trumpet.

ZU ZU BOLLIN is the sensational new guitarist who is "Lying 'Em In The Aisles" around Dallas.

T-Bone Walker golfing
Dallas, circa late 1940s
Photograph by Marion Butts

T-Bone Walker
Photograph by Jim Marshall
Courtesy Institute of Jazz Studies

"T-BONE" WALKER

Aaron "T-Bone" Walker was born in Linden, Texas, May 28, 1910. Walker moved with his mother to Dallas when he was two and stayed there and in Fort Worth, where his wife's family lived. As a boy his earliest memories were of his mother "singing the blues as she would sit alone in the evenings in our place in Texas." His first guitar was made from a Prince Albert can, which he strummed with a "'bluesy beat."

After moving to Dallas, he reminisced (in a 1947 article in *Record Changer* magazine), "I used to lead Blind Lemon Jefferson around playing and passing the cup, take him from one beer joint to another. I liked hearing him play. He would sing like nobody's business. He was a friend of my father's. People used to crowd around so you couldn't see him."

In addition to Blind Lemon Jefferson, Walker was influenced by the "boogie-woogie piano" and singing that he heard at the Holy Ghost Church in Dallas, as well as by the classic blueswomen Ma Rainey and Ida Cox, and by his stepfather, who played with Coley Jones's String Band. Walker's favorite singer was Leroy Carr, whom he recalled in an interview with Arnold Shaw: "I just loved him. I never met him, but he made a record of 'In the Evening When the Sun Go Down.' When I heard that one, it was dramatic — that was it."

While living in Dallas in 1929, Walker made two recordings for the Columbia label under the name Oak Cliff T-Bone. The songs "Trinity River Blues" and "Wichita Falls Blues" had limited success. T-Bone Walker did not achieve fame until he moved to California and recorded "I Gotta Break, Baby" and "Mean Old World" for the Capitol label in 1942. The popularity of these songs established T-Bone Walker as an instrumentalist and singer, and sparked the beginning of West Coast blues recording.

Between 1942 and 1974 T-Bone Walker recorded prolifically, appearing on more than two dozen labels and working with the top blues and jazz performers of his day in America and Europe. Despite the acclaim he received from his fellow musicians, none of his records from the 1950s on made the Billboard charts. His greatest commercial success came from his 1947 recording "Call It Stormy Monday." Like his contemporaries, Walker's career was eclipsed by the introduction of rhythm and blues-based rock 'n' roll. His career is well-documented in Helen Oakley Dance's biography (1987), though the extent of his importance as a musician and mentor is not fully established. The accounts of musicians in this book, however, attest to his profound influence in Texas.

Dallas, 1942
Photograph by Arthur Rothstein
Courtesy Library of Congress

Freddie King
Sweden, 1973
Photograph by Hans Ekestang
Courtesy Tommy Löfgren

ON FREDDIE KING
(1934-1976)

❝ Nobody expected to be writing obituaries for Freddie King yet. He looked too big and too strong to be anywhere near death, but on December 28, 1976, heart failure, a blood clot, and internal bleeding caused his death at Presbyterian Hospital in Dallas.

He was born September 3, 1934, and grew up in Gilmer, Texas. He received his first guitar lessons from his mother and from an uncle named Leon King, who died in 1945. He was sixteen when he and his mother moved to Chicago, where he almost immediately got work in a mill. His first jobs in a recording studio were on unissued Parrot sides by harmonica players Earl Payton and Little Sonny Cooper. In 1957 the El-Bee label released Freddie's first single ("Country Boy"/"That's What You Think"). He began gigging frequently and in 1958 quit work at the mill, surviving with ease on the cash he made playing clubs on the South and West sides. In 1960 he signed with the then-powerful King-Federal company.

This came about when Syl Johnson introduced Freddie to King-Federal A&R man Sonny Thompson. Soon after, he was in Cincinnati, recording the instrumental "Hideaway," a tune so popular that every bluesman with a band found it necessary to add it to his repertoire. Other successful recordings followed on Federal and though some were as dubious as "The Bossa Nova Watusi Twist" of 1962, his muscular guitar style was revealing its trajectory. [His songs that were issued on Federal 45s during this period are considered some of his best — "When Welfare Turns Its Back on You," "You're Barking Up the Wrong Tree," "She Put the Whammy on Me," "High Rise," "Some Other Day, Some Other Time," "Texas Oil," and "I'd Love to Make Love to You."]

King toured exhaustively during 1960-1963, and in 1963 moved to Dallas. He stayed with King-Federal until 1966, after which he signed with Atlantic and recorded two LP's for their Cotillion subsidiary. The label seemed bent on presenting him as a reinterpreter of standards, but his gut level playing wrenched new life from weathered classics like "Call It Stormy Monday" and "Ain't Nobody's Business If I Do," the latter of which always remained a staple in his act. Guitarists like Eric Clapton, themselves influential, revealed how their technique derived from Freddie's and he started to become known to a burgeoning rock audience. He was among the first performers to work the Fillmore in New York, and played there first in July 1971 on a bill that included Albert King, and to the disgust of attending blues freaks, Mott the Hoople.

In 1971 he signed with Shelter Records, an association that yielded the albums "Getting Ready" and "Woman Across the River." He also played on the largely unloved Jimmy Rogers Shelter album, "Gold Tailed Bird." Blues critics feared that Freddie's recordings were headed toward excessive pop flavor and a later association with RSO proved they were not entirely incorrect. King's live gigs, though, remained blues, despite what some regarded as excessive volume, and I for one thought he put on a satisfying show. I saw him work at many different places, including Cleveland's much-mourned Smiling Dog Saloon, and his Saturday afternoon at the Ann Arbor Blues Festival of 1972 triggered some of the most intense crowd mania I've ever seen.

The last time I saw him was at the Tomorrow Club in Youngstown, Ohio. I arranged to meet him the next day at Robert Lockwood's for a brief interview. He was playing at the Agora in Cleveland and was staying with Lockwood, as he usually did when he played that city. When I finally got there, hours late, Robert had just put on the LP he recorded in Japan and was preparing to go to the state [liquor] store. King looked beat and was not overwhelmingly talkative, he obviously wanted to have conversation more than answer specific questions, so when Robert returned with the booze, I put the recorder away. I wish now that a more detailed interview had gone down, because two years and three days later, Freddie King was dead. 99

Tim Schuller
Living Blues #31

66 Working in Chicago, that's where I first started playing in a band, but I been playing guitar since I was six. But I picked up the style between Lightnin' Hopkins and Muddy Waters, and B.B. King and T-Bone Walker. That's in-between style, that's the way I play, see. So I plays country and city.

It comes from the wrist, from the fingers here, and then I don't use any straight pick, I use two. I use fingerpicks, steel, on this, and a plastic pick on the thumb. And then I knock the tone down with the back of my hand. A lot of these rock groups, they hit wide open, whereas, you see, I can hit it open. I can turn it all the way up to 10, and it still won't be too loud, see, because I can keep the sound down with the back of my hand like that.

I never played with a straight pick, man. I used to play with my fingers and I met Jimmy Rogers and I seen he and Muddy Waters used those two picks, so they showed me how to. I used to use three, but then Eddie Taylor, he showed me how to get the speed out of it, see. He's fast, man, Eddie is. But in a way I'm fast in some things, you know. 99

Freddie King,
Living Blues #31

AL "TNT" BRAGGS
(1934–   )

Al "TNT" Braggs, circa 1960s; *Courtesy Al Braggs*

❝ I started out playing hillbilly. I listened to Ernest Tubb, Hank Snow. I'm particularly fond of Lefty Frizzell. I'm a pretty good yodeler. I loved all the yodeling cowboys. When I was real young I used to get behind the radio and take the back off and sing through the radio like I was on the air. Then I'd get a broom and pretend I was playing the guitar.

My mom taught me how to sing spirituals. First she taught me how to sing the lead. Then she would switch and she would sing lead, and she taught me how to harmonize. From there I joined this spiritual group and I started singing spirituals. We idolized the Soul Stirrers and that naturally meant Sam Cooke. After Sam Cooke we started listening to Bobby Bland, B.B. King and Little Junior Parker because we could get Duke records regular here, Houston, Texas, being somewhere down the street.

Don Robey owned the whole thing — Buffalo Booking Agency, Peacock Records, Duke, BackBeat, SureShot, Songbird. You know, he had an incredible array of spiritual singers, where he really got his business started. He had the Dixie Hummingbirds, The Five Blind Boys, The Mighty Clouds of Joy, all of the biggest. I could sing like them, but by this time I was more interested in blues.

All of my life I've been able to imitate people and my songs were Bobby Bland, B.B. King, the Five Royales, some Drifters. I was working at the Golden Duck across from Pappy Dad's Barbecue. That's when North Dallas was hot. We had the State Theater and all that stuff. Pappy Dad's Barbecue. Thomas and Hall. This is when North Dallas was *the* part of town. The Green Parrot was in North Dallas. When I first heard about the Green Parrot it was owned by George Parker upstairs on the corner of Thomas and Hall.

I was playing for Elmore at the Golden Duck, after hours, and what Elmore would do was whenever there would be an act in town at the auditorium or at the Longhorn, he would go by and get everybody to go by his club, all the entertainers, and have them make the announcement for whatever reason. And they would all come by, and he'd get me to sing these people's songs.

There was a big show in town — Jackie Wilson, Little Willie John, Sam Cooke — and they came over. Elmore wanted them to go on stage, but they wouldn't. So Elmore came over to me and said, "Al, start off with Little Willie John." I started off with Little Willie John's "You Better Leave My Kitten Alone." And then I did "Let's Go Steady" by Sam Cooke, and they wouldn't budge. They were standing over by a little round table set up for them with drinks, girls. Then I did Lloyd Price's "Have You Ever Had the Blues?" and every time I did a song, one of these guys would bump the other and laugh at it. "Hey, he really got you down." Then Elmore said, "Do 'Danny Boy!' " Jackie Wilson's "Danny Boy." Now I'm known for doing this song. All of my life I've been doing "Danny Boy." I started singing "Danny Boy" and in the middle of that song, Jackie Wilson jumped straight up, pulled me up from the keyboards and said, "C'mon, we're going to sing this together."

After that the owner backed me to form my own group. Al Braggs and the Organizers. Well, we played around town, was the house band at the Empire Room, all the clubs. Sometimes we'd play three gigs, a matinee on Sunday from three to seven. Then we'd have an hour to go and set up and hit it from eight to twelve. And then we'd have another hour to go set up again and play after hours from one to four. In two days, we'd do six gigs. That takes a toll, making big money, twenty-five or thirty dollars apiece.

By me playing at the after-hours places, Bobby Bland would come by, him and B.B. And oh, I could sound just like Bobby, still can to this day. He'd come by and I'd sing all his stuff. So one night he told me. He said, "How would you like to record?" And I said, "Fine."

He said, "Well, next time I come I'm going to bring Don Robey to the after-hours place, where I played the Golden Duck, for Elmore Harrington."

Sure enough, four or five months later, Bobby used to come about six times a year. Well, the next time Bobby came in. He brought Robey in. Here I am. Don D. Robey. This man is a legend. This is the man who is the creator of Big Mama Thornton, "You Ain't Nothin' But a Hound Dog." There's where Johnny Ace was made. And all these spiritual singers. And Robey looked like a white boy, all his life, and he took advantage of that. He didn't pretend to be white, but if you thought it, if you didn't know any better, you wouldn't know from him. He was shrewd.

So he came in and said, "Are you Al?"

I said, "Yeah..."

He says, "Bobby told me that you sing good."

"Well, I try to."

"I'm going to be around for a while and I want to hear you sing."

I said, "Okay."

So he sits down, and I go into it. I knew it was coming. I was really prepared for this. I did all of Bobby, B.B., I did everybody and show him that I could do all kinds of stuff. Back then it was all right to copy somebody's style. So after the show, he comes up and says, "How would you like to record?"

"Hey, I'd love it."

He says, "I'll tell you what to do. You give me a time and you be down in Houston at such-and-such time and I'll record you."

When the time came, he said, "I'm going to Chicago and I'll come through Dallas and pick you up, and we'll go on to Chicago and I'll record you."

I couldn't believe it. During this time I also had the opportunity to go see Mr. Berry Gordy at Motown. This girl, Joyce Coleman, who worked at the Golden Duck, she had a direct contact with him. But I elected to go with Don Robey. Berry Gordy was not the man he is today. Robey had more going for him. He had all these big stars, Gatemouth Brown, Junior Parker. I wasn't going to turn this down.

Al "TNT" Braggs
Circa 1960s
Courtesy Al Braggs

Mr. Robey came to Dallas and had Mr. George Parker bring me to Love Field. I board the plane and we go to Chicago. When I get there, they put me with Big Willie Dixon, bass player, still playing that upright bass, and he is the producer of my first record in 1959. The tune they gave me, I didn't think fit me and that's how I came up with "Don't Think I'm Going to Make It." On the other side was "An Angel You Belong to Me." And that tune came out and it took off immediately for me.

Then there's some talk about Bobby Bland and Junior Parker splitting up. And someone calls from New Orleans wanting to book Bobby Blue Bland. So Evelyn Johnson at the Buffalo Booking Agency tells him, "I'll tell you what I'll do. If you take a date on Al Braggs, then we'll give you a date on Bobby."

"Who? I don't know no Al Braggs."

She says, "Al Braggs is dynamite. He's going to turn flips. He dances, he sings, and he's dynamite. Tell you what, you take a date on Al Braggs and we'll give you a date on Bobby and Junior later on." Reluctantly, he takes the date and the man forgets my name. All he remembers is that I'm dynamite. So when I get to New Orleans to play the date I got three days. I see "Mr. Dynamite. TNT from Dallas." This is on the marquee. I say, "Oh, somebody else is here from Dallas." Then I see, "Plus Miss TNT, the dancer." Oh, this is his wife. That's what I'm thinking.

So on that same show was Joe Tex, Joe Hinton, Al Toussaint was the band leader over the musicians. All the way up to show time I was looking for TNT from Dallas, and then I was introduced, "And now ladies and gentlemen, a star from Dallas, TNT!" So Joe Tex says, "Hey man, you going on?" I says, "That's for TNT," and he says, "Man, that's you."

That's how I became TNT. I did "I Pity the Fool" and I turned a flip off the stage, I was almost falling, and just fell off into a split and just came up into something. I screamed. I crawled on the tables. And the next day the reviews said, "TNT is really TNT."

From there I went back to the company and Don

Al "TNT" Braggs and Bobby Blue Bland
Longhorn Ballroom
Dallas, 1984
Photograph by Alan Govenar

Robey said, "We'll have to do a record on that." And I guess a good year or two passed before I came up with the song "Take a Look At Me, I'm Doing the TNT." It became so popular. I liked it.

In 1961 Junior Parker and Bobby Bland were split up. When they split the band went with Bobby, and they gave Junior another band. So they said, "Who do you want, Junior?" and he says, "Joe Hinton." And Bobby says, "Give me that kid out of Dallas." So they called me, and I got to join Bobby in Indianapolis.

One time, about a year later, we were in Chicago and I wrote my first song for Bobby. I'm a night person and I always carry around a little tape recorder to get down my ideas. Well, our rooms were next to each other, and I get this idea around three in the morning, and I call Bobby and wake him up. I told him I've got this wonderful tune. He said, "Who is this?"

"This is Al."

"Boy, go to bed and call me in the morning."

"Oh, no, Blue. Just listen to it right now." So I sung it, beating on the table, "Love and affection, a heart so true. I'm yours for the asking...When you need a good loving"...all that.

Bobby says, "Okay, call me in the morning."

The next day it wasn't any better. Bobby just did not like the song. He says, "I hated it, Al, and calling me at three o'clock in the morning didn't help it none."

So I showed it to Don Robey, and he says, "How much do you want for it?" And I sold the song, which was named "Call on Me," for three hundred dollars. Well, Robey immediately decided to name Bobby's new album "Call on Me." That was a hard lesson. I sold the song and that's all I got out of it. That was one of Bobby's biggest hits.

Then I wrote another song for Sam Cooke, but he died before he could record it. So Bobby says, "I'll record it," and he gave it to Joe Scott. He was the arranger, who coached and taught Bobby. Joe Scott says, "Mr. Robey, we need to add strings." And they did, and the song "Share Your Love" came out in 1963.

One night we were playing the Regal Theater in Chicago and Aretha Franklin said she loved the song. She would stand in the wings and listen to Bobby sing "Share Your Love." And Aretha Franklin called me over and said, "Can I record that record?" I thought she was kidding, and a year or two later she did it. And when it came out, it really took off. But I never did receive any royalties for the song.

I stayed with Bobby until 1965, 1966 and then I went out on my own. He understood, but the company didn't like it. Bobby told me, "If you don't make it, you can always come back to me." But Don Robey, Evelyn Johnson, they didn't see it. So Evelyn says, "If you're going to go out and die, I may as well go out and book you." And she sent out a little flier and she didn't think anything was going to happen, and I got three months of dates.

Between 1959 and 1969 I had nine records released on Peacock. The last song I had was "I Like What You're Doing to Me." That came after "That's a Part of Loving You." I cut "Cigarettes and Coffee," "I Don't Think I'm Going to Make It," "We Belong Together," "The Earthquake," "Take a Look at Me, I'm Doing the TNT," "Joy to My Soul," "Chase Some Tomcat." Then I recorded about five or six that were never released. What hurt me so bad was that they took their time. If I got a release a year...the only ones that got good releases were Junior Parker and Bobby Bland. Junior was big, everything Elvis had was done first by Junior. Elvis' songs read like Junior Parker's, like "Train I Ride," "Drivin' Wheel," "Look on Yonder Wall," "Barefoot Rock."

Finally, I leave the company in 1969, and then I started working with Angus Wynne at his club called Soul City and with his company, Showco. So after a while, they asked me about "Share Your Love" and I told them that I never got any royalties. So they said they wanted to sue on my behalf, and won, but I didn't find out until I talked to Evelyn Johnson. They had to pay me all the back royalties. 99

R.L. GRIFFIN
(1943–   )

R.L. Griffin
Dallas, 1986
Photograph by George Keaton

" Everybody can understand the blues because there's a story. I was first introduced to the blues by my school director. Then I met a man by name of Freddie King and he really inspired me. I sang with Freddie King. We're both from East Texas. He was from Mount Pleasant and I was born in Kilgore. We were what you'd call home boys. The blues in Dallas isn't really different, though the people in East Texas seemed a little more into the music. In small places there wasn't as much pop music. More people were writing their own songs and singing blues.

I came to Dallas in 1967. I was on my way to Los Angeles and I had an uncle living here. See, I was a drummer at first before I was a singer. I stopped in Dallas and sat in with a group called Big Bo Thomas and the Twisting Arrows. They were the hottest group here, had been since the 1950s. When Bo heard me, he said he wanted me to join his group that had James Lynn Marsh, Fred Lowry, Don Williams. Not too long ago I got together with the old guys. Bo Thomas was a legend, "The Big Bo Twist." He was good in his time and he can still blow that horn, tenor saxophone. He was known for his song "Cornbread."

In the 1970s I started playing with Freddie King after Big Bo Thomas kind of faded out. Freddie didn't have a band and he used mine. I was a stand-up singer then, starting to work on my own music.

When you start writing a blues song, it may be at night, and then on the next day you get another idea. Sometimes when you're having lots of problems, you know, you sit down and you put something together. You go to thinking. Well, you can't pay a bill, it gives you the blues. You have to put your mind together. You got to be able to write a hook line. You would start out with "my baby" and then you'd have to go back to "my baby," every verse, you repeat it. That's the form. Take the song

Everyday, everyday I have the blues.
Everyday, everyday I have the blues.
When you see me worryin' it's you I hate to lose.
Nobody worry, Nobody worry, nobody seem to care.

It's telling the story over and over. It's about life.

My favorite blues singer at the time I began singing was Bobby Bland. He was my admiration. Every time I heard that Bobby Bland had a new record, I would run and get that Bobby Bland tune. And when I sang the songs, people said that I really sounded like Bobby. In time I put together my own style, but I drew on others. A personal friend of mine was Z.Z. Hill, one of the top blues singers from Dallas. We were good friends. He came over to my house and I went over to his. He said to me once, "Whatever you do, Grif, keep your own style." And that's what I've been doing.

Z.Z. Hill's "Down Home Blues" in 1981 was a turning point. In the 1970s everybody was bypassing the blues, but now it's changed. Disco came by and went fast. The people who really loved the blues never stopped listening to it. "Down Home Blues" was a real inspiration. I made it into my coming-on song, followed by Bobby Bland's "Nothing You Can Do." When you do those songs, you always get the audience going. Now the music trend is beginning to change on the radio. There's more of a white audience sticking with the blues.

When you're singing for a black audience you have to come up with one of the top songs, but with a white audience you can do your older songs. I think blacks are more up to date. They want to hear new material.

I started my own club, Blues Alley, in 1985. I had been working at the Classic Club in Oak Cliff when a couple of friends suggested it to me. I was doing such a good job of pulling people in for someone else. They told me, "Why don't you open your own club?" So I did, and it's going great. The audience for the blues is definitely coming back. Not too long ago I was in Tyler at the Climax Club and I drew two, three hundred people.

In Dallas, these days there are several blues singers. Johnnie Taylor is probably the leading performer. He's had several hit records with the Malaco label. His song "Still Called the Blues" is one of his big records now. He's done four albums with Malaco. Johnnie's one of

Beginning in 1982, Z.Z. Hill's "Down Home Blues" held a spot on the Billboard charts for ninety-two weeks. The success of this album (released on the Malaco label) signaled the resurgence of rhythm and blues and has become one of the best-selling blues albums ever. However, aside from the title cut, few of the songs are actually blues songs. Like Johnny Taylor, Z.Z. Hill earned his reputation as a soul singer who performed to a disco beat for Columbia records in the 1970s.

Born in 1935 in Naples, Texas, Arzell Z.Z. Hill began singing in the choir at Gethsemane Baptist Church. Following his graduation from high school in 1953, he moved to Dallas to live with an uncle. He continued to sing in local church choirs, though he also started working in small clubs performing popular tunes by B.B. King and Bobby Bland. In 1963 he made his first recordings for his brother's San Diego-based Hill label.

In an interview with Jim O'Neal (*Living Blues* #53) Hill identified Sam Cooke as his most important influence. For more than twenty years Z.Z. Hill recorded as a soul singer on the Hill label, as well as on Kent, Columbia, and United Artists. In 1980 he signed with Malaco and gained commercial success. As Hill liked to recall, "It was time for the blues to come back after all that disco." The phenomenal sales of "Down Home Blues" reflected Hill's understanding of his audience, his choice of lyrics, instrumentation, and the promotion of Dave Clark at Malaco. In his next album, Hill proclaimed "I'm a Blues Man," but his career ended unexpectedly a short time later. Z.Z. Hill died in April 1984 from a blood clot, the result of an auto accident two months earlier.

Johnny Taylor
Dallas, 1986
*Photograph by
George Keaton*

the best soul singers around. You just have to give it to him and he's got it.

Blues has a little different feeling than soul and is a little deeper, I think. The instrumentation might be the same, but the sound varies. I have a full show band, two guitars, keyboards, drummer, two horns (alto and tenor) and myself on vocals and harmonica. I was inspired to get into harmonica by Al "TNT" Braggs, who at one time was playing harmonica, too, and he told me, "C'mon and try it." So I started playing a little bit and everybody kind of liked it. Now, I'm including it in one or two tunes during my show.

Some of the other blues singers in Dallas are Little Joe Blue, Charlie Roberson, and Ernie Johnson. Little Joe Blue is out in Los Angeles now, doing some recording. His newest is "Dirty Work" produced by Leon Haywood. Charlie Roberson also plays in and out of town. Last week he was in Midland, Houston, and back here on a show with Vernon Garrett and Barbara Lynn. Charlie's latest song is "Let Me Do Something for You." Ernie Johnson has a different style. He's a little more explosive. At one time, Ernie was with Jewel Records, and they released his last record, "In the Mood for the Blues."

Al Braggs is still active, but he's mostly doing writing. He's producing my new record and doing writing for a new Bobby Bland LP. The new song Al wrote for me is called "Bad Blues, Bad Blues." All you have to do is call Al, and he'll let you know exactly what he's doing. He always keeps some new songs.

I have three records out now on the Classic label, "Something on Your Mind," "It Doesn't Have To Be This Way," and "I Don't Think I'm Going to Make It." "Cry, Cry, Cry" is on a new label in Dallas called P&P Productions. Right now, I'm shopping around my new record. I'm feeling better than ever. I'm forty-five now, and I get plenty of rest. I'm up late when I perform, but I don't make a habit of it unnecessarily.

My approach to the blues is almost the same as it's always been. Now you can do more in the studio, cut a whole LP with two musicians. The blues is what you put into it. **99**

Ernie Johnson
Dallas, 1985
Photograph by George Keaton

Charlie Roberson
Dallas, 1986
Photograph by George Keaton

LITTLE JOE BLUE

Little World and Little Joe Blue
Classic Club
Oak Cliff, 1984
Photograph by Alan Govenar

66 The blues is something that happens in everyday life. To my idea, the blues is something simple. It doesn't have to be about a lady. Sometimes your boss man makes you mad and you have to feel it on the inside, but you can't quit it because otherwise you wouldn't have one. When your lady makes you mad and you know you can't live without her, that's the blues.

The way I sing a blues song I have to feel it. When I play the blues I just see what's happening. I don't write blues. If someone else makes it up, I can sing it.

It needs to have a punch line. It has to have simple meanings to it, so that everybody can understand.

Sometimes blues songs have a repeating line. You give it in a certain way and then you come back. You may say, "Baby, I don't want a soul hangin' around my house when I'm not at home." You're kind of telling her. Then when you repeat it: "Baby, I don't want a soul hangin' around my house when I'm not at home," the emphasis is different. You're telling her like you really mean it. In the blues you need to set a foundation. You don't start at the top and then come down. You build a blues, and then you have a punch line with a special phrasing. That's the story, like the song I sing,

> I've been puttin off talkin' to you baby,
> About the things you do.
> I'm feelin' sooner or later, baby,
> It'll settle down to just me and you.
> But instead of slowin' down,
> You seem to be pickin' up speed.
> You used to tell me how'd you'd be back,
> But you don't tell me how you feel.
> I wasn't born yesterday.

That's the way it is. It builds up to a climax, "I wasn't born yesterday." In other words, she's doing all these things that you know she's changed, but she's not aware that you know.

Conditions started me singing the blues. I was always around a lot of singers. I was born in Vicksburg, Mississippi, across the river from Louisiana. A lot of blues singers would come through town. Jimmy Liggins, Lowell Fulson, T-Bone Walker, Howlin' Wolf, Muddy Waters, all of them used to come to our town to a place called the Green Lantern. I would take all my money that some people might spend on the movies, and I'd go to the dance for fifty cents. They wore nice suits, and a country boy like me didn't have no suits. So I watched them, and I always pictured myself doing that. 🍂

ANSON FUNDERBURGH
(1955–   )

❝ When I got my first guitar, it was a little old acoustic, and the woman I bought it from had a daughter who had a whole bunch of 45s. And in those 45s was "Hideaway" (by Freddie King), "Honky Tonk," "Sno Cone" by Albert Collins, some Jimmy Reed, "Big Boss Man," and a few of those kinds of things. There was a Roy Rogers, a little fake guitar. I was in grade school, six, seven, eight years old. I didn't know exactly what was goin' on, but I knew I liked it. It kind of hit my ear.

I've been playing in nightclubs since I was fifteen, fixin' to turn sixteen. I've had little bands on and off since grade school. I'll be thirty-three next month.

Boz Scaggs was from Plano, where I grew up, but I never really met him until the last two or three years. I never really saw him. I knew his brother.

Most of what I've acquired out of the music has been from records. I've seen Freddie King a lot, but I never saw Muddy Waters, though I did get to play with Lightnin' Hopkins at the Granada Theater. That was in 1976, 1977. That was fun. He was a grumpy old coot. I guess he had heard it all. I can imagine it feeling like it's a repeat. I know what it's like for me now. Sometimes I wonder what it would be like with another forty years tacked on. Lightnin' Hopkins, though, could really play. He was great. He played electric guitar and had a band: drum, bass, him, myself, and Marc Benno.

In a way I'm more influenced by the Chicago sound, Muddy Waters, Magic Sam, Buddy Guy, B.B. [King]. I like that harmonica a lot; Little Walter, Robert Jr. Lockwood, Luther Tucker, they're all big influences, too. I kind of pulled something from everybody. I do what I do and go on. I don't think about it too much. [So much of the Chicago sound is the immediacy of the performance. It's a live sound]. Any time you use a harmonica you have to relate to what they did in Chicago.

Anson Funderburgh
1987
*Photograph by
Randy Jennings*

Sam Myers
1987
Photograph by Randy Jennings

Sam Myers is from Mississippi and played in Chicago. He really added a lot to my band. [Anson and the Rockets] were started about nine years ago, October 1978, with a basic harmonica, bass, drums, and lead guitar. We stayed with four pieces for about a year and then we added a piano. The band has gone through a lot of personnel changes to get to where we are now: Sam Myers on harmonica and vocals, Randy Simmons on bass, Matt McCabe on piano, Mark Wilson on drums, and myself. We've been together since about 1986.

I met Sam Myers in Jackson, Mississippi. I was playing with the old band and Sam was living there. So we were playing and a guitar player that worked with Sam, named Pete Cushie, came up to us. He was a young white guy and told us about Sam Myers, and I said, "*The* Sam Myers?" I had a lot of his early records, but I didn't know that he was still alive. As it turned out, Sam didn't get a chance to come to see us that time, but the next time he got up and played. I flipped over him and I tried to get Hammond Scott from Blacktop Records (my label) in New Orleans to do a record with Sam, and finally he agreed. That's how the "My Love Is Here to Stay" album came about. The newest album, released this year, is called "Sins." Sam plays on that, of course, though I did use a different band on "Love Is Here to Stay." I didn't want it to sound like a Rockets album. It was for Sam. We did his tunes mostly, "My Love Is Here to Stay," "What's Wrong? What's Wrong?" "Poor Little Angel Child." Some he had recorded before, but he redid them. A few were covers, a Little Walter tune.

Earl King wrote two songs for the new album, "A Man Needs His Lovin' All the Time" and "Leftovers."

Sam Myers wrote three songs, one was a cover of "Sleepin' in the Ground," one of his early songs. I only wrote one of the tunes, an instrumental, called "Chill Out," a tribute to Albert Collins. In putting together the album, I work as a kind of arranger to make the tunes sound a little different.

I'm just now starting to develop my own style. I pulled some of what I do from various influences. Now when people hear me, I hope they think, hope it sounds like me. I don't really want to sound like someone else. My biggest influences in my solo work were B.B. King, Freddie King, and Magic Sam.

The blues is something I really enjoy doing, I wouldn't know how to act without it. I've been doin' it a long time. There was a time I mostly played black clubs. That was in the mid-1970s, with a group named Delta Road. I played all over South Dallas, on Metropolitan, the Jade Room, Forest Avenue, the Spider Lounge, and the New York Ballroom [which was the old Ascot]. The black people we played for loved us, most of the older blacks, because we did something special for them.

Sometimes you listen to the lyrics of the blues and you get tickled. It makes you feel good. It makes you happy. In this way the blues is like country and western. It's about life. Sometimes you'll hear the lyrics and it will just make goose bumps go up on you. The blues is something that anybody can relate to if they really stop and listen. I see people out there who I think might not really understand what they're hearing, but they're tapping their foot. People like the beat. A lot of people who grew up on rock music are finally starting to figure out the roots. I had a hard time making it in Dallas for a long time. Austin had a lot more going for it, the early Antone's days, and there was another place, called the One Night, where I used to hear Jimmie [Vaughan] in a group called Storm, and they used to pass the hat to pay the band. Times have not always been great. The blues can make you sad. It's a very emotional music. It moves people in one way or another. The blues is simple, but very honest. It seems the more complicated you make it, the further it gets from the true sound. **99**

Roy Milton
Fort Worth, circa 1940s
Photograph by Calvin Littlejohn

Little Richard
Black DJ in Fort Worth
Circa 1950s
Photograph by Calvin Littlejohn

Old Fiddlers Contest
Fort Worth, 1901
*Photographs by C.L. Swartz
Courtesy Fort Worth Museum
of Science and Industry*

T-Bone Walker
Fort Worth, July 1944
Photograph by Calvin Littlejohn

ROBERT EALEY

(1924–   )

❝ I've been playing the blues since I was about fifteen years old. I was quartet singer in Texarkana. It was a church spiritual group and I wanted to do something different. I was working for God, but I had to change over a little bit.

My mama and daddy didn't want me to sing the blues. They wanted me to stay with the good Lord. Well, I told them this, I said, "Look, mama, I have to do something different."

And she said, "No, son, you sing this gospel. I don't want you singin' no blues."

I say, "What's the difference between singin' gospel or singin' blues?"

"Well, you serving the devil one place and you're serving God."

I said, "Look here, I got to come up. I got to get grown one day and do what I want to do."

So, she said, "Go ahead on."

"I'm not doing anything different than I was doing. Fact of the matter is you're going to church and I'm singing the blues and I'll go to heaven quick as you will. God forgive you for some things."

My daddy went to one church and my mother went to another. Do you see what I'm saying? I wondered why they never went to church together. I couldn't figure it out, what was going on. Why couldn't they both go to the same church? And I still don't know why today. The way I feel, they must not have had the same God.

I remember one day a long time ago, I was twenty when I left home, I was singing to myself and it was blues. But I sing church songs. But I used to listen to Lightnin' Hopkins, Lil Son Jackson, Frankie Lee Sims, T-Bone Walker. He played the Bluebird not long before he died back home in California

T-Bone was great, and he would sing the blues. He would upset the crowd the way he was on stage. And he was a singer.

I didn't start singing the blues professionally until I moved to Dallas. Then people got to liking me so well, coming more and more, and I got a big crowd.

And that made me get on up in the world. When I moved over here to Fort Worth, I got with another band. We were the Boogie Chillen Boys. That made me famous, and I must of played at the Bluebird for another twenty or more years. And when Miss Mamie died, the owner, these white boys wanted me to get the Bluebird. I've had it for eight or nine years, and I got a lot of white folks coming out there.

So when I first started out I got with some white boys. They called me one day at the house. They say, "Robert, you want to come out and do something with us tonight?"

I say, "Where you all playin' at?"

He says, "At The Hop. We're just going to get something together."

I had been playing with another group for two months, and I quit. I got together with these white boys and we practiced. Everybody was liking us. Then when we left there and we got placed out of town. That's when the blues was coming back in, in the 1960s. We played Soap Creek Saloon on Sunday, and then Antone's on Monday, and everybody went wild over us. That was the band before the Juke Jumpers. We were called the Five Careless Lovers [with Sumter Bruton]. When we started out it was three coloreds and the rest was white. And we had a ball, man. We really turned things out. White people started liking me. And they would rather hear me sing than anything else. They wouldn't come out to the club if I wasn't there. I was the king of blues.

Right now, they're still crazy about the Juke Jumpers. A lot of folks still say, "You could of kept Robert Ealey. You had a good thing going. But with Robert running the club, he couldn't go nowhere. He had to stay at the club." They travel all over the place.

A lot of people try to do away with the blues, but it don't work that way. As long as I'm in Fort Worth, the blues is going to stay here. And people are still crazy about the blues. There's something inside the blues that make people start wondering. ❞

the Mellow Fellows. It wasn't much of a band. A whole bunch of us would get together and we didn't know how to play. The drummer had a snare drum and a ride cymbal.

And we played the Big D Jamboree on Jerry Lee Lewis' first night there. For the show, my drummer went out and bought a bass drum, a big old marching band bass drum. The band was myself, my brother, and a friend of his, and his brother. There were four guitars, no bass, a sax and a drummer. None of us could really play, but we went over to the Big D Jamboree and signed autographs and all that stuff. From that day on, I have had my own band. It was the year Jerry Lee did "Crazy Arms," about '55 or '56.

Myself, the drummer and the sax player went on from there and put together more of a real band. It was about the time I went to visit my aunt and uncle in Florida and there was a motel there called the Starlight. Every Tuesday of the month they would have a talent contest and on the last one of the month, the winners of the previous three weeks would go on. So my aunt rented me a guitar from a music store in Cocoa Beach. And I entered the contest and I was there for a month and I won singing "Goin' Steady," the old Tommy Sands song, and "That's All Right, Mama," the Elvis thing. That night, there was a woman in the audience who came up to me and said she was from Capitol records and wanted me to send her a demo tape. Well, I thought, "This is it." So when I got back home we went in a studio in the basement of KFBJ radio and we cut "Mean Woman Blues" and the first song that I wrote, called "Who." Course, I haven't heard from that woman yet.

Right after that my drummer, sax player, and I put together a group called the Straightjackets. There have been so many names and so many bands since then. I don't know where that one ended and the next one started. But that's when we started playing blues.

We got into listening to KNOK. Man, that was a great station back in the mid-'50s. I remember hearing "Honest I Do" come on the radio, and that's the first time I was ever really caught by someone playing harmonica. That was Jimmy Reed and then shortly thereafter, we were the only white band that played at the old Skyliner Ballroom in Fort Worth on Blue Monday. It was black night out there and we were the only white band playing on that. And one night Jimmy Reed was there on the show, and the next day I bought me a harmonica.

A little after that we went into a studio over on River Oaks and recorded an old Sonny Boy Williamson song, "Wake Up, Baby." And Jimmy Clemmons, who was a DJ on KNOK, he booked a lot of shows. He played that record, "Blues at Sunrise" six o'clock in the morning. I'd be up to listen to it, and then he'd play our song "Wake Up, Baby." As far as I know we were the only white band back in those days that was on that radio station. It was mostly Little Milton, B.B. King, Jimmy Reed, Howlin' Wolf, all that stuff. The only time we'd be on the air would be at sunrise.

At that time we did some Sonny Boy Williamson, Elvis, ballads, Jerry Lee Lewis. Whatever we considered to be happening we played. Back in those days, every guitar around here went to play with Cornell Dupree at the White Sands Supper Club, an after-hours joint. Cornell lives in New York now. He's not more than four or five years older than me. I'm forty-seven.

Cornell Dupree and Ray Sharpe were the two who people went to listen to. Ray is a dynamite player and he was back then, very innovative and full of a lot of energy. Ray was the guy everybody went dancing to, doing the Push. He's always had his very unique style. He was doing country music, a vocal stylist, but also is a powerful and unique guitar player. Now, Cornell, he was called C.L., he had a different approach. He would sit up on a bar stool on the bandstand with his legs crossed and just play his butt off.

T-Bone Walker in Fort Worth
Courtesy Sumter Bruton

Then there were the Duke/Peacock people that came through here, Junior Parker, Bobby Bland. They were always a package deal at the Skyliner. We did his songs then, and I'm still doing "Turn on Your Love Lights" in my show every night.

Sonny Boy Williamson used to work at a place called Jack's Place, out on the Mansfield Highway, right outside the Fort Worth city limits. It was a notorious place where kids could get in. He had a deal with the police out there. The neon sign [in front] was a big old jackass and the unwritten law among everybody, all the kids, was that if the jackass wasn't kicking, there was going to be a raid. So it was a pretty safe place for young people to go.

We'd go out there and sometimes get to play with Jimmy Reed, Howlin' Wolf, Joe Tex, Sonny Boy Williamson. So when Sonny Boy came through here, we'd work out there with him Friday and Saturday. Sunday, we'd drive with him up to Lawton, Oklahoma, and play up there. We'd go out there and do fifteen or twenty minutes, and then Sonny Boy would come out. I learned a whole lot from those guys.

I remember one night they were having Buster Brown and Jimmy Reed and, hell, I was about nineteen. I was in the dressing room, sitting between those two guys with a brand new harp. I was going to learn me something. And they were passing a fifth of Old Grand Dad and I was in the middle. I didn't drink and I was hittin' it double. I never even saw the show, man [laughs].

We worked with Joe Hinton at the Tracer Club. It was one of those clubs that had telephones on every table, and on the wall, there was a diagram where you'd see some gal sitting at some table and you could call. It was a big hit around here. We were the house band out there for two years, and we worked with Joe Hinton, Barbara Lynn, T-Bone Walker. That was in the early 1960s. I always enjoyed playing in black clubs. I was learning, playing with people who were just magic to me. Freddie King was great and he came out to the Tracer Club. He was a ball of fire, the

hardest working guy I ever saw. He'd get up there and blow it all out.

The first recording we did of any consequence was a song that I wrote, "If You Really Want Me To, I'll Go." It came out on one of Major Bill Smith's labels around here. And it did so well around here that it was picked up on Smash. But Major Bill and one of the guys who worked with him got into a difference [of opinion] over who owned what. So the record ended up sittin' and dyin' on the floors of Big State distributor because Smash couldn't ever get any satisfaction from anybody.

Because of that record, the Straightjackets kind of busted up because the band that made the recording had different people and that caused some animosity. So the next band I had was called the Ron-Dels and we were kind of a big deal around here [in Fort Worth] and then that finally came apart. I stayed around and had any number of bands. Every week I'd call it something else. But finally everything turned to shit for me, my personal life, everything else was chaos.

In 1970 I took off and went to California. A friend of mine, Glen Clark, was already out there. Well, he and I got to writing songs. We went to see a friend of ours that we met, Danny Moore, and T-Bone Burnett. We did a spec thing at Paramount studio. This guy came by and heard us, Earl McGrath, and he had contacts at Atlantic. Earl had started his own label, called Clean records, and we signed a deal with him. They never amounted to much, but they were good albums, "Delbert and Glen," and "Subject to Change." They were all originals and were very unique. Some of it was progressive country before its time. The players were all excellent. We got great critical acclaim but never really sold anything. After we did those things, Glen and I went our separate ways, not as friends, but musically.

Then I signed with ABC and that very week everybody from coast to coast got fired, all the bigwigs. So nobody knew I was on the label for the first year. But I ended up doing three albums for them.

I was going to be their Progressive Texan. The first one was "Victim of Life's Circumstances," which is all songs that I wrote. The second one was "Genuine Cowhide," which was some songs that I'd written, plus old R&B things that I love and want to do forever, like "Blue Monday," "Please, Please, Please" by James Brown, "Lipstick Powder and Paint." After the third release, ABC went out of business. So I went with Capricorn. They had been big business with the Allman Brothers, but that was petering out. But I had two albums, "Second Wind" and "Love Rustler," and within two weeks after "Love Rustler" was released, I had a song go into the *Billboard* Top 100. That week Capricorn declared bankruptcy and all the telephones were disconnected.

So I did this thing with MSS Capitol and I did an album called "The Jealous Kind" and had my first hit, "Givin' It Up for Your Love." And after the second album, "Plain' From the Heart," Capitol went bust. I was going on forty years old and I was pretty disenchanted with the whole business, and I had a little bit of a drug problem. I gave up on recording. I'd had a lot of heartbreak. I started working the road and since then I've done a pretty good job of cleaning myself up. In fact, I've done a damn good job. And I think it's starting to sound better than it ever has. I have a lot more stamina. Most of all, I feel real lucky that I had people to encourage me to go on, when I just wanted to forget about it. I moved back to Fort Worth about five years ago. Then I went through a divorce, which was just over two weeks ago. It was going on and on and has pretty much kept me from doing anything. I didn't want to do any record deals until I got that straightened out. Right now, I'm writing songs, putting a new band together. Next month we start serious rehearsals. I've got a lawyer in L.A. that's pitchin' some of this stuff around and is trying to get me the best record deal I can find. And I'm going back into the record business. I have had a couple of re-releases come out, and I did a guest appearance on the Roy Buchanan album that came out last year.

I'm going to stick with whatever sound feels right at the time. Lately I've been writing stuff at the piano, and I haven't done too much of that, but it comes out different than when I write on the guitar. I wouldn't begin to call my music traditional blues, but there's no doubt there's a lot of influence there. I couldn't go through a day without playing a shuffle here and there. I don't know exactly what the next album will be. I'm moving to Nashville. I've written about five songs, and I'm still looking. I just don't want to put out a record, I want to put out something that I like. I've gone through a lot of band changes in the last few years. Working without a record deal is hard on musicians, a lot of it is just that, work. When you don't have a record out there happenin' there's not much goin' on but the club circuit and that will just wear them out. They drop like flies.

Bill Campbell is playing lead with me now. He's been dried out for two and a half years, and he's a hard playin' son of a bitch. He's the one who some say taught Jimmie Vaughan and Stevie Ray to play. He was from the early Antone years in Austin. Right now, he and I are the mainstays of our operation. We are going to keep horns. It's not quite right if there's not two to five horns. It's hard to carry that many people around, but I'm going to have at least two horn players, tenor and trumpet. I'm playing piano, guitar, and I've just started playing harp again in the last year. I was getting away from it for a while, but I brought it back and it's feeling fresh. I'm having a lot of fun and I'm looking forward to the next year. I've a good attitude, and I've got a lot of things behind me that I really needed to get behind me. You might say I'm in the pink. Blues is reaching all the way down and expressing it. In that way blues and country are the same thing. It's about getting up in the morning and making it through the day and managing to go to sleep at night thinking you'll never be able to. **"**

The Longhorn Ballroom
Dallas, 1984
Photograph by Alan Govenar

Johnny B and Sumter Bruton
Fort Worth, circa early 1970s
Courtesy Sumter Bruton

SUMTER BRUTON

(1944–   )

❝ I'm originally from Fort Worth, born here in 1944, and moved back here after the War. My dad's from New Jersey, and we moved from there in 1948. I grew up listening to the music. My dad's a jazz drummer, been doing it for fifty-three years. He played in big bands when he was younger, but now he plays in five or six bands.

I started listening to the blues radio stations, KNOK in Dallas and Fort Worth, WLAC in Nashville, when I was a kid in '53, '54. I didn't start playing music until 1962 when I was in high school. I had been collecting records, but I wasn't playing. Then I went out to a frat rush party. I saw a band playing and thought I should do that, too.

The first band was a little group over at TCU, a few football players, a couple of frat guys. We played rhythm and blues. We played what was happening at the time, "Louie, Louie," all of that typical college stuff. Then in 1967 I got in my first full-time group with Robert Ealey. At first it was Robert Ealey, Ralph Owens, Johnny B and me. You ask Johnny what it was and he'll tell you Johnny B and the Tornadoes, and ask Robert Ealey and it was whatever he came up with at the time. We formed two bands together, Robert, me, Ralph [Owens] on piano, Mike Buck on drums, and Freddie Cisneros, which became the Five Careless Lovers in 1968. It was a mixed band, and we played The Hop and places on Camp Bowie, a lot of black clubs off Evans and out in the country. I can't remember the names, but we worked quite a bit, three or four nights a week.

The Bluebird opened originally as a barbecue stand around World War II, and the guy kept building onto it. It may have started in the 1930s, but in the 1940s it really started happening. Cecil Gant played there. T-Bone didn't come to the Bluebird until the time he sat in with Robert Ealey and the Five Careless Lovers.

The biggest rhythm and blues and jazz place in Fort Worth was the new Jim Hotel, opened up in the 1930s, first black hotel in Fort Worth. It had a barber shop, restaurant open twenty-four-hours a day, after-hours club. T-Bone was the house band there in the mid-1930s. There were pictures of T-Bone with Count Basie, Lena Horne, Charlie Christian.

Anyway, the Juke Jumpers didn't form until June of 1976. The original band was me and Jim Colgrove, Mike Buck, and Jack Newhouse. Buck went with The Thunderbirds after about three months. Then we got Mike Bartula, and Jack Newhouse left to join Stevie Ray Vaughan. So we got Jim Milan. In '79 we got Johnny Reno and after that Craig Simichek. He'd worked with other bands I'd been in. Johnny Reno left in 1983, '84 to form his Sax Maniacs. But he still plays with us every now and then.

We want to play that Texas R&B and a little rockabilly. Jim is into rockabilly, but I'm into R&B, Goree Carter. Duke/Peacock, Freedom, Macy's kind of stuff. So we put that together with a little jazz, rhythm and blues, and rockabilly. We have that Texas swing style, and a little Louisiana, too. You go down the road about thirty miles from Port Arthur and you're in Lake Charles — Gatemouth Brown, Johnny Copeland. T-Bone played Houston; he also played Lake Charles, Port Arthur, Beaumont, and Clifton. He went the other way into Houston.

When we were playing in the late 1970s the music was kind of dying out. They threw away all those Duke/Peacock 78s. The company had been sold, and well, what are you going to do with them? [laughs] But those albums are being reissued now. I've got a lot of the 78s, but the sound quality is better on the "Strutting at The Bronze Peacock" album reissued by Ace. And those 78s sounded good.

My guitar style comes out of that period, but includes everything from T-Bone to Charlie Christian, the Texas swing style and, of course, people like Bob Wills. We have two guitars, two saxophones, tenor and alto — they can switch off — piano and drums. We've done four albums now by ourselves and one with Robert Ealey. The first was "Panther City Blues" on Flying High records. The next was "Border Radio" on Amazing. That had Johnny Reno. And after that

Johnny Reno, 1983
Photograph by Tracy Hart/Heights Gallery

was "The Joint Is Jumpin'," and on the last one is "Jumper Cables" on the Varrick label, which is part of Rounder.

I still like the same basic sound and there are some other groups in Fort Worth getting into it. There's an interesting Spanish band these days out on the North Side. They're doing some James Brown soul stuff, but then they're doing Roy Milton, T-Bone, they're even covering some of our stuff. Their instrumentation varies, sax, two guitars, drums, but the bass player also doubles on sax. So one of the guitar players can play bass. The three brothers are the leaders: Steve Coronado, Joe Coronado, John Coronado, bass, drums, and guitar.

Fort Worth has had some great ones. Finney Mo was one of those. His hit song was "My Baby's Gone." He was in his early 50s when he died. I have a bunch of tapes of him from KCHU, the station that was pre-KNON. He used to have a radio show he was on with Dave Liggins, Chops Arrendondo, three guys from West Dallas who sat around and talked about the West Dallas days. And I heard ZuZu Bollin on the radio in those days.

In the 1950s in Fort Worth there were Robert Ealey, Ray Sharpe, and C.L. Dupree was in town. Two of the best bands were Little Al and the HiFis and Louis Howard and the Red Hearts. Al was a pretty good-sized group, probably had three to five horns, congo player, piano. He had a left-handed Fender guitar. He played all the frat parties. That was when the black bands played all the white frat parties. They did all over the South, the blues and soul music. Look at "Animal House," that's exactly the way it was, everybody doing the "Gator." There was a lot of wild shows. Lee and His Jolly Five. Aaron Watkins was a black booking agent in town, and he booked most of the frat gigs. You'd call him at four o'clock in the afternoon and say, "We need a band at eight." And he'd have a band there.

King Curtis left Fort Worth in the mid- to late '50s, Ornette Coleman, Prince Lasha. The guy who taught

HOUSTON

With the growth of Houston as a shipping and industrial center in the early 1900s, the black population increased rapidly. By 1920 there were an estimated 35,000 blacks in Houston, and by 1940 there were roughly 86,000 blacks.

Houston's black community congregated in four segregated wards: the Third, Fourth, Fifth, and Sixth. It was in the Third Ward that Lightnin' Hopkins in the 1920s accompanied his cousin, Alger "Texas" Alexander, and where Hopkins returned by himself in the 1940s to play on Dowling Street. The Santa Fe Group gathered in the Fourth Ward. They were a loosely knit association of traveling black pianists in the 1920s and '30s that included Robert Shaw, Black Boy Shine, Pinetop Burks, Rob Cooper, and Buster the roadhouses and juke joints along the Santa Fe railroad, playing their distinctive style of piano that combined elements of blues with the syncopation of ragtime. In the Fifth Ward there were also black pianists, but according to Robert Shaw, their style of performance was even more eclectic. Probably the most well known of these were members of the George W. Thomas family. The eldest, George Thomas Jr., was born about 1885, followed by his sister, Beulah, better known as classic blues singer Sippie Wallace, and brother, Hersal. Their style of playing involved more fully developed bass patterns than were used by the Santa Fe Group and it integrated the influences of other performance styles that they acquired after moving from Houston to New Orleans and then to Chicago in the mid-1920s.

In Houston there were fewer opportunities for recording than in Dallas until after World War II when several independent labels were started. The earliest to record blues was Gold Star, founded by Bill Quinn in 1946 as a hillbilly label to record Harry Choates. In 1947 Quinn decided to enter the race market by recording Lightnin' Hopkins, whom he found singing country blues on Dowling Street. Although the sides recorded by Hopkins were successful, Quinn was unable to keep him from recording for other labels, and in 1952, after the death of Harry Choates, Quinn ceased operations and sold or leased many of his masters to Saul Bihari.

By the early 1950s competition among independent record labels in Houston was intense. Macy's, Freedom, and Peacock (as well as Bob Shad's New York-based Sittin' In With label) were all involved in recording local and regional blues musicians, including Lightnin' Hopkins, Goree Carter, Lester Williams, Little Willie Littlefield, Peppermint Harris, Grady Gaines, and Big Walter

Clarence Foster, Black-faced comedian;
circa late 1940s; *Milton Larkin Collection*
Courtesy Metropolitan Research Center, Houston Public Library

Price. In addition, there were countless other black blues, jazz, gospel, and zydeco musicians, who were active in Houston clubs. They came largely from the segregated wards of Houston as well as from the surrounding areas of East Texas, Beaumont, Orange, Port Arthur, and areas of Louisiana.

Of the Houston-based independent labels, Peacock emerged as the most prominent. Started in 1949 by Houston businessman Don Robey, Peacock Records was founded to record Gatemouth Brown, who was the headliner at Robey's Bronze Peacock club. Robey's biggest early success, however, came with his gospel recordings of the Five Blind Boys of Mississippi, the Bells of Joy, and the Dixie Hummingbirds.

Robey was a well-known entrepreneur, born in Houston in 1903, and rumored, because of his light skin, to be a racial mix of Negro, Irish, and Jewish ancestry. Robey was a self-made man, tough and hard-nosed, known as a gambler and aggressive businessman, and reputed to have pistol-toting bodyguards.

The first rhythm and blues singer with whom Robey made the charts was Marie Adams, whose song "I'm Gonna Play the Honky Tonks" was a hit in June 1952. With this success, Robey was able to expand his recording interests by acquiring the Memphis label, Duke Records, from WDIA disc jockey James Mattis. Through this acquisition Robey secured the rights to the musicians who were then under contract to Duke. These included Johnny Ace, Junior Parker, and Bobby Blue Bland, all of whom had hit songs during the 1950s.

Much of Robey's success with these musicians resulted from the brass-dominated arrangements of Joe Scott and the talented sidemen he assembled for the recording sessions. Pluma Davis, Hamp Simmons, Clarence Holloman, Wayne Bennett, Johnny Brown, and Teddy Reynolds were among the core group of sidemen who worked regularly for Don Robey and helped to create the distinctive Duke/Peacock sound.

Dixie Humming Birds
Peacock promotion, circa 1950s
Courtesy Doug Seroff

Tap dancer
Circa early 1940s
Milton Larkin Collection
Courtesy Metropolitan Research Center
Houston Public Library

In addition to Peacock and Duke, Robey started the Songbird and Back Beat labels, as well as the Buffalo Booking Agency, which was operated by his associate, Evelyn Johnson. The Buffalo Booking Agency was designed to promote Robey's recording artists and to coordinate the bookings of other musicians, such as B.B. King, who performed often in Houston and elsewhere in Texas. He also co-owned a record shop with Johnson, had controlling interest in the Club Matinee, and marketed a patent brand of hair straightener.

Don Robey was both respected and feared because of his aggressiveness and violent temper. At the peak of his career Robey had more than 100 individual and group recording artists under contract to his label, and over the course of one year he was known to use the services of more then 500 studio musicians. Robey's business began to wane in the early 1960s, but benefited greatly from the influx of British rock 'n' roll and the revival of interest in rhythm and blues. In 1973, however, when a court decision in litigation with Chess records went against him, Robey decided to sell his recording and publishing interests to ABC/Dunhill Records, under the condition that he remain as a consultant, which he did until his death in 1975.

Despite Robey's efforts to dominate rhythm and blues in Houston from 1949 to 1973, he was never completely successful. Many musicians distrusted his business practices, which involved claiming authorship of many of the songs he published, under an alias Deadric Malone. The accounts in this book raise questions about the manner in which Robey dealt with others, and the way he was regarded by those who worked for him.

During the mid-1950s a new generation of Houston-bred rhythm and blues performers began their careers, but they were not recorded by Don Robey. Living in the Third Ward within walking distance of each other's houses, they were the first generation of black musicians in Houston to grow up listening to T-Bone Walker in live performances and on the radio. When they got their first guitars, they imitated the T-Bone Walker sound and then developed their own styles. These musicians included Albert Collins, Johnny Copeland, Joe Hughes, Johnny Guitar Watson, Clarence and Cal Green, and Pete Mayes. Playing at the Club Matinee, Shady's Playhouse, and other nightspots in the Third Ward and around Houston, these musicians slowly gained popularity in the black communities. They recorded for small labels in Houston and Los Angeles in the late 1950's and '60s, but did not achieve widescale acclaim until they were discovered by a white American audience and by Europeans, who eagerly reissued their earlier recordings and offered them contracts and concert tours.

Vaudeville troupe
Houston, 1925
Milton Larkin Collection
Courtesy Metropolitan Research Center
Houston Public Library

Leon Hughes, Joe Hughes' grandson
Juneteenth Blues Festival
Emancipation Park, Houston, 1987
Photograph by Alan Govenar

Johnny Copeland and Kathy Whitmire, Mayor of Houston
Juneteenth Blues Festival Proclamation
Emancipation Park, Houston, 1987
Photograph by Alan Govenar

Since 1980 there have been more than 100 reissue albums of Houston blues by Ace Records, Interstate, and Charly in London; Mr. R&B and Route 66 in Sweden; Double Trouble Records and Diving Duck in the Netherlands; and by Houston producers Roy Ames and Huey Meaux. With the Grammy-award-winning success of Gatemouth Brown, Johnny Copeland, and Albert Collins in the last decade, the demand is swelling for Houston shuffles, the big band beat, heart-rending ballads and hard-rocking rhythm and blues.

Houston blues artists are reunited each year at the Juneteenth Blues Festival, founded in 1977 by Lanny Steele and SumArts, a community-oriented performing arts oganization. Today the festival is the most widely attended celebration of its kind in the state. The aim of the Juneteenth Festival is to recognize Houston-born blues artists in a series of free concerts with a mix of local and nationally known performers at Miller Outdoor Theater and at Emancipation Park in the Third Ward. Each year a blues artist of the year is selected and honored. Honorees have included Sippie Wallace, Milton Larkin, Clifton Chenier, Eddie Vinson, Gatemouth Brown, Albert Collins, and Johnny Copeland.

Juneteenth is a holiday in Texas that commemorates June 19, 1865, the day Texas blacks learned of the Emancipation Proclamation, signed two years earlier. Freed men and former slave-owners began observing the anniversary with picnics, speeches, and reminiscences in verse and song. For blacks in Texas, Juneteenth remains a time for celebration and reflection on the progress blacks have made since that day in 1865, in the areas of education, politics, economics, and the arts. However, it was not until 1979, when Gov. Bill Clements signed a law declaring June 19 Emancipation Day, that Juneteenth was officially recognized.

THE HONKERS

Joe Houston
Los Angeles, 1987
*Courtesy
Pentakelion
Management*

In the Variant Zalen of the sprawling *Congresgebouw*, which houses the North Sea Jazz Festival in The Hague, Joe Houston is making his first European appearance as a soloist in front of a Dutch rhythm and blues group called De Gigantjes. They have never played together before, though Rob Kruisman, tenor saxophonist for De Gigantjes, has studied Houston's vintage recordings on 78 rpm sides that are now available on European reissue albums. The general musical sophistication of De Gigantjes is impressive, but for the first few numbers there is a cultural collision in the sound. Then the raw strength of Joe Houston's tenor solo takes control, a surge of repetitive low notes that unexpectedly scream to a close.

Though he is mainly known as an instrumentalist, Joe Houston is equally as exciting a singer with his powerful shouting voice. Well-groomed and mannered on stage, wearing dark glasses, he jolts his body as he plays and sings, jumping and twisting to emphasize every phrase. Houston embodies a style of performance that began in the 1940s and 1950s and had the raw energy of rock 'n' roll before that expression spread to a white audience. Thirty years later, it's regaining popularity.

Joe Houston grew up with the "honkers," the wild men of jazz who broke open the standards of the day and defined the idiom of rhythm and blues. They played their tenor saxophones with abandon, relentlessly honking single notes, making sudden changes to freak high tones, blowing low and dirty, igniting their audiences with crazed stage antics and crude sounds. Tension is built through repetition with slight shifts in emphasis.

The basis of this kind of playing, Leroi Jones observes, is "the saxophone repeating the riff much past any useful musical context, continuing it until he and the crowd were thoroughly exhausted physically and emotionally. The point, it seemed, was to spend oneself with as much attention as possible, and also to make the instrument sound as unmusical, or as non-Western, as possible. It was almost as if the blues people were reacting against the softness and 'legitimacy' that had crept into black instrumental music with swing."

Honking was a music of disassociation from the smoothness of jazz and white popular song. Honking challenged the established order and in so doing, was a response to the abysmal conditions of postwar segregation and incipient racial tensions. For black musicians, there were few opportunities for commercial success. Discriminatory practices were imbedded in all facets of the entertainment industry, from dressing rooms to radio broadcasts and recording sessions. In honking and screeching tenor solos, musicians mocked expectations and created a sound that was more stylized than personal. Lying on his back, kicking his feet in the air, blowing rowdy notes, the honker did more than simply

Buddy Tate
North Sea Jazz Festival
The Hague, 1987
Photograph by Alan Govenar

express his personal feelings. Honking was a burlesque performance that separated jazz and rhythm and blues from the past, both musically and socially, and that influenced the advent of rock 'n' roll.

At the time that honking was introduced, the Texans' — Buster Smith on alto, and Budd Johnson and Buddy Tate on tenor — were widely recognized as major saxophone stylists. Buster Smith was the mentor of Charlie Parker, and Buddy Tate was a cornerstone in the Count Basie Band. Of these, Buddy Tate at age seventy-three is still active today, living in New York, playing the big band sounds he originated in the 1930s and 1940s, and touring in Europe six months a year.

When asked about the honkers, Buddy Tate forces a smile. "I didn't like it the first time I heard it, and I'm still skeptical. You can't hear the changes," he says, "It's too loud and distorted. The great rhythm and blues saxophonists had a more complicated sound — Louis Jordan, Big Jay McNeely, who was the first tenor to move off the bandstand into the audience, playing wild solos, standing on tables and sometimes honking with his back on the floor."

Buddy Tate's tenor style is more refined and introspective. The changes are deliberate and smooth, and strongly rooted in swing-era jazz, though he says he did play rhythm and blues with T-Bone Walker in 1933 and 1934.

"It was in a placed called The Big House, on the outskirts of Dallas, built by a gangster, who had us play dressed up in prison uniforms. T-Bone had a jazzier sound. I played a high-energy tenor, but it wasn't honking. The sound I was after told a story for T-Bone's guitar to follow. Honking was something else. It was more associated with Houston bands."

In Houston, Milt Larkin's big band was a breeding ground of Texas saxophone giants. It featured Arnett Cobb, Eddie Vinson, and Illinois Jacquet. In 1940, Jacquet was lured away by Lionel Hampton on the condition that he play tenor, but until that time Jacquet had only played clarinet, and sometimes soprano and alto saxophones. With Cobb's help, Jacquet was soon playing tenor and went on to become an important stylist in the Lionel Hampton Orchestra, where he is credited with introducing honking in his 1943 solo on the recording "Flying Home." The success of this tune sparked a nationwide interest in honking. Even Jacquet's friend and teacher, Arnett Cobb, started to honk, but the life of honking in jazz was relatively short-lived. In 1943, Jacquet left Lionel Hampton and was replaced by Arnett Cobb. Jacquet returned to more mainstream jazz, joining Cab Calloway and then Count Basie. Today, both Illinois Jacquet and Arnett Cobb, who were two of the great honkers of their generation, say that "honking is a gimmick, a novelty" and that they prefer straight-ahead big band jazz, where the saxophone solos can be developed with more subtlety.

Lionel Hampton and his band
Longhorn Ranch House
Dallas, March 1953
Photograph by R.C. Hickman
Courtesy Barker Texas History Center

(Right) Eddie Vinson
Houston, circa early 1950s
Photograph by Benny Joseph

EDDIE "CLEANHEAD" VINSON

Eddie "Cleanhead" Vinson has been performing professionally for more than fifty years. He was born in Houston in 1917 and grew up in a musical family. Both of his parents, Sam Vinson and Arnella Sessions, played the piano, but in high school, Eddie had a friend who had an alto saxophone and that became his instrument of choice. His parents bought him an alto sax and he took lessons at Jack Yates High School, where he soon attracted the attention of local band leaders.

Around 1935 he joined Chester Boone's band, which had also included T-Bone Walker. Milton Larkin — a Territory band leader whose orchestra included Illinois Jacquet, his brother, Russell, Arnett Cobb, Tom Achia, Cedric Haywood, Bill Davis, and by this time, T-Bone Walker — persuaded Vinson to join his orchestra. They played at the College Inn in Kansas City and the Rhumboogie Club in Chicago. In addition to alto sax, Vinson became a featured vocalist.

In 1941 Vinson left the Milton Larkin Orchestra, which was then led by Floyd Ray (Larkin was in the military). Vinson joined the Cootie Williams Orchestra in Houston and made his first recordings on the Okeh label in 1942. These included "When My Baby Left Me" and "Stars at the Apollo."

His next recording session wasn't until 1944, when he played alto sax with the Cootie Williams Sextet, and sang the vocals with Williams' orchestra on "Cherry Red" and "Things Ain't What They Used To Be," issued on the Majestic/Hit label. The Majestic/Hit recordings were followed by additional sessions with Cootie Williams on Capitol, but by 1945 Eddie Vinson had formed his own band and signed with Mercury records. Between 1945 and 1947 Vinson produced some of his best work, including four instrumentals and twenty-six vocals, featuring remakes of "Cherry Red" and "Somebody" as well as his new material, such as "Kidney Stew," "Cleanhead Blues," "Oil Man Blues," and "Lazy Gal Blues."

From 1949 to 1952 Vinson recorded under the King label and then returned to Mercury in 1954. Since then his recordings have been sporadic, though he did front the Basie band for a brief period (1957) and worked with the Adderly brothers (1961).

Over the years Eddie Vinson has built a solid reputation as an instrumentalist and singer with a wheezing vocal style. He has recorded both jazz and rhythm and blues and has involved a wide array of musicians in his bands, including Tyree Glenn, Slide Hampton, Buddy Tate, John Coltrane, and Red Garland.

The scope of the discography of Texas tenor and alto saxophone stylists is complex and vast. Herschel Evans, Buddy Tate, Jesse Powell, Budd and Keg Johnson, Buster Smith, Illinois Jacquet, Arnett Cobb, Eddie Vinson, John Hardee, Adolphus Sneed, David Newman, James Clay, Henry Hayes, Grady Gaines, and King Curtis are some of the major Texas saxophone influences in modern jazz and blues.

The enduring influence of honking, which constitutes only a small area in the overall history of saxophones in Texas, is most evident in white crossover rhythm and blues and rock 'n' roll. In the 1980s, honking has been repopularized by saxophone stylists, such as Mark Kazanoff of the Angela Strehli band, Johnny Reno and the Sax Maniacs, and the Juke Jumpers in Fort Worth. In their performance styles the rudiments of honking combine with modern techniques to create a contemporary music that has few distinguishing regional characteristics. However, the role of the saxophone or horn section has retained its basic presence as the cornerstone of rhythm and blues. The single string runs of the electric guitar solos often follow the saxophone riffs and emulate the horn sounds. There is a call and response between the saxophone and the electric guitar that shapes the Texas style. How this is articulated empowers the solo and distinguishes the attack of the sound.

(Above) Arnett Cobb; Capitol Radio Jazz Festival; London, 1979
Photograph by Val Wilmer/Format

Eddie Vinson shaving his head
Berlin, West Germany, 1974
Photograph by Val Wilmer/Format

Eddie "Cleanhead" Vinson
Los Angeles, 1985

Since his appearance with Johnny Otis at the Monterey Jazz Festival in 1970, Vinson has been active on the festival circuit. He has made numerous tours in Europe, working with foreign and American groups, and in recent years has recorded with Roomful of Blues.

Aside from his alto saxophone and vocal style, Eddie Vinson is also well-known for his bald head, the origins of which he explained in a 1975 interview with Norbert Hess. "In those days black boys used to try to keep their hair straight. So, I put some of that stuff on my head one day and it had so much lye in it, it ate all my hair out. So by shaving it off rather than letting it grow back I got a little attention. When I got bald, everybody wanted to feel it, play with it."

"Well, I'll tell it like it is. I was sneaking off on maid's night out. So I was up there as close as I could get, and T-Bone comes out in his white suit with big diamond rings. He comes out there and strikes up his guitar, v-room, v-room. Oh, Mister T-Bone! He couldn't even get through the first song before the purses started flyin' with everyone goin', "Play my song, Mister T-Bone!" Then they started goin', "Take all my money!" and he was so cool, but then after he got hot, he put that guitar behind his head. Then he'd start to really pluckin'. He'd turn around and swing. And then everything went: shoes, rings, bracelets, everything. Honey, he'd play them blues all night long. But sometimes the men got mad at the girls for throwing their money and purses or whatever else they could on stage. T-Bone would back out and start playin' again and they threw anything they could get loose."

Mariellen Shepphard
1984

MILTON LARKIN
(1910–   )

Milton Larkin Orchestra
with Arnett Cobb and Eddie Vinson
Houston, circa 1940s
Courtesy Sumter Bruton

66 My dad played violin and my sister took it up. I wanted to play violin, but I liked so many instruments, I didn't know which one I wanted to play. When I was about ten or twelve years old I saw a picture of Noble Sissle in a magazine and I told my mother that I wanted to be a musician. I was born in 1910 in Navasota, but we moved to Houston in 1923. I started playing the trumpet, but I changed over to valve trombone after I went into the service. My mother didn't want me to play because she thought I'd get into trouble, but I showed her I was different.

A lot of musicians have gotten their start with me: Eddie Vinson, Tom Archia, Wild Bill Davis, Cedric

Maywood. Illinois Jacquet played alto with me in one of my first bands, and then he switched to tenor with Lionel [Hampton]. I've had my own band since 1936. Arnett Cobb was another of the greats who played with me. We'd have saxophone battles, whoever had the chair next to Arnett would battle with him. That's what led to honking. It's in the phrasing, the repetition of notes, squealing.

The Texas sound has more feeling, melodic syncopation and a different beat. You can hear it in Louis Jordan, even though he wasn't from Texas. Any time there's a Texas band, blues and jazz fit together.

In my early bands I had a banjo in the rhythm section. Guitar started later, around the time of bass violin. At first there were tubas, no bass violin. Then the guitar came along, electric guitar. T-Bone played with me when he was in his early thirties, at Joe Louis' Rhumboogie Club in Chicago. I went for two weeks and I ended up staying nine months. T-Bone would come in and go out on the road some of the time. T-Bone was wonderful. He was a picker; he used his fingers, sometimes with a pick. He was in my sixteen-piece band. He played blues and other things. There were five reeds, four rhythm, five saxophones, myself, and a vocalist. We were playing swing, big-foot swing, which is what I still play now.

After several one-record deals with small labels, I worked as a sideman on sessions, playing trombone or piano, with Eddie "Lockjaw" Davis, Hal "Cornbread" Singer and Eddie "Cleanhead" Vinson. Around 1949 I cut some sides for Regal with Howard Biggs' Orchestra and two years later for Coral, with the former Erskine Hawkins sideman, piano player Ace Harris, whose band included Count Hastings on tenor. I was with my own vocal group, the X-Rays, but that didn't last that long.

In the 1960s I played at the Celebrity Club in New York. There was two rooms there. I played one room, and Buddy Tate played the other. Well, that lasted into the 1970s and then I went back to Houston around the time I cut my album "Down Home Saturday Night"

with a group I called Milt Larkin and His All Stars on my own Copasetic label. The record had Wild Bill Davis on organ, alto man Jimmy Tyler [from Boston] who played with Count Basie for many years, trumpeter Johnny Grimes [from Birmingham], and Johnny Copeland from Houston.

It seems like people are beginning to like what they're hearing of it again now. A lot of it is through the ear. It's playing chords that are more melodic, chords that will stick with a person. Well, you took that solo, you can hum the whole song. You appreciate what you heard.

I'm in a group now with the city called Get Involved Now, a non-profit organization. I play for shut-ins. It don't matter what language they are, how old, they all react to music. **99**

GRADY GAINES

(1934–   )

Grady Gaines
Houston, 1986
Photograph by Tracy Hart/Heights Gallery

66 I was about twelve years old when we first moved to Houston from a little town called Waskom, Texas. Louis Jordan was real hot then, and I'd listen to him playing the saxophone and that's who inspired me to get a saxophone. I got a paper route and started throwing papers for the *Houston Chronicle* and I saved up enough money to buy me a saxophone. And I took lessons from a lady named Miss Punch, who lived a couple of blocks from us. Another guy who taught me a lot was R.P. Wallace. He lived third door from me on the same street in Fifth Ward.

From there I played the saxophone at E.L. Smith Junior High School and there I met Calvin Owens. He was the student teacher. He would take over when the band director wasn't there. Calvin Owens taught me how to hold a saxophone mouthpiece and he stayed with me for hours at a time until I got it together.

In senior high school the band director was Sammy Harris and he taught me for a few years. During that period I met Little Richard. He came to town with a group called the Tempo Toppers, and I played with that group for a while. That's how I first met Little Richard. We were working at the Club Matinee.

Little Richard did some recording for Don Robey at the Peacock Recording Company, where Joe Scott was the arranger, got everything together. From there, Little Richard decided to quit the Tempo Toppers and he met Bumps Blackwell, that was his manager. They recorded "Tutti Frutti" in New Orleans, but Bumps lived in Los Angeles. They released "Tutti Frutti" and it was a real big hit for me. After that "Long Tall Sally," [and] "Lucille." So Little Richard called me and asked me if I wanted to come on the road with him and lead his band for him. I told him I would, and I took another saxophone player with me. His name was Clifford Wirtz. Well, Clifford and I went to meet Little Richard in Washington, D.C., and from that night on we were gone. We never did look back from then on. We stayed with Little Richard up until the time he quit. We were with Little Richard from the last of '56, '57, '58.

Roy Gaines
Holland, 1977
Photograph by Sem van Gelder
Courtesy Marcel Vos

When he quit the business we were on the Australia tour, and we stayed over there for about a month. We were on our way one day, we were on a bus on a ferry and Little Richard said, "I'm quittin'. God's calling me and told me throw away all my jewelry." So he started pulling his rings off and getting ready to throw them overboard. So the other saxophone player grabbed him and I jumped up to grab him. We tustled with him to stop him, but he overpowered us and threw those rings, four or five diamond rings, in the ocean.

When we got back to America, Charles Sullivan, a promoter in San Francisco, had a lot of dates set up for Little Richard to play in Los Angeles and all up the coast, San Francisco, Portland, and even into Vancouver, B.C. But Little Richard quit, and we had to play those dates. That's when we named the band The Upsetters and we had to play those dates on our own. We sent to Chicago and got Dee Clark, who made "Raindrops" and several other hits, "Girl With the High School Sweater," and we got him and he took Little Richard's place. He had his own voice, but he could sound just like Little Richard. We made those dates and the tour went over real well because the band was so powerful. We only had six pieces, no piano, guitar, bass, drums and three saxophones and the vocalist. We were good showmen.

After we got off of that tour Charles Sullivan had some dates booked on Little Willie John, and Little Willie John didn't have a band. So we picked up Little Willie John and played the dates he had set up in the California area. Dee Clark was still the vocalist for the band. We toured with Little Willie John and he wanted the band to play with him permanently, and we accepted it. We worked with Little Willie John for maybe four years through all his greatest hits, "Fever," "Talk to Me, [Talk to Me]" "Leave My Kitten Alone," "Heartbreak," "Let Them Talk If They Want To," "Unforgettable," a lot of them, some with the band, some with a studio band.

While we were working with Little Willie John, Sam Cooke got hot. He had been trying for a long time. He had three songs in the top ten, and Henry Wayne, the promoter from Atlanta, Georgia, contacted us, and we toured all through Georgia, Florida, the Carolinas. We even played dates in New York and New Jersey. He set up a little tour with Little Willie John and Sam Cooke. We played that tour, about twenty-five days, and after that Sam Cooke talked with us and he wanted us to come with him. We had a talk with Little Willie John and Sam together. We were all good friends.

We went with Sam and worked with him until the time of his death in '63 or '64 [December 11, 1964]. Then we took Sam's brother, L.C. Cooke, and toured the country for maybe a couple of years with him. After that things started dying down. I came back home and formed me a band. I did real well recording a song "Something on Your Mind" on John Green's label. Then we released "Let Your Thing Hang Down" and "Midnight Sensation," and I kept that tape for about eight or ten years and then I released it myself on the Leo label about a year ago. It did real well and caused me to get a contract with the Black Top label for a new album. I use my brother, Roy Gaines, on guitar and vocals, Clarence Holloman on guitar, Teddy Reynolds on piano and vocals, Walter Joseph on the drums. My bass player is Michael Doggan, I use him on some of these things. I also had a bass player from New Orleans, Lloyd Lambert. He used to lead the band for Guitar Slim.

My brother Roy and I hadn't really played much together since we were little. He went out on the road with Roy Milton in 1956, I believe, and he's never lived in Houston since. He comes back, but he never stays for more than a few months. After Roy Milton, he went to New York and he stayed in New York and that's where he ran into Chuck Willis. He helped Chuck put his band together.

Roy was more influenced by T-Bone Walker than anybody else. He liked Barney Kessel, but T-Bone was his main resource. T-Bone was great. I played his last Houston dates. He called me and asked me to put his band together. He was coming to La Bastille for a week down in Market Square. We played that date and he went back to Los Angeles and died about a month later. T-Bone was an inspiration to everybody, whether they played guitar or whatever instrument.

Through experience my music has changed a little bit but not too much. I quit playing for about five years in the '70s because the only way I could make a decent living was to travel, but I didn't want to travel no more. So I stopped playing and got me a job working for United Airlines and also for Holiday Inn. I did real well with the jobs, but my friends, Elroy King, a blues singer around town, Milton Hopkins, a guitarist, and V. Weiser Turner, another saxophone player, they kept after me to start playing again. I had gotten to the point where I didn't play no more. They said I had too much going on my horn to give it up.

So I started with Milton Hopkins' group out to Etta's Lounge, Milton Hopkins and Julius Miller and the Blues Untouchables Band, and I played with them for about a year. That brought me in to where I am right now with my band Grady Gaines and the Real Thing. In this group I got Teddy Reynolds at the piano, Floyd Arseneux on trumpet, Michael Doggan on bass. I've got two vocalists. One is Big Robert Smith, a real good blues rockin' singer. He tears the house up everywhere we go. He shouts, but he gets down and sings the blues, too. Our other singer is Joe Medwick, wrote most of the Peacock hits for Bobby "Blue" Bland. He wrote "I'll Take Care of You," "That's the Way Love Is." I can't remember all of them. But he wrote a tune for me called "I Been Out There," and it tells about all the artists that I worked with. It's a rappin' thing, but it's hot.

At one time, a lot of people said I sounded like King Curtis, but King Curtis sort of got a lot of his style from me. He was from Fort Worth. When I was playing with Little Richard, when we did "Keep A Knockin," I did a lot of that chopping up of notes. He worked a show with me over at the Paramount Theater in Brooklyn with a big band. So he hung with me after the show and before I knew anything that yakkety yak saxophone was out. He was doing it. I was working with Little Richard, and he stayed there in New York. So he made it with it.

I love the blues, but I can play hot rock 'n' roll. I don't call my saxophone playing a real honking type. Some people might consider it that, but I don't try to play like nobody. I only play my own self.

I always keep a guitar close to me. The saxophone determines all the drive and rhythm with the guitar. Teddy puts a lot of fire to it on piano. The saxophone in jazz is more like a singer, more out in front. In blues I can stand out in front with a guitar player, singer, or anybody else. I try to prove that to myself and to the audience. That's why I let both of my singers sing, and do the best they can possibly do. Then I come up after them and see what kind of reaction I get from the people. I can do what a singer does by playing my horn.

Sometimes I even go out in the audience. We call that walking the flow, pleasing the people, where I play at now they call it the Grand Finale. That means I have to walk that floor. If I don't do it, they're not satisfied. I seen Big Jay McNeely. He inspired both me and Albert Collins. We worked a show together. There were about ten acts together when I first saw Jay McNeely and he inspired me to do a lot of walking. I had done it before, but I didn't do it as well until after I saw Jay.

Musically, I was influenced by Louis Jordan, Gene Ammons, Earl Bostic (I liked his highs). I don't sound like Gene Ammons, but I think about him when I'm playing, when I do my builds. A lot of my notes and feeling come from Louis Jordan. He was an alto player; I played alto, too, but mainly tenor. Louis Jordan was my biggest influence — "Let the Good Times Roll."

I don't write out my music. I just play from feelings. I think I can get more out of it that way. In fact, I know I can. 99

El Dorado

BALLROOM

"Featuring Houston's Top Jazz Personalities"

- - - - - - - - - -

FRI JULY 5th

GUITAR SLIM
LLOYD LAMBERT

AND

ORCHESTRA

SAT JULY 6

JIMMIE REED

ETTA JAMES

CLIFTON CHENIER

GUITAR SLIM

JULY 8TH

CHARLES BROWN

RETURNS

Presale Tickets $1.25
At Door $1.50

(*Top*) Eldorado Ballroom; Houston, circa 1940s; *Milton Larkin Collection*
Courtesy Metropolitan Research Center, Houston Public Library

(*Above*) Nathaniel "Pops" Overstreet; Houston, 1986
Photograph by Alan Govenar

(*Left*) Eldorado Ballroom
Houston Informer advertisement
July 6, 1957
Courtesy Dallas Blues Society

Sippie Wallace
New Orleans Jazz and Heritage Festival, 1985
Photograph by Michael P. Smith

BEULAH "SIPPIE" WALLACE

(1899–1986)

66 Oh, yes, I knew them well [Ma Rainey, Bessie Smith, Ida Cox, and Alberta Hunter], but I never thought I was going to be a blues singer, because I was nothing but a gospel singer. At seven years old [in 1906] I was the organist of my church. Instead of going to Sunday school classes I would go up to the organ and start playing the piano. The pastor said, "Let's give this child a music lesson, or lessons." So when Mama came in, they told Mama — "Sister Thomas, the members of this church have decided to give Beulah music lessons." Mama said, "Thank God." When Mama got home she told my oldest brother what the church had decided to do and said, "George, why don't you go give Beulah music lessons, so that'll help the church out." So he did, believing that I'd sing his songs and the church songs, too...Mama died, and the city bought her property in Houston. I went to Chicago and lived there for about ten years because my brother George was there.

After Mama died, I thought my brother was going to take care of me, but my brother told me to get a husband — I never had any company. It caused me to look dumb — I didn't know what sex was, even after I was grown and married. Children today are born knowing what sex is.

After I made "George, George," [her first recording success on the Okeh label] I had twenty-eight hits! One right after the other! That gave me a contract — so, when I got the contract, Clarence Williams wanted to play for me. He played one song for me [on Okeh]. Then my little brother, named Hersel, began playing for me. He was in Chicago, at the time, with George. Hersel made about 150 records with me.

I wrote a song called "Special Delivery Blues." My husband, Matt, had gone to the Army and he told me he was going to send me a special [special delivery package]. He never did send me a special — so, I wrote a "Special Tune," and Louis [Armstrong] helped me to make the song a hit. I had King Oliver playing with me and Sidney Bechet, too. That's one of my greatest songs!

I talk — I tell a story behind every song and why I wrote it. I wrote a song about Adam and Eve. I said, "When God made man, he loved man. He loved man so, he made him in his own image. He told man he would never have to work because this garden would furnish food for him. He said, 'You can eat of all the fruit, but don't touch the fruit tree in the middle of the garden.' While he was gone, Eve saw a snake near the tree. The snake said, 'Did I hear him say that if you eat that fruit you would die? Don't believe that — you won't die, but you'll be as wise as God.' Well, God came back. He called, 'Adam—Adam! Adam!' Adam said, 'Here I am Lord.'

'Where art thou?'

'I was naked, God, and I tried to hide myself.'

He said, 'Who told you you were naked?'

He said, 'Eve told me I was naked.'

He said, 'For your disobedience, you shall earn your bread from the sweat of your brow. For Eve's disobedience she will bear nine.' And so, he drove Adam and Eve out of the garden. And that's how we came to have the blues. Eve was the cause of it. Now, if Adam had been a man and did what God told him to do, we wouldn't have the blues. Since that day, everybody has had the blues."

I could sing the blues after the man I had started wanting liked everybody but me, so I sang the blues about the way the man treated me. When I sing the blues, I am talking about myself.

I'm a mighty tight woman and there's nothing I fear. When I'm singing to the audience I make them tell me how I'm doing. Say, "How am I doing?" Then, I tell the women something. I say, "Women be wise, keep your mouth shut and don't advertise your man." Because I declare I'm going to take him away with me. I know that from experience.

Not a bit [of difference between gospel and blues]. I play for a church right now. I have an adult choir and a junior choir. I played last Sunday. You don't see any place in the Bible that says you'll go to hell if you sing the blues. If you can sing gospel, you can sing the blues. The only thing that divides the blues from the gospel are the words. Where you say "Lord" in gospel, in blues you say "daddy."

Even now, they advertise the blues, but they won't advertise the gospel. When I go up there and sing the gospel, they will say, "Sippie, you ain't doing nothing but preaching." But they won't advertise it.

The music [gospel] uplifts me. I believe if I were dying and someone played [starts singing]:

Ain't you glad
You've got good religion.
So glad
I've got good religion.
So glad
I've got good religion.
I've got good religion.
Asleep in His arms, but not in the grave.

I believe I would stop dying to hear that song sung. I love to sing. 99

Interview by Christopher Brooks
Austin, 1985
Courtesy Barker Texas History Center

Esther Phillips was the show name for Esther Mae Jones (1935-1984). She was born in Galveston, but grew up in Houston and Los Angeles. As a young girl, she listened to the records of Dinah Washington, Sarah Vaughan, and Billie Holiday. They inspired her to begin singing. Esther moved to Los Angeles with her mother and sang in church choirs until she was discovered by Johnny Otis. Otis was so impressed by her singing that he presented her, at age thirteen, at his Barrelhouse Club in Watts. In 1949 he produced Esther's first hit record, "Double Crossing Blues" and took her on the road with his Johnny Otis Rhythm and Blues Revue.

Esther Phillips' success was marred by personal problems and addiction to alcohol and drugs. Her performing career was often interrupted by hospitalization and periods of recuperation, and she admitted that her addictions prevented her from achieving the acclaim she might have received. After her last hit record, "Release Me" in 1962, she was invited to appear on British television with the Beatles.

B.B. KING

(1925–   )

(*Above*) B.B. King
New Orleans Jazz and Heritage Festival, 1972
Photograph by Michael P. Smith

(*Left*) Esther Phillips
London, 1980
Photograph by Val Wilmer/Format

B.B. King in Houston
Houston, circa late 1950s
Photograph by Benny Joseph

n the white light of the stage at the Venetian Room, the blues of B.B. King are larger than life. The institution of contemporary blues stands in the spotlight of hard-won success. To be a blues singer, B.B. King says, is "like having to be black twice," once by birth and then again by the music he performs.

The next day in a suite at the Fairmont Hotel, B.B. King looks tired. Circulation problems in one of his legs have slowed him a little, but his face still radiates a dynamic energy, even behind sunglasses. He is wearing a yellow shirt with a tan suede sport coat. Next to him is a radio producer from Los Angeles, planning a series of syndicated programs called the B.B. King Blues Hour.

B.B. King stands up slowly and extends his hand, "It's a pleasure to meet you," and then motions me to a table off to the side. As he talks, the words seem tireless, spoken with a genuine sincerity. Being a blues legend begets a responsibility, which B.B. King accepts with dignity. He is as generous with conversation as time permits.

❝ Our booking agent was in Houston. Buffalo Booking Agency. Evelyn Johnson used to book us. We used to spend a lot of time there, but I never did live there. Evelyn Johnson is a remarkable lady, one of the great women of her time. I don't think she gets enough recognition, because to me she was one of the pioneers, she helped a lot of people. Not only in the blues field, but jazz, soul and rock as well.

She worked with Don Robey, who owned Peacock Records, the Eldorado Ballroom, and the Club Matinee. I never did record for Robey, but I almost did, if the Bihari Brothers didn't give me the money I wanted. Robey was just as fair as the rest of them that I ever worked for. I was very happy with the booking agency. I didn't see any difference between what they were doing and what all the other booking agencies and record companies were doing.

Evelyn booked us into white clubs, but that was not a lot of them, because at that time in the 1950s and 1960s I was not at the point what they call crossover. There were not a lot of white clubs that would have

me. The crossover for me didn't happen until the latter part of 1968, early '69. It started with the song "The Thrill Is Gone."

My producer at that time was Bill Szymczyck. He was just starting on the scene, and his ideas reminded me of the old Bihari days. He wouldn't interfere with you while you were recording. There's a big mistake a lot of people make; they try to coach a guy and record him without letting him be himself. Don't misunderstand me. I know this was a different time, and some of us need coaching. I'm one, but only to a point. Make sure I say the word right, make sure I don't break a verb or something, but the sound, allow me to express me as I am. Let me play as I do. Don't say, "Sound like this person," or, "Do you remember hearing the record so-and-so?" Well, that kind of attitude makes me not want to be on record because I like to be myself.

Bill Szymczyck was a young producer and he understood me, one of those types that bring out the best in you. They tell you when you're not close enough to the microphone, and says, "Would you please play that again?" With that kind of coaching, the artist is going to do his very best to be himself. That's the way it was the night we recorded "The Thrill Is Gone," one late night. I had Hugh McCracken on guitar, Herbie Lovell, on drums. The bass player was Gerald Jemmott, and a keyboard player [Paul Harris].

I told Bill, "I've got this tune I've been carrying around for about eight years. Every time I record I've never been able to do exactly what I want with it, and this rhythm section is cookin'! I think that I want to try this!" He said, "Fine, go ahead." And we went into "The Thrill Is Gone" and man, it was just like hand-in-glove. It clicked for me, but not for him. So we finished about two-thirty in the morning. I said, "All right, we're gonna knock off." Bill said, "Fine." He thought it was a good session. But I knew

B.B. King
Montreux International Jazz Festival, 1987
Photograph by Edouard Curchod

it was a good session. So I said, " 'The Thrill Is Gone' is that tune." All of my career, I'd never thought of Top 40, Top 20, like producers and record companies do. I think in terms of a good record. And I knew "The Thrill Is Gone" was a good record. So I said, "Man, think about it," but Bill wasn't too into it. I went to my apartment, we were in New York, and he went to his. About two hours later, I get a call and he's all excited, "Man, B! This is Bill Szymczyck!"

I said, "Yeah, Bill, what's happenin'?"

And he said, "Man, 'The Thrill Is Gone'. That's a song. That's a good record!"

"I agree."

"What do you think about adding some strings? I think strings will help it."

"Fine."

He said, "Man, that's a good pop record."

I didn't really think too much about it because I like strings. So he got a guy called Bert DeCoteaux to do the strings. About three or four days later I went down to hear the strings being put on and they did give it a different flavor from what began on record. I liked it, and when "The Thrill Is Gone" was released, my crossover began. It was soon after that the Rolling Stones invited me to tour with them.

My audience had started mixing before that, of course, but that really pushed it over the top. A lot of people heard me on that Rolling Stones tour that hadn't heard of me before. I remember once in Baltimore, one white lady came out, she had teenagers who seemed to be impressed with what I did. She came up to me and asked, "Have you made any records?" I'd made a whole lot of albums. I don't remember [how many] I had in 1969, but I have about sixty-seven albums now.

When I first went to Europe, my first country was England. I remember when my group and I was getting off the airplane. For years they had tried to get me to come over without a band, but I would never go, but this time it was good. I had my own group.

We came through customs and there were about 2,300 people waving American flags. Well, I knew that the Beatles had been over here and everybody was crazy about the Beatles at the time. So I was thinking. Well, I don't know what was running through my head, but I had no idea these people were welcoming us to England. And as we walked through customs, everybody started hollering, "B.B.! B.B.!" By God, I was frightened. I almost turned around! But my manager was with me and he said, "This is a greeting for you, B." And gosh, my hair was almost standing up on my head. I'd never seen anything like that before. Never ever! I was actually like a superstar to them, at least, that's the way they treated me.

The first press conference I ever had was in London, and everybody wanted to know what I think. It was sort of weird. What differences does it make? Who wants to know? Everybody was so polite. We must have had reporters from most of the countries in Europe and they had their photographers. My manager said, "A lot of this, whatever happens in London, will go throughout Europe." In other words, he was reminding me that if I didn't go over well there, it wouldn't go well anywhere else. That started it. Now I've been all around the world two or three times.

One of the keys to being able to stay out there so long is playing to the audience. I wouldn't play in the Venetian Room what I would play across the street where you got a lot of teenagers. They're more conservative downstairs, even the young people that come down there. I like to keep it where I'm still doing blues, still being B.B. King, but that's the other side that I try to portray, a type of blues that can be humorous in some of it, and have feeling in some of it, kind of in between, not just hard-core blues. But if I go across the street where you got a disco atmosphere, I'll do "Big Boss Man," "Into the Night," and songs like that.

Teen hop
Eldorado Ballroom, circa 1950s
Photograph by Benny Joseph

B.B. King wall mural
Third Ward, Houston, 1987
Photograph by Alan Govenar

In the Longhorn Ballroom they have such a mixed audience there, even when it's full of all blacks. There's a mix among them. So I need to play different things. I'd do "Three O'Clock in the Morning," but I wouldn't do that in the Venetian Room because I feel the audience couldn't relate to it as well. But "Sweet Little Angel" they can. I'm the quarterback. I figure out the plays.

What I do depends on the audience and who's on the bill with me. Anytime I got to follow a female, any female, talented or not talented, or a teenager or a kid, it's murder. Most of my things are upbeat, and I don't shake my tail like a lot of guys do. You've got to start thinking about David and Goliath, and I'm David. You got to think how to maneuver your way in. So I try to think of myself as a guy with long rubber arms that I reach around the audience and try to make them dance with me, swing with me.

If I'm following Millie Jackson, I try something that's going to draw attention from the audience. The guys, they don't want to see you at all, but the ladies might be a little relieved, but you still got to give them something that's going to take their mind off what just happened.

When I used to do the early rock shows, the original rock/soul shows, where the kids didn't know me or think much about me, you'd have people there that didn't want to be associated with the blues, I would do things like "Sweet Sixteen" because there was a line, "Treat me mean, but I'll keep loving you just the same." See, I was living that while I'm on the stage, "But one of these days you're going to give a lot of money just to hear somebody call my name." I used to belt it out, because that's the way I used to feel on stage sometimes because kids back in the early 1960s, they'd boo me. They heard Mom and Dad talk about me. So when they heard blues — these were black kids — they didn't want to be associated with that at all.

Black kids weren't exposed properly to blues. Blues never had the presentation of rock or soul music. I remember once when a guy introduced me in Chicago. I was on a show that mixed jazz and blues — Sarah Vaughan, Dizzy Gillespie — and some people in rock, Jackie Wilson, I believe. So the emcee got right to the point when introducing other people, "Ladies and gentlemen, here's Sarah Vaughan, the lady of jazz," but when he got to me, he said, "Ladies and gentlemen, you can bring out your turnip greens and blackeyed peas and cornbread because here's B.B. King. You can get your watermelon out and your chitlins." That didn't flatter me a bit, but I went on with one block that he had set in front of me. I thought, well, I'm already a blues player, and the way he made me sound is like being black twice [laughs]. I went on and worked as hard as I could, and afterwards I went over to the emcee and said, "You know, I like chitlins and cornbread and eat watermelon, but I know a lot of blues players that don't. So why do you have to introduce me like that? You didn't do it to the rest of them."

This is the way kids have been presented the blues, like it's something that should be thrown away and that you shouldn't be associated with it. They take a "that was then" attitude. Well, if you're black, probably so was your grandfather and your grandmother. They're still a part of you. I've tried to change things through my music, but I can't do it single-handed. You need a family.

A lot of blues purists don't really dig me. There's an argument there. You know, I'm almost in the jungle by myself because blues purists say I'm not playing true blues and jazz don't really claim me, nor soul. So I'm just there. **99**

EVELYN JOHNSON

66 James Mattis (of WDIA in Memphis) found Johnny Ace. He was one of the Beale Streeters. He had recorded him, had already made "My Song." But then it fell to our lot [Don Robey purchased the Duke label] to record him from then on. Four of his big things, well, everything Johnny did for us was big. "Pledging My Love" was his last and biggest. He was a real giant at the beginning, a real giant at the end, and in between was smooth sailing. He was a natural and yet all day long you could find boys who could out-sing him. But they didn't have that certain something that he had. He was a very unassuming person. He would pick up a lyric, not read it, just look at it, and say, "I don't want to do it." "Why, Johnny?" and he'd say, "I don't want to do it. It's too many words." [laughs] And he said very little. He played a lot, which is why he's dead. He was playing. He was no more aware of what happened and that was the worst sight I ever seen. I hope never to see it again.

It was Christmas of 1954 in the City Auditorium that has been demolished and replaced by a fabulous building now. He'd just come off stage, singing. It was in the dressing room, sitting on the dresser, surrounded by people, friends and musicians, and playing with a little twenty-two revolver with one bullet in it. He had the very bad habit of pointin' that gun. He was playing with that gun — all of this is hearsay but everybody says the same thing — Big Mama Thornton said to him, "You're always pointing that gun at somebody. I notice that you never point it at yourself." He pointed it at her and snapped, just constantly playing, and after a while he said, "I'm gonna point it at myself." And he put it to his temple. The bullet was there that time. And that little bullet made a small opening right there and his hair stood on end like horror movies. His brain oozed out of that little hole. He bled so immediately and so profusely until it was like a river. And it coagulated [snaps fingers] just that fast. He had

a little smirky grin on his face and his expression was, "What I'd say?" When you looked at his face, you'd see, "What I'd say?" It was horrible! He was twenty-six years old.

That was a very sad death, and another one was Joe Hinton, who, I assure you, had untold talent. But very few people knew that he had had a very rare skin cancer. As a matter of fact, they wouldn't accept him in the clinic because they said they couldn't treat it. They said he was the first Negro that had been there with this particular disease. So they sent him to Boston because they were working on some treatment there. Once it hits the bloodstream, it's some form of leukemia. Now the name of it is twelve syllables. I can't remember it.

(*Above*) Evelyn Johnson and Don Robey
Houston, circa 1960s
Photograph by Benny Joseph

As often as he could, Joe went into seclusion for about three months. That was when the reaction was keloid-looking things and they hit his face at that time. Now, he had lost his hair several times. But he would wear wigs. But when they hit his face, it was more than he could bear. It originally had been on his back and arms. He always wore long-sleeved shirts. I doubt that there were two people who had seen him other than the doctor and myself. His mother didn't even see him. But when they hit his face, he stayed inside with the shades drawn and wouldn't face anybody. So he was successful in kind of getting them off and he had gone to work. He did a club engagement, and as soon as the club engagement had ended, he had to rush on up to Boston. As fate would have it I was in New York when he was at his worst. So they called me and said he asked for me. I couldn't get any [transportation] out of New York until seven o'clock the next morning. They called me at four o'clock and told me, "Don't bother. He's gone." He held up all the way, his absolute decline didn't come until he went into the hospital. And he drove [himself] to the hospital. "Funny How Time Slips Away" was his biggest hit.

I booked Joe Hinton, B.B. King for nine years, Bobby Bland, Junior Parker, Johnny Ace, Willie Mae Thornton, Lloyd Price, Little Richard from scratch, Little Richard and the Tempo Toppers, one of the most terrific male groups that there ever was. I had the Buffalo Booking Agency. That was just my thing. It started with Gatemouth Brown. I finally gave it up because it was very unrewarding. It was a tough row to hoe. However, I can boast that I kept their heads above water until their time came. When I first met B.B. King, he couldn't move to the next town. I wasn't even interested in a contract on him. But we had nine nice years together. I remember them. I don't know who else remembers, but I do, and the United States Treasury, they remember very well.

There were certain clubs I couldn't go into, couldn't get a foot in the door. But the acts I booked worked more than any other show on the road. Maybe for less money, but they were working for two reasons, not only for their living, but for mental stability. This was their life. So the more that they did, the better off they were. And they worked more than anybody on the road. Every now and then we'd get a decent job here and there. We did the theaters. And that was the thing then, because at that time these people weren't going into these other clubs. Who was going to Tahoe? No black entertainer but Nat King Cole. You just didn't cross those lines and you stayed in your own back yard.

When we first went into the record business, the record companies didn't want us in. It was unheard of that a Negro group would come through this way. There were only one or two black owned recording companies who had floundered around with a record now and next year. But we went into like, here we are, a record company with a full catalog. This was unheard of. Now that stigma didn't last too long. Then we didn't grow to a competitive status except with product. So your product couldn't go any further than your internal situation could make it go. Then in later years we had the problem of the disc jockey; we couldn't get our records on the air. So you see, our problems came in stages.

So many of our records (Duke and Peacock) were ahead of the time. They're more popular now than they were then. This is the strength of our catalog. We've got a great "repeat catalog." All these dates they're bringing back now, rather than delete them. They are meeting the demand, and they are cutting the pirates off at the pass. 🙶

"BIG MAMA" THORNTON

Willie Mae Thornton left on a West Coast tour with Gatemouth Brown and eventually settled in the San Francisco Bay area. In the 1960s she relocated to Los Angeles, where she recorded for several different labels, including Sotoplay, Kent, Movin, Speed, and Galaxy.

Horst Lippmann invited Thornton to appear with the American Folk Blues Festival in 1965 on a tour throughout Europe. In England, Chris Strachwitz from Arhoolie records produced an album, "Big Mama in Europe," that presented Willie Mae Thornton with a Chicago back-up band of Buddy Guy, Walter Horton and Freddy Below.

In the late 1960s and '70s Thornton appeared often at blues festivals and concerts and released albums on Mercury, Pentagram, Buddah, Vanguard, and Crazy Cajun. Due to illness and excessive drinking, Willie Mae Thornton dropped from 350 Big Mama pounds to a skeletal ninety-five pounds. She died embittered at not receiving the popular and financial success she deserved. The covers of her songs, most notably "Hound Dog" by Elvis Presley and "Ball and Chain" by Janis Joplin, were never as good as the originals, but always outsold them: Willie Mae Thornton's versions of "Hound Dog" and "Ball and Chain" sold thousands, while the covers by Elvis Presley and Janis Joplin sold millions.

Willie Mae Thornton
Peacock promotion in Houston
Circa 1950s

Originally from Montgomery, Alabama, Willie Mae Thornton (1926-1984) came to Houston in 1948 on a long southern tour as part of The Hot Harlem Review. She liked the city so well that she decided to stay and try to further her career. A self-taught musician, singing and playing drums and harmonica, she had already developed her own style by the time she arrived in Houston. In a short time she got a job in Joe Fritz's band and was discovered at the Eldorado Ballroom by Don Robey, who signed her to a five-year exclusive contract and booked her into his club, The Bronze Peacock.

In early 1951, Robey took Willie Mae into ACA Studio with Joe Scott's Band to produce her first records. "Mischievous Boogie" and "Partnership Blues." These were followed by "Let Your Tears Fall, Baby," which became successful enough that Robey had Evelyn Johnson book her on the road with B.B. King and Bill Harvey.

Johnny Otis, on tour in 1952 with his band in Houston, negotiated a contract with Don Robey whereby he would record his band and vocalists in Los Angeles and send the masters to Houston for pressing on Robey's Peacock label. Included in this deal was Willie Mae Thornton as vocalist. Later that year Thornton recorded eight sides with the Johnny Otis band, including "Rock A Bye Baby" and "Hound Dog," which Robey did not release until 1953.

With the chart success of "Hound Dog" Robey added Willie Mae Thornton to his blues package show that included Bobby Bland, Junior Parker, and Johnny Ace.

In 1954, after the death of Johnny Ace, Thornton joined the Johnny Otis Band and toured with them until 1955, after which she returned to Houston to reunite with Bill Harvey. She recorded three sides with Harvey and his band, featuring guitarist Roy Gaines.

In 1956, after her contract with Don Robey expired,

Gatemouth Brown
Houston, circa 1950s
Photograph by Benny Joseph

CLARENCE "GATEMOUTH" BROWN

(1924-   )

n his room at the Hilton Hotel, Gatemouth Brown is with his family: Yvonne, his wife of eight years, and their daughter, Renee. Yvonne is from Baton Rouge, where she recalls she didn't know much about the blues until she heard Gatemouth in New Orleans and later met him by chance. Yvonne is warm and friendly, Renee is watching Saturday morning kid shows, and Gatemouth is uneasy. My presence seems to make him anxious, though he tries to be nonchalant. He leans back against the side of the full-length mirror across from the bed and says, "The last man that interviewed me wrote a book. He called me at home and asked me questions for an hour and a half. And then when the book came out I saw him in New York and he asked me if I wanted to buy a copy. I don't do interviews any more for books. I'm writing my own book."

For a sixty-three-year-old man, Gatemouth Brown has a lifestyle that belies his age. He wears a bright floral shirt and blue jeans, but his teeth are decayed and when he smiles the blues beams forth. He puffs on a tobacco pipe and the space in front of him fills with smoke.

When I show him Benny Joseph's Duke/Peacock photographs, Gatemouth grows more irritable. "Man, these are worth a million dollars," he says as he turns his head away. "What am I going to get out of this interview?" His tone is surly and muttering, "Am I going to get a royalty?" Then he lowers his face and says nothing. The silence is deadening until he unexpectedly looks up and declares, "I feel like I've been crushed in a vice of bullshit. Call me tomorrow, maybe I'll feel like talking then. I'm not mad at you. It's just the way the system works."

I looked at Gatemouth with a kind of disbelief, shaking my head and smiling. I left the room quietly, saying, "Hope you feel better. I'll call you tomorrow. Maybe we can get together. I'll bring my daughter. She's the same age as Renee."

Later that night during a long conversation with Jim Bateman, Gatemouth's manager and time-worn friend, the source of the morning's conflict became perfectly clear. The photographs of the 1950s Houston scene had an intensity that conjured up the past with an unforeseen power. Those were the years of Gatemouth's youth and national success as one of the hottest rhythm and blues sounds, but today there is little to show for it. The recordings have been bootlegged and reissued, and the publishing rights were innocently signed away to Don Robey, who often took or shared the authorship with an alias, Deadric Malone.

Gatemouth Brown's early recordings on Robey's Peacock label are classics. The electric guitar sound is modern: quick single string runs with a driving rhythm backed by tenor saxophone and trumpet. On some of the early sessions the horn section is enlarged to give a big band sound with swing era solos in a call and response pattern with the progressions of the electric guitar.

At present there are three important reissues of Gatemouth's earliest recordings, one on Rounder in the United States and two on Ace in Britain. His first sessions appear on Ace and appropriately mark the beginning of Ace Records' multi-album reissue series of the Peacock and Duke catalogues owned by Don Robey. Together these reissues establish Gatemouth's stature in the history of rhythm and blues, but bring few monetary benefits. The licenses are bought directly from the present owners of the original contracts in which Gatemouth signed away virtually all the residual rights to his music. There is, however, some contention over the assignment of royalties, and in time, Jim Bateman hopes to help secure for Gatemouth some of the compensation to which he is rightfully entitled.

On the next day Gatemouth was more relaxed. Jim Bateman had called and said that I was all right. I brought my daughter, Breea, and she and Renee went swimming and played together. Gatemouth and I sat by the side of the pool; Yvonne joined us and ordered coffee. For the next hour Gatemouth recalled his life with a sincere tone, mocking his early inexperience with hoarse laughter, reminiscing about the past with a looseness that did not belie his story's coherence.

Gatemouth Brown was born April 18, 1924, in Vinton, Louisiana, where he lived for only three weeks. Then his family moved to Orange, Texas. His early musical influences were as diverse as the interests of his father, Clarence Brown Sr., who worked as an engineer for the Southern Pacific Railroad and played in a string band on weekends. He played fiddle, banjo, mandolin, and guitar at house parties, dances, and fish fries, performing in the songster tradition the popular country blues, zydeco, and fiddle tunes of the day.

At age ten Gatemouth began playing the fiddle under the tutelage of his father, though he was also interested in the instruments played by his brothers. Bobby was a drummer and

Gatemouth Brown
New Orleans Jazz and Heritage Festival
Courtesy Hans Kramer

James 'Widemouth' Brown was a respected blues guitarist and vocalist. As a teenager in Orange, Gatemouth worked as a drummer with Howard Spencer and his Gay Swingsters and later went on the road with William M. Bimbo and His Brownskin Models. In a 1979 interview with Ray Topping, he recalled, "I was about 16 or 17. I went all the way to Norfolk, Virginia. I worked at the Eldorado Club on Church Street in Norfolk. I played drums in a little house band until the outbreak of World War II."

Gatemouth served during the war, and after his discharge returned to Texas and joined Hort Hudge's 23-piece orchestra at the Keyhole Club in San Antonio. After hearing of the success of T-Bone Walker at Don Robey's Bronze Peacock, Gatemouth began playing electric guitar in a style that challenged Walker's virtuosic abilities. His first encounter with T-Bone Walker was in Houston in the mid-1940s. He remembers the experience vividly.

"I hitchhiked to Houston to see him and went into this club called the Bronze Peacock. He was the hottest stuff on guitar in Texas, but he was sick with a stomach ulcer and he laid his guitar down on the stage and walked off to his dressing room. I got up and went up to the stage. No one knew I was a guitar player, but I just picked up T-Bone's guitar and started to play, inventing a little boogie — 'My name is Gatemouth Brown. I just got in town. If you don't like my style, I won't hang around.' Well, they loved it, but T-Bone didn't. He came back out on stage and snatched away his guitar and told me that I was in big trouble if I ever fooled with his guitar again."

Don Robey, the owner of the Bronze Peacock, intervened, realizing Gatemouth Brown's raw abilities to play in the style of T-Bone Walker, who by that time was quite successful. Robey bought Gatemouth a new Gibson L5 guitar and some new tuxedos from a custom tailor on Dowling Street. Later he flew Gatemouth out to Los Angeles to sign a recording contract with Aladdin Records. In November 1947 four sides were recorded, including "Gatemouth Boogie" and "Guitar in My Hands." However, Robey was dissatisfied with the timetable and the promotion the records received and decided not to renew his contract after the first year.

Convinced that Gatemouth Brown could be a big hit, Don Robey started Peacock Records, named after his club, the Bronze Peacock. Gatemouth Brown's recordings for Peacock have an undeniable energy. His first sessions included at least three slow blues, the rarest of which, "Ditch Diggin' Daddy," is still unavailable. His first song to achieve regional success was the uptempo "Mary Is Fine." This motivated Robey to switch his recording operations to the A.C.A. studios in Houston. Even then, as Gatemouth recalled in a 1983 interview with Dick Shurman, the conditions were much different from today's.

"We had maybe one mike for the big band. That's when a man walked out and soloed. We had one mike for me to sing. They would put a mike out in front of my amp...If everybody played and tried not to overplay then everybody could be heard."

From 1949 to the mid-1950s Gatemouth worked regularly and cut standard four-song sessions. The Ace and Rounder reissues follow his development as rhythm and blues stylist and show the importance of studio arrangements. The horn charts were put together by Bill Harvey, Joe Scott, and Plummer Davis, who also contributed heavily to the shaping of the overall sound. Many of the individual session players, however, were selected by Gatemouth and included two hometown friends, George Alexander on trumpet and Wilmer Shakesliner on alto and tenor saxophone.

Gatemouth's music from the Peacock period combines slow blues, like his perennial "I've Been Mistreated," with uptempo guitar instrumentals, like "Ain't That Dandy," which he still uses as a set opener and re-did for his "One More Mile" album on the Rounder label. In addition, the early recordings included jump blues like "Okie Dokie Stomp," the influential "Boogie Rambler," reflective blues ballads like "Sad Hour," "Depression Blues," and "Mercy on Me," and the intense vocal shuffle, "Midnight Hour." Together, these recordings are considered some of Gatemouth Brown's best, though it is clear from talking to Gatemouth that he has worked since then to develop a new sound that brings together his regional influences into what he calls a "true American music."

-rence Gatemouth Brown His Vocals & Guitar

Recording exclusively for
Peacock Records, Inc.
4104 Lyons Ave.
Houston 10, Texas

Peacock promotional photograph
Courtesy Hans Kramer

““ I don't think that nobody alive put more into Peacock records than I. I suffered the growing pain. I went in there as a young child. It was an adventure to me. I didn't think about money. I put trust in people. That's why today it's hard for me to trust anybody, and yet, I have to trust somebody. But who is this somebody? Sometimes it's the most wonderful people who do you wrong.

Robey was a gambler. The world knows that, but he had a friend in San Antonio who I started dealing with before I met Robey. He did some gambling, but it wasn't the kind of thing Robey was into. He was more forceful. He got it all at once or nothing at all. That's the kind of man he was. I'm grateful for one thing: everything that happened to me wrongfully worked out rightfully in the future. I'm doing real well today, thanks to him. For years, there was no one doing anything.

The problem with Robey was that he had a fictitious name, D. Malone, Deadric Malone, that claimed authorship to things he didn't write. It was his way to get the royalties. As time went by it was clear my feelings for him deteriorated. I started out feeling like he was a father of mine. I respected him that much, and after I got in there, I considered Evelyn Johnson a mother figure of mine in business, meaning I would trust these people with my life, because I figured they would never do me wrong. Poor Evelyn, I feel sorry for her. She was caught up in the Robey web and couldn't get out of it. Me, I walked out of it.

I left in the early '60s. I walked into his office and looked him right in the eye and said, "Look, Mr. Robey, I'm splittin'. Don't try to do anything to me." I went to free-lancing around to different companies. For years I couldn't find a company. He had it so no one would record me. I don't know how many sides I

Peacock promotional photograph
Courtesy Hans Kramer

get a chance to stop in the twilight zone, a rest period, but the ultimate part of this trip is the nine giant steps. You got to go at supersonic speed and not many can get there. What I'm talking about is my idea of music. You listen to all of my records from the time I started to today. I don't go back and try to sound like I did ten years ago. I may take one of those tunes, but when it comes out to be heard again, it's another piece of music. I'm still growing. I won't stay in my place. I've heard this all my life. "Stay in your place." Well, where the hell is my place? I'm talking now about the prejudice in my life. You know what makes a good colored man? What is it? Stay in your place. My ideas go beyond music. I have the greatest love for the human race any man can ever have, but what burns me is to see one, just one put himself up on a pedestal in front of a crowd of five thousand and say that he's good and I'm not.

My music is explanatory. I don't have a college education, but I've got sense. Texas is where I grew up, where I learned to play white country music, French music, and blues. The blues depends on what you're feeling, but it's also supposed to be an explanation. How can I tell you what I'm doing if I can't explain it? You heard what I did, but can you ever truly know if I don't tell you? Anything I do is an explanation, otherwise it's a mystery. The idea is to make people feel better when they leave than when they come in. I try to record and create the positive ideas for the people around me, black and white. I don't want to make my audience feel guilty. Nobody owes me anything. But I'm a threat because I'm trying to tell the truth. **99**

recorded for Don Robey. A lot were never issued and a lot got lost in the shuffle. Robey was a cold man. He sold the company and cut music away from his life. Then one night awhile later, Evelyn [Johnson] told me, he was up watching TV and got up, turned the set off, and dropped dead on the spot. I don't know how he had died, but he did. He turned the music off in his life.

I've been together with Jim Bateman since 1976. We've gone through so many ordeals that we made it. He's the cause of me getting some royalties today on some of my past records.

I've done three albums with Rounder. They're all right. I don't really like record companies. Where I see my music going is where the modern blues player has never been able to go, to a vortex on the other side of Mars, beyond that. In order to get there, you have to suspend the G-force. Then if you do that, you might

Teddy Reynolds (piano) and Frank Robinson (drums)
Clarence Green recording session
Houston, 1987
Photograph by Alan Govenar

TEDDY REYNOLDS
(1932–   )

❝ I started to listen to people like Amos Milburn and Charles Brown. I loved their style of playing, and I just started playing by ear at first. Everybody said I sounded good. Then I had Joe Scott as a music teacher, and from there I started working in a studio for Mr. Don Robey. Joe Scott was the arranger, and he started teaching me chord structures and different things. I played behind a whole bunch of Peacock artists, Joe Hinton, Big Mama Thornton, Gatemouth Brown, all of them, but Joe Scott was the one that started me playing. I'm from Houston. I'm fixty-six, and I started working in the studio at sixteen, about 1948.

Don Robey was a wonderful man. He was good to the musicians. He loved us all. Once he wanted something done he wanted it that way and that was it. My close friend, Joe Medwick, who wrote the songs for Bobby Bland, we'd get together. I'd be on piano, he'd come get me and say, "Hey, Teddy, I got some songs I want to put on tape. Let's go over to Mr. Robey. So we'd catch the bus and go over to Erasmus and Lyons Street. Joe would hum the melody. He'd say, "Teddy, go like this here," and I'd sit at the piano and I'd play the melody along with him and he start putting the words to the song. From the arrangements he hummed to me I took it on from there and put the songs on tape. Next we hear them, it'd be Bobby Bland singing them or Junior Parker.

The biggest sessions were Bobby's sessions. They were beautiful. That was the thrill of my life to be able to put these patterns that Joe Scott taught me behind Bobby Bland. Joe would put the sheet music, the chord structures, in front of me and tell me, "Teddy, put your own feeling into these chords." And I would play my own feeling, something from the heart. The blues is everything in my life, you know. By me having all these artists at my piano, I put all these styles together and that's why I can change to any pattern you want. That's a gifted thing. You play the blues from your heart, you know that. I've been playing for more than forty years.

BOBBY BLAND

Bobby Bland
Peacock promotion, circa late 1950s
Courtesy Hans Kramer

Junior Parker
Houston, circa late 1950s
Photograph by Benny Joseph

I went on the road with Bobby Bland, from 1957 to 1959. During that time we cut "Drivin' Wheel" and "Two Steps From the Blues," and "I Pity the Fool." Oh, there were so many during that time. Bobby was a very hot artist. Still is.

Mr. Robey had a package with Bobby Bland, Junior Parker, TNT Braggs and Miss Eloise. One of the greatest shows you've ever seen. It was just beautiful, and the musicians were just great. Hamp Simmons on bass, Wayne Bennett on guitar, Joe Scott on trumpet, Plummer Davis on trombone, Melvin Jackson on trumpet. Jabo [Starks] played drums and I was on piano, and we had L.A. Hill, the boy who left home with me, on tenor. We had about three tenor players. We had such a big sound.

We'd all worked in the studio together; we'd been exposed to discipline. When you go into the studio, you have a creative mind. You create the lyrics like the singer is singing, and music is made to fit what he sings.

When an idea came to you, Don Robey would never get in the way because he knew that when you'd straighten it out, it would fit those lyrics. Sometimes he'd look through the mirror in the studio, through the big glass mirror and you'd see him with a big grin on his face. Yes, I know the old man was very satisfied. Joe [Scott] would get the musicians for the sound, that bunch of musicians for that sound. It would all blend in for the blues. Each musician played the blues, and though each might play it different ways, it was still the blues. Miss Evelyn Johnson was the producer, and we had Robert Evans, who played tenor and alto, and was also the engineer, But sometimes Joe [Scott] would engineer. He would tell the engineer what to bring up, what to bring down. He played trumpet, French horn, any brass. And he played a lot of piano, and that's where I got a lot of my knowledge at. Joe Scott.

We recorded records in the studio and Mr. Robey pressed them in the back of the studio building. He had his own pressing company and everything. We just struck a groove and whatever pattern fit what the artist was singing, we'd go on and cut. Next thing you know the record was out there.

The only big thing I did live was with Bobby Bland and B.B. King together. That was a live thing in L.A. It was the first time Bobby and B.B. were together. I did the LP with them. I think it was in '72 or '73. That was great. I really loved that. James Brown and all of them were there at the session at Sunset Studios. It was live and it was wonderful.

I also played with Gatemouth Brown, Nappy Brown, Percy Mayfield, Junior Parker. Junior liked to kid all the time, something like Johnny Ace. Junior played wonderful harmonica, and sang, man. I'll never forget when we did "Drivin' Wheel." It was a ball. Junior kidded with all the musicians, joked with them, tell them about their hair and all different stuff. But he got serious when it got down to business.

We worked hard in the studio, but on weekends we'd play in the clubs: Shady's Playhouse on Sampson and Simmons Street, Club Matinee. And people like Albert Collins, Johnny Copeland, they were youngsters, but they'd come around with their guitars. They didn't have electric guitars, and they'd come around and watch some of the professional guys and learn from them, and the other guitar players were glad to help them out. Now, today they're steppin' out with it. **99**

LESTER WILLIAMS
(1920–   )

66 I've been singing all my life — elementary school, high school, church choirs. I was born in Groveton, Texas, in 1920. As a boy we moved to Houston, and I remember hearing those records by Blind Lemon Jefferson and Lonnie Johnson.

After the war I heard T-Bone Walker and liked that guitar sound. His phrasing and voicing was fantastic. He was my inspiration. I said to myself, "I could learn how to play guitar and pull in some of that money that T-Bone made." I had been singing with Ike Smalley's band at the Eldorado Ballroom, and I quit. I applied to the New England Conservatory of Music in Boston and I went up there. Blues guitar was not in vogue, so I studied piano and voice. Then when I came back to Houston, I got myself a guitar and studied diligently for six or seven months. I had these songs in my head and I made a couple of tapes of "Winter Time Blues." Before long I cut it as a record with a band I put together and it took off. That was in 1949 on the Macy's label, produced by Steve Poncio. All of a sudden everyone wanted to hear Lester Williams play blues. Later, in the early 1950s I went [to] Art Rupe's Specialty label, where I cut "I Can't Lose with the Stuff I Use," "Trying to Forget," "Lost Gal," and "If You Knew How Much I Love You."

It was my interest at that time to prove that a blues musician could have academic training and didn't have to be someone sitting on a stump. I didn't graduate from the New England Conservatory, but I did get my fundamental training there. And when I got home to Houston I worked on my guitar and applied those principles. I started playing at Don Robey's Bronze Peacock. And I later cut a session for Robey on the Duke label in 1954, "Let's Do It" and "Crazy 'Bout You Baby". But I never did sign a contract with him, though his (Buffalo Booking) agency got me several different touring dates.

For me the blues is a way of telling a beautiful life-like story. It's like country music, about what someone has lived and knew. When I wrote "Winter Time

Blues" my wife and daughter had gone to Los Angeles for the summer and I was going to Texas Southern University. Fall was coming and the house became so lonely. I wrote asking her to come home, and this thought came into my head, "I'm walking down a track, winter time is coming and my baby has gone away. Ain't nobody's told me, but I believe she's gone to stay. I sure do get lonesome here by myself, but I guess I'll have to take it, can't use nobody else." I was a family man and those were true lyrics. The neighbors were talking. "They don't think I can make it. That's what the neighbors said. Winter without your baby, you might as well be dead."

Blues can be just as sophisticated as any other form of music. I'm kind of an oddball entertainer. I don't drink or smoke. I don't fool with dope. I love my family, my wife, children, grandchildren. I'm a different kind of blues singer. 99

Lester Williams
Houston Informer advertisement
January 16, 1954
Courtesy Dallas Blues Society

QUEEN OF HITS

Macy's Recordings

5000-B
(ACA-1225)

Vocal by
Lester Williams

WINTERTIME BLUES
(Lester Williams)

LESTER WILLIAMS

2631 OAKCLIFF ST., HOUSTON, TEXAS

WHISPERING PINES NIGHT CLUB
8002 Hirsch Road
Trinity Gardens

For Your Dancing Pleasure

COME TO THE

WHISPERING PINES

HOUSTON'S FAMOUS DANCE HOUSE
DANCING EVERY SAT. & SUN. 9 P. M. TILL 1 A. M.

Featuring

LESTER WILLIAMS
And His
ORCHESTRA

SPECIALIZING IN CREOLE DISHES
FINE FOODS
FOR CLUBS-DANCES-PARTIES AND BANQUET ENGAGEMENTS
CALL MY-9391 or OR-9197
SERVING BEERS AND SET UPS
DANNY GUERRA, Owner

111

Johnny Brown
Houston, circa early 1960s
Photograph by Benny Joseph

JOHNNY BROWN

(1928–)

66 My father was a musician. He was a blues player, his name was Clarence Brown. He played the ol' natural blues, say like the Lightnin' Hopkins-type country blues, though he did play that bottleneck style. I tried it in my early years. To be honest with you I don't play it any more, but it wouldn't be a problem for me to play. It's a certain way you tune your guitar. You tune your guitar cross, natural. You tune it in the key of E natural and that leaves it open. Say, you take a person that doesn't know the guitar that well, they use what you call a clamp. They can move that clamp up and down the board, just like positions, and still get that same thing goin' on.

My name is John Reilly Brown. My professional name is Johnny Brown. I was born in Choctaw County, Mississippi. My father was blind and we traveled around a lot. I was very young then. He worked at the railroad before he lost his sight, and [they gave] him this pass where he could travel around on the railroad for either half-price or no ticket. My father was shot with buckshot and then we traveled from place to place. I was playin' guitar and tambourine. We played little clubs. Sometimes we played street corners. He never did any recording.

Let me tell you a little story. Okay? We used to play these things around Natchez, Mississippi, what they'd call the Pilgrimage Fair. They have these old colonial homes, this is in the first part of the year, like April, May, and we used to play around those different homes for the tourists coming around. We'd play on the street and collect that money. And one time there was a producer from Hollywood that came there. This is a true story. My father had a dog that played guitar. Really, he [my father] would hold the guitar on his knee and he'd make the chords and the dog would sit down and paw the strings with his paws. My father had a couple of little tunes he would sing and the dog would paw the strings. So this producer came by and saw this. It was in the early '40s and we got a letter from him to come to Charlottesville, Virginia. They were shootin' a movie and we had a little short in the movie, *Virginia,* with Sterling Hayden, Madelyne Carrol, and I think Marie Wilson.

In 1946 I moved to Houston with my father. It was there that I met up with Amos Milburn and the Chickenshackers. I toured with them for a while and then went into the service, the Army, from 1950 until 1953. Then I went back with Amos. Amos was gay, but easy to get along with. He recorded "Chickenshack Boogie," "Took a Long Time, Baby," "Operation Blues," "Two Steps From the Blues."

During the late '50s I started working with Peacock Records and the Buffalo Booking Agency. I went on the road with Bobby Bland and Junior Parker during the years of "Wishing Well," "Further on Up the Road," "Cry, Cry, Cry."

I recorded with Peacock during 1959. Most of the recordings I did with Peacock were with Bobby Bland, Junior Parker, and for myself. I did some tunes, "Two Steps From the Blues," "What Can I Do," "Screaming Please," "Suspense," "Snake Hips," "Red Pepper in Pie" [with Don Wilkerson]. Some of them weren't released.

I worked as a session musician just about every day, from 1959 through part of the '60s. And during the time I was workin' in the studio I was also travelin' at the same time, mostly with Bobby Bland, Junior Parker, Buddy Ace, Joe Hinton. They had a package. We'd travel, then come back in and record, and then go back out. I played lead guitar.

Workin' with Don Robey I can't say was all that good, but I can't say it was all bad. We did some good sessions. But as far as the touring part, it was existence, but there was no big money in it. That was one of the problems. He was hard-nosed, but he was fair in his way. But he was a hard man to get that money from. As far as the studio part, he wasn't really in the sessions that much. He had this A&R man, Joe Scott, and to me he was a beautiful person to work with.

Robey had a certain sound that he wanted from particular people. Say for instance, Bobby, Junior Parker, he had a particular sound he wanted from them, but I think more, he was just trying to get a good record out. Bobby was his most successful artist. Then Junior Parker. I played on "Look on Yonder Wall," "Annie Get Your YoYo," and "Next Time You See Me." Clarence Holloman worked on that, too.

Well, I came back to Houston in '63 off a tour, and decided to leave Peacock. I just played local and started workin' a day job, the first was for a delivery service, workin' for a uniform company. Did that for about three years and then I became a shipping/receiving clerk for Memorial Baptist Hospital for about five years. Then I left that and was self-employed for a while, had a dump truck. Now, I work for MKI as a forklift operator. I still play. I got a four-piece band — guitar, keyboards, bass, and drums. I'm playin' the blues, doing some writin', too. But I haven't done any recording since the 1960s.

Charlie Christian was a big influence on my guitar playing. I never met him, but I remember his playing. This goes back to the time of my father, and there was a little cafe that had those records on the jukebox. But I like a variety of music. I play the basic sound I've always played. I do a little jazz, blues, C&W, we do it all. But the blues always kicks it off. What you call the real gut, man, straight-out gut. We do "Every Day I Have the Blues," some of Lowell Fulson's tunes, like "So Long," and maybe "Next Time You See Me," "Look on Yonder Wall." I do Bobby's songs, but I don't do the vocalizin'.

Now, I'm doing the things I've wanted to do, that I've always wanted to do with my instrument. The guitar that I'm playing now has these attachments, modules that you can plug in to get different sounds. But it still has the natural tone. **99**

CLARENCE GREEN
(1937–   )

66 My mother worked for a white lady who taught her how to play guitar. She always had a guitar around the house. My brother, Cal, and I — Cal was the guitar player for Hank Ballard and the Midnighters — but when we were little boys we used to make guitars out of cigar boxes and little sticks stretched with screen wire that was on the frame of a window. And by my mother having her guitar around we would slip in and pick it up. She finally let us have one with two or three strings on it and we would bang, bang. My first guitar cost twelve dollars. My mother picked it up from town for me. It was a Stella. I started to strum on it in church, and it happened one night that I could play. Mama said, "Wait until we get home." And I picked up the guitar and showed her I could play. I was about ten years old. I've been playing ever since. I'm fifty-one; my brother is fifty. We're a year apart.

First I learned how to play hillbilly. It was real popular. There weren't any black stations to hear much else. My mother worked for a disc jockey and he found out that she had two sons that played guitar. We used to play church music on the radio. My brother broke away and went out first, and I came out after him. That's when we were swinging into the blues.

A young man found out that we lived over in Frenchtown [in Houston's Fifth Ward]. I was working at the Rice Hotel and decided to go to play an engagement at another place. We just had one guitar and a rub board. We called ourselves Blues for Two and then we added drums and another guitar. We played big halls and clubs, different functions. But after a while we busted up. I kept playing and soon joined a group with Elmore Nixon and Dave Fisher at a club called the Silver Spur. And I left from there to play with Ted Taylor. He came through one night and he needed a bass player. You know how sometimes guys get in bad shape and they want you to hold their instruments for a few dollars? He left his instrument with me and I said, "I'm gonna take advantage of

Clarence Green
Houston, circa 1960s
Courtesy Clarence Green

this." Most guitar players can play bass, and that's what I ended up doing with Ted Taylor. Later, I formed my own band, the Cobras.

I had the experience of working some with Chuck Berry. I went on the road with him and did a few engagements in Louisiana. And one night Fats Domino came in, and Mr. Berry's nephew, who was a guitar player, took sick, and I got to play on stage with Fats Domino. From artist to artist that I met, I got more knowledge about my box.

In the early 1960s I worked with Don Robey, in the studio, more or less in the background. I was the rhythm guitar player on sessions behind Bobby Blue Bland, Little Junior Parker, Joe Hinton, and so many artists I can't remember. I had one record myself, and had more in the hole that were never released. "Welfare Blues" was one of the tunes and "Keep on Workin' Baby" was another. Some of the other ones I can't recall. The only one that was released was "Keep on Workin' Baby" and this other tune I can't think of the name of it. It's been quite a while. It was an experience for me. I really enjoyed it. I learned things about recording and mixing and what to listen for. It was a great experience. It was very inspiring for me. But working for Robey was another thing. I won't go into that too much [laughs]. He was a cold man. He just got mad at me one time, because I cut a song not exactly as he wanted. It was a tune that Roy

Head had cut and I was supposed to have done the thing over and I didn't. I did one of my tunes, so boom, it shot me out of the saddle with Robey. But other than that everything was straight. I didn't have any problems with him.

My brother, Cal, worked on one session with me at Robey's studio. We did about six numbers and he played on those. Mr. Clarence Holloman couldn't make it. He was a guitar player that Don Robey used for recording. He never did any recording that was released under his name. He was a studio guitarist.

I never went out on the road too much. I did five or six engagements with Percy Mayfield, Z.Z. Hill, Little Richard, Sonny Boy Williamson, Johnny Nash. I think I was influenced by B.B. King, Gatemouth Brown, and also Barney Kessel, the jazz guitarist. I've done jazz things, sentimental things, whatever it took to satisfy the public. That's what I got off into. Now the blues is becoming more popular. So I jumped into that.

I think blues is taking off. People at first didn't understand the blues. A lot of people don't realize that the blues is not just playing music. You might get up one morning and you're late to work. You jump in your car and that rascal don't want to start up. You know how you just get frustrated and angry. And you got the blues! People had the blues all along, but didn't know it. They thought it was just music. You're disturbed because your ol' lady done burnt up the bread or you forgot something that you left at home and you got the blues. Sometimes you can't do nothing about it so you just start humming or moaning or whatever. You might be like a man that's got a problem and he takes a drink. He's out for a while and gets back up when he's sober. The blues works on you the same way. You just keep playing the blues and you get a release for a while. Next thing you know, you singing more blues. The problems are always around, and it don't take much for you to have blues now. **99**

BIG WALTER PRICE

(1914–   )

66 I go by Big Walter, the Thunderbird. No one ever calls me Big Walter Price. I was born in Gonzales, but I was raised in San Antonio, and I've been in Houston off and on since 1956. At that particular time I had a chance to get with a bigger record company. I started off with TNT, that's Texas and North Town. So after talking with Mr. Don Robey, he told me that if I got my release from TNT he would record me. TNT wasn't really too interested in blues anyway; they more or less recorded Spanish people. So that was a pretty big step for me, as far as rhythm and blues was concerned, because they didn't have rhythm and blues anyway. And they just wanted to get me started. I was recommended by the man they call Red River Dave. Red River Dave had a radio show on WOAI, Channel 4, out of San Antonio. So when I got on Channel 4, I got to record for TNT and TNT recommended me to Peacock.

Rightfully, I'm seventy. There is a three-year difference from my birth certificate. So we're talking about sixty-seven. It's not really true. But we have to go by what we know.

There was only one blues player in San Antonio when I was there and he moved out. That was Gatemouth Brown. He used to room with my auntie. So he was a roomer. He was little ahead of me as far as Peacock was concerned. I started as a spiritual singer, The Lord of Wonders out of Michigan, and one day I was just hummin' a song when a friend of mine was workin' with me on Texas-Pacific railway says, "As good a voice as you got you should sing blues."

I says, "You got to be kiddin'."

He says, "Try it anyway."

Well, he kept nagging me about it for a month and a half. He says, "If you don't get head on and start singing' the blues. Your voice is beautiful."

I says, "I singin' spirituals now."

And he says, "I'm not knockin' it, but I don't think you'll be too good in that field. You let somebody else stay in that field like Sam Cooke. So I kind of laughed it off. I didn't think much about it, and then one day it kind of dawned on me. I'll try it. So they had a club in Fort Worth called the Zanzibar, and I came in one afternoon and I asked the lady, "Can I sing?"

And she says, "Yes."

I says, "Can I sit in?"

And they said, "No."

So, I went back and told her what they said and she said, "You tell them that if they don't let you sit in, they don't have a job." What that lady didn't realize was that I played in one key and that was in C, and I played all night in C. [laughs] I got the job.

I have had the question asked many times [how Texas piano is different from other styles], but it's really hard to explain. You need to have a music expert or lover, an arranger to answer that question for you. But as far as me, I couldn't answer that. You have to have feeling as well as sound because if you don't feel what you're doing there's no point in foolin' with it because you're not going to be able to get it over to the public if you don't feel it. You can't get it over to them. This is what I am saying. Of course, somebody else might have a different version of it.

The blues really tells a story, the past as well as the future. It depends what you got your mind on. Playing the blues will kind of prevent you from doing things. Well, that's fine, but if blues is motivating you to do other things, then you ought to do something else.

The only change in the blues I play today that I ease in differently than when I started is the beat. The beat is different on certain songs, but some songs that beat don't work regardless of how you do it. Blues is just blues, but the precious Lord may step the tempo up, and put a different beat to it.

Louis Armstrong said there wasn't any difference between blues and jazz. When you're listening to jazz, you are listening to blues. You might have to slow it down or back it up, you still got it. The only little change in it is in the tempo. I just have to give it to you the way he gave it to me. I had a talk with him several years ago when he was down here and several people asked him that question, but when I got my

own personal chance, he told me that they were
the same.

I perform myself and also with my own unit. That's
how I made my European tour. I went over by myself.
I got paid thirty-eight dates. Thirty-seven were
standing ovations. I don't know what happened to the

Big Walter Price
Houston, circa 1950s
Courtesy Walter Price

other one. The European audience is great. The European people, fans, great. They accept blues more than they do in the U.S.A. You'd have to talk to a European about that. They have records on blues artists we don't even have in the United States. Anything anybody ever did before, ninety-eight percent, they have it. I met one German piano player who had won all of the high awards, and I asked why he doesn't play more and a high official related to me, "Because he wasn't black." As far as playing piano, any type of instrument, they walk over you like hot water, but they can't get the credit because they're not black.

Most of the places I played in Europe, there wasn't even standing room and the most exciting crowd that I had, everyone was there on bicycles. Man, I never seen so many bicycles in my life. I don't know whether I was in France or Germany. It was one of the two. It could have been Holland, or maybe Switzerland, but I can tell you that, thousands and thousands of bicycles. They were all stacked on top of each other. I don't know how they figured that one out. There was nothing strange about seeing a young lady riding down Main Street on a bicycle with a mink coat and diamond rings. That's the number one mode of transportation over there.

I got a hundred and sixty-nine original songs, and three hundred instrumentals. I got fifty-two records on the market and I'm credited in three different movies, and one of them is *Sugar Hill*. I played the role of the drunken preacher. That was a production out of Beverly Hills, California. I did a courtroom scene with Muhammed Ali, the Greatest. They didn't give me a talking part on that because at that time, I didn't have my license. My license hadn't come back. So I did an instrumental.

I got a lot of music that I almost done forgot. My albums are still available, but I couldn't tell you where to find them. They're collector items. **99**

PEPPERMINT HARRIS
(1925–)

66 My full name is Harrison D. Nelson, from Texarkana. I've been playing blues professionally since 1947. Peppermint is just a moniker I made up. Everyone had one, so I got one too. When I started, I wasn't doing this professionally. I just liked it. I went around with guys that played and one night I went with some friends of mine to a studio. I was just going as a spectator, and that was when there was the recording ban. So nobody was recording anything. There was a lot of bootlegging going on in Houston. As a matter of fact, there was only one studio, and I just went out there to fool around and they asked me if I wanted to make a record. I had played a few gigs around town at the old Eldorado [Ballroom] and it seemed to me that it was just something to do.

I got the name Harris from the Sittin' In With label. They brought several of us in for an audition, and I was the last one they recorded. And when they edited the tapes, they found out I had the best songs and they made it into a record. They knew they called me Peppermint, but they didn't know the last name. The confusion was because my first name was Harrison. So they just called me Peppermint Harris, and they released the record and the name stayed with me.

I had bought my first guitar overseas. I was nineteen years old and I bought it from some guy aboard a ship in the South Pacific. I'm fifty-nine now, and I've lived in Houston off and on since 1943.

When I started playing the blues, the blues was as big as rock 'n' roll is today, maybe not as big, but it was the predominant music from the early 1940s on up to the late 1950s. Louis Jordan was the one who started the thing with small groups. Before then there were mostly big bands. Then there was Johnny Moore and the Three Blazers. But compared to today, the blues is basically the same, the same patterns, but the beat has changed to keep up with the times. The tempo is different. They might try to change the songs, but they keep the basic pattern. Look what the Rolling

Stones did to Tampa Red songs, and what Elvis Presley did to Big Boy Crudup. They didn't change that much with rock 'n' roll. The people are different, but it was a continuation of the basic chords.

The blues is very complicated. You have the Mississippi blues and they play quite a bit differently than people in Texas. It's a different sound. Take people like T-Bone Walker, Lonnie Johnson, or Lightnin' Hopkins, Smokey Hogg; they are significantly different from B.B. King, Muddy Waters, Elmore James. They use the sliding effect. Elmore James put a cylinder on his finger, but B.B. King says he couldn't handle the cylinder. So he developed a style with his tremolo. Well, Texas bluesmen very seldom use that kind of sound. You can hear the whining in the guitars of people from the Delta. Even the Louisiana blues is different. The Texas bluesmen tend to pick more. They don't use as much tremolo. It's a subtle difference.

It's hard to compare T-Bone, because basically he was a jazz guitarist. Like Charlie Christian he brought the guitar to a different plateau than where it had previously been. At first, people only played rhythm guitar in bands. T-Bone, you might say, had a revelation, and he had a great impact on blues guitar and singing. He made the guitar into a lead instrument.

Every blues that I recorded I wrote myself, except for a couple of classic blues, like Muddy Waters' "Key to the Highway." I've done very few tunes that I didn't write myself, but everybody wants the blues singer to do some tunes by other people, like "Backwater Blues" and "Going Down Slow."

I don't write just blues. I write lyrics and by the time they get to the arranger there are a lot of changes made. There's a song now that Buddy Ace is doing called "Check It Out." The way I wrote it was a traditional blues, with basic changes, but Joe Hughes has changed it to something else than I originally intended. That's the peculiar thing about the blues because it can easily be changed to fit another pattern. The form is changed, but the lyrics usually stays the same.

> *I kicked the habit of being a fool for you.*
> *I kicked the habit of being a fool for you.*
> *I was so hooked on you, baby,*
> *that I don't care what you do.*

That's something that I wrote that Buddy Ace is doing on a new album, but you probably won't recognize it. Buddy Ace is in Oakland, and the sound there gets more into urban blues. There's a different interpretation. There are a lot of Texans out there. They're the ones that brought the blues to California when they migrated there, while the people from Georgia, Mississippi, and the East Coast, they go to New York and Chicago. I think that probably the biggest blues place today is in Chicago because a lot of different singers have gone there — Jimmy Reed, Muddy Waters, Elmore James, John Lee Hooker — but there you have a melting pot of the blues and you hear all of them. But in California, you hear more of a Texas big band influenced sound.

GOREE CARTER

(1930–   )

Several blues are improvised. My friend Percy Mayfield wrote songs on his way to the studio. A lot of times I'll be singing a song and there are so many different lyrics that will fit the music. I have forgotten lyrics, but because of the pattern of the music, I can always make something. Most of the records I made with Aladdin records were with jazz musicians, but they could play my blues. I've written maybe a thousand different tunes and recorded for more than fifteen different labels, between 1947 and 1984, and there hasn't been a year gone by that I didn't work with somebody. You can just imagine how many records that might involve, but in fact, I can't remember half the records I've done.

What I like best about the blues is the feeling. I compare it to country music, because probably just about every country record you hear can be applied to everyday life, what really happens. I think the blues is like a reporter. You're not making up anything when you write blues songs. You're writing about what you're doing. You're writing about society and you're singing about the truth. It's nothing that you dream up. It fits any situation in a person's life. It's like when I was a kid, and I was seventeen years old, in Wichita, Kansas, alone, when I started singing, "Please write my mama and tell her what shape I'm in." That was the song "Going Down Slow." It hit me right away because this was happening to me. I have written songs about just about everything that happens in life, or relationships between man and woman, hard times, good times. The word "the blues" is just a label, but everything goes into it. I don't know where it ends. I pick up the guitar and start singing. The biggest song I ever had was "I Got Loaded" and I never intended it to be a song. There was a stigma on marijuana, so I changed it to a drinking song because drinking is more permissible, but the story is the same. In the early 1940s and 1950s they wouldn't let you record suggestive songs, but times have changed now. People say anything now. 99

66 I'm from Houston, the Fifth Ward area, 1310 Bayou. I've been playing the blues since about twelve years of age. I had a cousin that was going to California and his daughter used to play guitar. He left his guitar with me. So I started pickin' on it. I couldn't get no help with it because there weren't too many guitarists around during that period of time.

I had a wind-up Victrola that I used to take out in the park. There were certain artists that I liked and I'd listen to their music and I'd try to pick string by string. This is how I learned because I had no teacher and no one to show me. So I would get along and play. Finally, I learned a few chords, listening. Then I went and bought a book, a chord book, and I started finding my chords from there. This is the only thing I had to go by.

I'm fifty-four now. Let the public be the judge. I can't judge myself because the public is the one who makes you.

The blues is a feeling that you have within yourself and other people. You see other people and you see yourself, too.

I figure it this way, every town has the blues and I couldn't say whether California has its own blues, or Washington, whatever, New York. The blues is within a person and the life that you live, the things that you go through with. That goes with the richest or the poor.

Most of my records were my own songs. "Rock Awhile" was probably my most well-known piece, but I could call a lot of songs. I had one song that was even written for me, Johnny Copeland's "Working with My Baby." Most of my songs I wrote myself. Then I had a lot that I just tore up and they were good songs. I tore them up because they wouldn't let me cut them. They said I was ahead of myself. So I destroyed them. If I can't perform them, then I'll do like Moses did with the Ten Commandments. Can't live by it, die by it.

I had to do what they tell me to do. I was young, didn't know anything about going out in the world. I had always just stayed at home. So I got to the studio and I had to do what they tell me to do.

I don't have anything to go by anymore but what I feel. I sit there and sing. I talk with people. They tell me their problems and then I put mine in with it. And this is the blues, because as long as you live you're going to have a problem. So I listen to other people and I see people. I see myself in them. Some people are doing worse than myself. That helps me because a lot of times when you think you're really down, you're not. You look around you, there's always someone doing worse.

The blues is experience. What you know, you try to get out of, you know, if you're down, if you're in a hole and you want to crawl out of it. And once you get out, you want to stay out of it. Okay? So, the blues comes from a person that had it hard, have lived this, plus he meets people that have the same problem. You see, you never walk alone with anything. It doesn't matter if you're rich or poor. Whatever life you live, there's always someone with you, and this is the music. You have all different fields of music, ballads or whatever you want to call it, or symphonic sounds or rock, but it all adds up in a way speaking to the same thing. It's all about the world. Music is just life. Without music, I don't think the world would make it.

It's a biblical thing. The blues is a task in life, I mean, hard living. That's why the bluesman never died, because there was a foundation.
It comes from hardship. **"**

PETE MAYES
(1938–   )

" I've been playing the blues professionally for more than thirty years. I started when I was fourteen and I'm forty-six now, but I've wanted to play since I was four years old. I remember hearing the sound of T-Bone Walker. I used to hook little strings on doorknobs and pick on them. That was the beginning and from there I got a little Gene Autry guitar. My uncle bought it for me when I was about thirteen or fourteen and within a few months I was playing blues well enough to compete in a school talent show. I played a couple of T-Bone Walker songs, "T-Bone Shuffle" and the other was "Blue Mood." And it went so well for me. Everybody like it so well, I guess that's why I'm still playing blues. If it had gone bad, I might have quit at that point.

I was raised out in the country and I listened to battery radios, and T-Bone Walker was the music I heard. That guitar stuck in my ear, and even today that sound stays in my work. No matter what happens, I always got some of it in me. It's just there. T-Bone Walker was the first man to play the amplified electric guitar as a lead instrument. He was the greatest. Next was my man, B.B., and Gatemouth Brown, and on down the line. But when I heard T-Bone it would send chills over my body, even as a little boy, and it still does lots for me.

I grew up in Anahuac, Texas, between Houston and Beaumont, Texas, about sixty miles away, but actually where I lived was a little community outside Anahuac called Double Bayou. I was raised by my grandmother and grandfather and they didn't think a whole lot of blues. They were religious people and they were from the old school and they liked that religious music, but never once did they ever try to stop me from doing what I wanted to do. I always admired that, and I still don't know how they put up with me, practicing six or seven, maybe eight hours a day. They would fuss at me, and how they stood me making all that noise I will never know. I stayed at home and started practicing in the afternoon and continued on into the night. They never said anything bad about it.

Manuel Rivers
Double Bayou, Texas, 1985
Photograph by Alan Govenar

My uncle, Manuel Rivers, owned and operated the Double Bayou Dance Hall from 1947 to 1983. It was there that I first met Joe Hughes in the mid-1950s in a battle of the guitars that my uncle arranged.

When I was young I did T-Bone Walker songs mostly, but since then I've also written my own blues, "Moving Out," "Crazy Woman," "Texas Jump," "I'm Ready," "The Word Is Out," "Peace," "Honeysucker," and others I can only think of when I'm playing. The blues is an expression of something that may have happened to you or to someone else. It could be good or it could be bad, sometimes it's sad. Where I was raised up in the country, the blues had to do with some depressing things in my life and other people's lives that I saw. That's the way I see it, someone else might think of it another way.

There's a Texas style of blues that's played with a kind of modern sound and a whole lot of expression. It's not jazz, but it's not like the Delta. Texas blues has class and is played with deep feeling. For instance, I was playing in France in 1978 touring with Bill Doggett and Illinois Jacquet, he didn't really know me, but he heard the way I was playing and he came up to me after that and he said, "I knew when I heard you, you had to be from Texas. I could tell by what you were putting in the music." Texas blues has a clean sound with a lot of feeling.

In 1954 I met T-Bone Walker at Walker's Drive-In in Barrett Station and got my first opportunity to play with T-Bone on stage after staring long and hard. And from that day on I played with T-Bone whenever he'd come into this area. Sometimes he'd play piano and sing, but I did his style on guitar. Even back in the '50s I played in a lot of the smaller towns with T-Bone. It was fun. He was a real good musician, but he was easy to work with. He could help you so much, tell you things and he'd never make you look bad in front of an audience. But afterwards, he might tell you about the things you did wrong.

T-Bone told me that he was a banjo player and that's why he played with the guitar flat out in front of him. The way he came up with that style, he said that it wasn't something he tried out, but it just came out that way.

I moved to Houston in 1960. There was more work there. In the late '50s I had played with Big Joe Turner, Percy Mayfield, and Lowell Fulson. From 1966 to 1970 I was the lead guitar for Junior Parker and got to record four sides with him for the Mercury label at Universal Studios in Chicago.

Today blues has a larger white audience. You see, they picked it up later, while the black people knew about it all the time. In Houston I work different clubs where the audience is about ninety percent white. It's mixed slightly. Often times the white people who come to hear are there to just enjoy the music, while a black audience might come out just to be going somewhere. The blues is the truth. If you start doing blues and there's something about it that isn't true, there's no way for you to sell it to the people. If you're telling the truth, the people can feel it, but if you're telling a bunch of lies, it's not going to work too well. When I do the blues I'm at my best. The blues takes everything away, even bad feelings, even if I'm feeling bad. I have to be awfully sick to not make a gig. The blues makes me feel better because I'm getting totally involved in what I'm doing. 🙶

JOE HUGHES

(1937–)

66 The blues is a derivative of spiritual music because it comes from suffering. When you're in a depressive mood and you play the blues, it's sort of relaxed. It's sort of like taking an aspirin, a tranquilizer, or something. It helps relax you. It kind of lifts you up. It comes from the spiritual, the other feeling.

In the cottonfields all us Negroes, I say Negroes because that's what we were classified in those days, all they had was their music to ease the pain. Blues is nothing but a spiritual that uses the praises of love of another person instead of using God or Jesus or what have you. You use "I love you" or you refer to a person instead of the Creator. Basically, you express your inner feelings and the heart of life that you've led. The more suffering you had, the deeper your feeling is. Blues is emotions, like Goree Carter says, it doesn't matter if you're rich or poor, there's some point in life, you're going to suffer. If you're suffering and you're rich, it might come from the feeling that you can't watch over your money. Somebody is trying to take your money away. Suffering is suffering. The feeling is the same. It's just that the poor man, all he has is his music for relieving his pain.

When I was coming up, a guy would work ten hours a day and he was living for the weekend. The only time he had enough money, after he paid his bills and what have you, the money he had left over, he could go out and party Friday and Saturday night. And he more or less lived for the weekend. Just as long as the week made it seem worth it. Because, "Hey, we're waitin' to the weekend. So I can relax so I can enjoy a little life." And you would basically relate to music that was something about you, about your problems, about your way of life, or maybe some lady broke your heart, and though you might not be in that situation now, you still like to relate to those issues, because your memory is what motivates you today, what you've been through. And you don't want to forget what you've been through because if you forget what you've been through, you forget your knowledge because this is where your knowledge come from.

When I came up, T-Bone Walker was my biggest influence. I refer to him as the grandfather of the blues guitar because he was one of the first to play with an electric instrument. T-Bone expressed his feelings through different melodies played on the electric guitar like no one else. As far as I'm concerned he originated it, and after him, as far as Texas was concerned, was Gatemouth Brown.

I would relate to the both of them. And I learned the way that Goree did. I learned by myself. I had always had a good ear for music. So I could hear you play something now and I could play it, you know, just from the sound. And when I started I would do Gatemouth, Lightnin' Hopkins. One of my favorite tunes was the original "Rock Me, Baby," which was done by Lil Son Jackson. You know, B.B. later recorded it, but I loved the style of Lil Son Jackson, the way he delivered it.

T-Bone was the main man I listened to, because we didn't have a Victrola, and my aunt had one and she was crazy about T-Bone. So I'd go out to her house and start listening to T-Bone.

I'm forty-six now, but I started in the business young. At sixteen I was on the bandstand. When I was fourteen I bought my first electric guitar with money I earned as a dishwasher. In 1953 I saw my first electric guitar in the hands of my back-door neighbor, Johnny Watson, and six months later I was on the bandstand with a group I called the Dukes of Rhythm. In this band were James Johnson, Hubert Henderson and another Third Ward neighbor, Johnny Copeland, whom I taught to play electric guitar song by song. Johnny left the Dukes of Rhythm in 1960, and in 1964 the Dukes of Rhythm disbanded with me going on the road with Grady Gaines and the Upsetters [Little Richard's original band that stayed together after Little Richard left].

Early in 1965, I got to play at the Apollo Theater with T-Bone Walker, whom I had first met ten years earlier. Then I was hired as a sideman for Bobby Blue Bland, and in 1967 I left Bobby to work with Al "TNT" Braggs, who had also split from Bobby Bland and was touring with his own group. Over the next three years I worked on and off with Al, and in 1970 I took the job of lead guitarist for Julius Jones and the Rivieras.

Between 1971 and 1981, I worked with several Houston area bands, including We Four, Soul Brothers, and The Music Good. Since then, I've been mainly developing my own music. In 1985 I was asked to co-headline with Johnny Copeland at Blues Estafette in Utrecht, Holland.

Now, today you have a mixed audience, but I'd say blues now has a bigger white audience than black because blacks have grown too accustomed to it. It's just like any other kind of you music you listen to, if you've heard it all your life, then you want to reach out for something different.

The bluesman is like a preacher. He's delivering a message. He isn't going to tell you something you haven't heard. But he's told enough people that he's made an art form out of it. **"**

Joe and Willie Mae Hughes
with T-Bone and Vida Lee Walker
Houston, circa 1965
Courtesy Joe Hughes

Guitar Slim (Rayfield Jackson)
Guitarist with the Clarence Green band
Houston, 1986
Photograph by Alan Govenar

JOHNNY COPELAND
(1937–   )

D riving to Navasota from Houston, the road is black, straight, and fast. Johnny Copeland and I are squeezed together in the back seat of Robert Turner's Cadillac. Next to Robert in the front seat is Johnny's wife, Ethel. I am in the middle, on one side is Robert's wife and his small baby, on the other is Johnny, his face still dripping sweat from the fervor of Juneteenth in Emancipation Park. Johnny is singing in a scat voice, "Turn the radio down and let's get going."

66 I thought the show tonight was great. I liked the way Joe Hughes performed and I liked the way I performed. I didn't have long enough, due to circumstances as they are, but maybe next year I'll get enough time. This is my third time at the Juneteenth Festival. It feels great coming home. You talk about these things everywhere and you tell everybody about Houston and to be accepted by your home in your own community like I was accepted tonight makes it great. Houston let me come home. I appreciate the honorable mayor being out and giving me my proclamation, and the kind words, telling me that I was one of the few that pushed that music from this area and that she was proud of me. That's a good feeling.

I'm from Haynesville, Louisiana, born in 1937, the son of sharecroppers on the Prentice Meadows Farm. When I was six months old my parents split up and I moved with my mother to Magnolia, Arkansas, where I did not get to see much of my father. I got to see him one time, and I guess about six months later he died. And they gave me his guitar. When I went to see him I heard a lot of playing. I spent two weeks down there. The night I got there he took me along. I'd been around other guitar players. I stayed with another guitarist named Son Beal when my mother went to

Michigan once. He played at home, but he loved music. He'd play all day long, all them old blues, and he even had a record player with records by Lightnin' Hopkins and Louis Jordan.

Blues right now is in all the colleges, all the elementary schools and junior high schools. I see where the kids are going to have a wider knowledge of blues and they're going to be able to put songs with faces, songs with names. That's something that our generation hasn't been able to do.

I'd like to think that I've had my part in the blues coming back. I've been out there hammering my brains out trying to get it did. I like to think me and the other representatives out there like me are really doing something. That's what brought Texas blues back. The uprising is the Texas blues.

It was a strange feeling going to Africa because before going I only had knowledge that I was from Haynesville, Louisiana, down on Prentice Meadows Farm to Third Ward, Houston, Texas. That was as far as my thing went. But in Africa I got to go past that in reality and I went to a country where eighty percent of the blacks in America come from. And I traveled from country to country and I saw the similarities among people. I left from Paris, and went into the Congo. The picture on the cover of the "Bringing It All Back Home" album was from that first day. There were two or three hundred musicians playing their music on the field, and they were dancing all on top of their houses, in the trees. You can't hear nothing but music, nothing but the beat, and it was like the whole world was moving, whole world shaking, and funny as it may seem, I kind of felt the effect the drums had had on our people, to make us want to dance and move. It transferred me to another frame of mind. You're not with yourself, you're right there with the music. It was like you were floating right into the music, and the energy level never changed at one point, it moved all the time, but it stayed in one place.

I got an African band together and played up and down the East Coast, ten countries, and we got great reviews in the *New York Times, Boston Globe, Washington Post,* but it was only a trial. We wanted to see if it could work. We had four African musicians, a guitar player, two horn players from the Cameroon, and a percussionist. They all came in from Paris [where they record].

Africa made me realize the worst thing we could have ever done was disband the music due to the fact our young people [in America] felt that it was a disgrace, the moan out of the people. We have to accept ourselves, we have to be who we are.

I travel to Europe about three times a year. I don't see much difference in audience. Blues audiences are really great. All of the settings are pretty much the same, and the faces, they are there to have a good time. That's one thing that the artist has in his favor every time [in Europe]. I like to work with that little edge. You got to look like you belong there, not like you're borrowing some time. If you can do that, you fare all right because that's what they come to see.

I'm always working on a new album. I'm always working on my material, but the business is another thing. Whenever they call and say it's time to cut another album, I'll be ready. I want to have a choice doing my material. I like to do ninety percent of my own. I'm writing all the time. Life isn't nothing but one big song. It works out. I wrote a song for this show today, but I was afraid to do it. You know how you write something and you say, "I'm not sure if this is what I want to do, or say," and then you go back to the drawing board. I worked hard on it, but I never did get away. I have to go back and do some more.

When I was in Spain I was writing all the time. I would sound-check songs and if I didn't feel what I wanted to feel, I didn't use it. As I go along, I do lots of research. Living in New York, Harlem is the greatest place to be, by yourself or around four million

Fans at the Juneteenth Blues Festival
Houston, 1987
Photograph by Alan Govenar

people. It's given me time to think about what the blues really is.

With my first album in 1981, though I had been working on the music all along from 1978 up, I realized, hey, this is a brand new world. Now we're dealing with a liberated woman, a lady that gets up every morning and goes to work and doesn't feel like she's mistreated about it. She goes home and helps pay all the bills. You can't put all the blame on her anymore. You have to balance it off. The blues had a tendency, if it talked about the lady, it tended to put the man on the top and the lady on the bottom. So I thought the blues could use a new message. I wanted to have the same feeling, but a better idea.

I'm helping people through my music. Blues is what happens in life, it's trying to be happy. That's what I want to bring in my music. The vibes of the music come from God. It's an inspiration. When you're making music, you can't make trouble. And if you make music and trouble at the same time, it's turmoil.

I've been in New York twelve years. I was in Houston, and disco was moving. My friend, Robert Turner, he lived up in New York and he kept telling me to come to New York. Well, he was in Houston in October 1975, and he said, "You got to go," and he picked me up and took me there. I got to New York and started looking around. I don't like this big old town, and he kept talking to me about the city, explaining things. He made it comfortable enough to sit there and try to work my music, made it so I didn't have to be rushing to where I wanted to be. I never felt the roughness of New York. He was okay there, and he helped me dearly. Through that I was able to start doing things through the community in which I was living in Harlem, and started building from there. He tried to set everything up for me, and there we met Kenny Vangel and Danny Doyle. Then things started happening, the "Copeland Special" album with Rounder. Now I've done four, "Make My Home Where I Hang My Hat," "Texas Twister," and "Bringing It All Back Home."

Then last year, there was the Grammy album with Albert Collins and Robert Cray. Albert and I have been friends for a long time [since growing up together in the Third Ward in Houston]. We've always talked about doing an album. We're like brothers. We work together out here with this Texas music because he feels the same way I feel. We love the same people, the same community. We have so much in common that when we meet up on the road, it's like a family, Stevie, the T-Birds, we all have a good relationship going toward trying to help each other and push each other forward. I did ten dates with Stevie Ray Vaughan on his Midwest tour last year. It was very comfortable. We hope to do more.

Robert Cray got involved because he was a pupil of Albert. He had been playing jazz on the guitar and he got to hear Albert at his prom one night in 1971, I think, and that's where he fell in love with Albert. He wanted to play the same music and he was lucky enough to do some things with Albert. I got a chance to meet Robert, out in Portland, with Albert later on. I thought he was great, a great little brother who's loyal to where he came from and where he's going. We had a wonderful time making that record together, though at first we were to use Gatemouth Brown on it, but the business got in the way.

When we were growing up, we all knew each other real well, and we knew Mr. Robey. He made Gatemouth Brown. Robert Turner used to work for Robey, take his records out on the road. Robey once lent us his truck and we wrecked it. We said we were going to buy it and tour. So we did the weekend with the truck and the last night it got wrecked and we had to try to get it back to Houston before Mr. Robey knew. It was all messed up, but we were friends. Mr. Robey was a nice guy in that manner, down to earth, and real with anybody who was real with him.

Johnny Copeland
Juneteenth Blues Festival
Houston, 1987
Photograph by Alan Govenar

I don't think he really understood the music
business, because he came from an area where he was
the only one [black person to own a record company],
so he had to tie everything up as much as he could to
deal with it. That was his business tactic. If he had
given anybody any room to sue him, his business
would have ended twenty years before he sold out. He
was trying to protect himself. I don't like the way he
did it in a lot of ways, but I understand where he was
coming from. He wasn't doing anything worse than
anyone else in this business.

I met Robey when I was seventeen or eighteen. I did
one session over there with Miss Lavelle, only one,
under the direction of Clifton B. King. I did have one
song, though, that got caught up with this stuff.
Johnny Guitar Watson came into Houston and came
by the club, Shady's Playhouse, where I was playing.
It was 1956. He said he was going back to Los Angeles
and try to get me a contract from somebody and he
went back and he got me a contract with an actor that
had a label in California.

So he said, "I'm going to fix it so that you can stay
in Houston and cut the record with my friend, Don
Robey." And sure enough he called Don Robey and
he told me to come out. I signed the papers and he said,
"Let's go looking for material. You have to choose the
songs carefully." I didn't know nothing about writing
at the time, so I get my friend Joe Medwick, and we
sit down one night after hours. We started writing a
song called "Further on Up the Road." We finished
the song that night and Joe went out to the studio the
next day to submit the song to Mr. Robey because that
was what Mr. Robey told me to do. I said, "You take
it out there. I'm not going with you," because at the
time I was married and I had little kids and my wife
was working during the day time. I was home with
the kids and it was hard for me to move around. Well,
when Joe got to the studio, Bobby [Bland] was cutting
an album and they needed one more song, and that
was it. I'm not identified on the record because Joe
tied the song up with Don Robey, just as he did with
every song. Joe sold Mr. Robey maybe five hundred

songs, ten, fifteen dollars apiece, and he cut maybe five, but they were big hits. You understand what I'm saying.

I understand Joe Medwick is back, singing, sounding good. He's maybe five years older than me, maybe fifty-five years old. We all grew up together, Pete Mayes, Clarence Holloman, who was a little ahead because his brother taught him. He taught the kid how to play all of Charles Brown lick for lick. After Clarence reached twenty or twenty-one he got to go out on the road with Charles Brown and stay with him until he retired. He was one of the great guitar players. He played all of Junior Parker sessions, Bobby Bland. It was Clarence Holloman or Johnny Brown. There was Milton Hopkins, who played with B.B. King. Then Wayne Bennett. There's so many good guitar players in Houston, Joe Hughes. I always thought that Joe was someone special. We played together in the Dukes of Rhythm.

I've always been a T-Bone Walker person. Joe Hughes was always into Gatemouth Brown, and we'd have guitar battles and fist battles, too, all kind of battles. Joe and I used to be on stage and he'd say something I didn't like and I'd say, "You better not step outside." Of course, he'd put the guitar down and we'd go outside and he'd say, "Say it again!" And we'd fight, then go back inside and start playing again. We were just kids. It wasn't really a fight. It was playing around. We didn't have enough intelligence to know we were messing with these people's money. We were once locked up in Galveston for being on the streets too young, and we were at the jail house fighting [laughs].

I once got a chance to record with T-Bone Walker. It was in '66 or '67, for Huey P. Meaux. We did a lot of playing together, Club Matinee, Eldorado, all up through the counties outside of Houston. My guitar style was influenced by his, those hot cuttin' licks, but it took me a while to start to like my singing because I couldn't sing like everyone else. I always liked to go to church and sing. There's a little bit of that preacher in me on stage. You got to use everything you got. 99

Maxine Howard
Juneteenth Blues Festival
Houston, 1987
Photograph by Alan Govenar

AMOS MILBURN

(1927–1980)

❝ As a young boy about five years old my parents rented a piano for my eldest sister's wedding. The following morning, they told me I went to play the piano and did "Jingle Bells." My father said, "We better keep this piano and get him lessons." I took only very few lessons, I was too fast for music. I said, "Just let me play, teach me the keys, I go ahead and play the song." It sounds stupid but it carried me through. So I get a little older and I start to listen to the jukeboxes and local taverns from the outside, 'cause I couldn't go in. They played so loud, you could hear them on the outside, and I remember hearing Billie Holiday, Louis Jordan, and I could go back and copy. I had a brother that influenced me with the old standards, "Body and Soul," "Stardust." I found out, when I went to New York later, that if you couldn't play those numbers you couldn't get into the union, you wasn't a musician.

[In 1942, at age fifteen, Amos joined the Navy and after three and a half years overseas he returned to Houston in 1945.] After leaving I decided I would get a little band, we played all around the little towns around Houston and suburbs. Finally somebody heard me. Mrs. Lola Cullum offered me to come to rehearse at her house. She had a big baby grand piano and that was something new to me, after playing in these little joints, you know. I recorded "After Midnite" and she took me to Los Angeles on this train. We submitted the number to Modern Records, they refused it. Well, they didn't actually refuse it, but they offered me so little money 'til she refused it. She said, we heard of another company, that had Charles Brown. At that time they were the Philo Record Company, what was made at Aladdin. At the time the president of Aladdin, Eddie Mesner, was at the hospital. So my manager [Lola Cullum] took the record and a record player and took it up to the hospital and let him hear. And he told his brother Leo, the vice president of the company: "Sign him up right now, he's good. I like him!" And that started it all. **❞**

❝ The first session took place September 12, 1946, and Milburn stayed with Aladdin for twelve years, recording about 125 numbers, until the company went out of business. Most were arranged by the famous Maxwell Davis, who blew the sax solos. During the late '50s the company released two albums on Aladdin and one on a subsidiary label, Score. Another album followed after Aladdin was bought by Imperial. Milburn's first record, "After Midnite," sold over 50,000 copies and in 1949 he was Billboard's best selling R&B artist.

Milburn's "Bad Bad Whiskey" reached No. 1 in *Billboard's* R&B charts in November 1950, and [he] continued to use either a happy-go-lucky enthusiasm or a sad, almost crying, voice on other drinking songs, such as "Just One More Drink," "Thinking and Drinking," "Let Me Go Home Whiskey," "One Scotch," "One Bourbon," "Good Good Whiskey," "Vicious Vicious Vodka," and "Rum and Coca-Cola."

In the late 1970s five labels reissued albums of Milburn's early Aladdin material, [among them] United Artists (USA), Riverboat (France), and Route 66 (Sweden). **❞**

Norbert Hess
Living Blues #45/46

ALBERT COLLINS
(1932–   )

Albert Collins; guitar walk at the Hard Rock Cafe; Dallas, 1987
Photograph by Alan Govenar

The blues is the bus, getting a flat tire on the way to Dallas outside Waxahachie, swinging through Texas in ten days, playing dates in Houston, Austin, San Antonio, Fort Worth, and Dallas. The bus is running hard, belching smoke. Albert Collins, 1987 Grammy Award winner, drives this bus with an understated determination. At age fifty-four he is going strong, but there are still obstacles, the most immediate of which is the flat tire. His sister, Marie, lives in Fort Worth and he knows he can take care of his engine problems there. It's getting to Dallas that's on his mind now, to the Hard Rock Cafe. He played the Hard Rock, New York, last year, and he's hoping to get dates soon at other locations in the burgeoning Hard Rock chain.

The sky brightens and they find a mechanic who loves the blues. They get to Dallas early. In the parking lot off McKinney Avenue, Albert begins to wind down. "The blues have never been better," he says with a calmness that belies the pressures of the day. He looks out the open door of the bus and nods. The lines in his face are drawn tight, but suggest a smile as the crowd overflows from the Hard Rock steps onto the sidewalk.

"Today they know what they're listening to. They understand the music," Albert Collins says, "In the 1960s, when white kids first started hearing blues, they didn't really know what it was. It sounded like rock 'n' roll but it wasn't. It took them a while to figure out that blues is the root."

Inside the Hard Rock, Dallas, the memories of the past are everywhere. Vintage electric guitars line the domed ceiling of this self-proclaimed "Supreme Court of Rock 'n' Roll." Photographs of Jimi Hendrix, Mick Jagger, Buddy Holly, and more stars than you could ever count are mounted in gilded frames. A back-lit glow emanates from a stained glass portrait of Elvis Presley at the rear of the stage. Hard Rock, Dallas, is completely self-conscious, a shrine to popular culture since the advent of the electric guitar.

A man who says his name is Brick sits next to Albert Collins on the bus and laughs loudly, remembering his first meeting with Albert in the mid-1970s in Austin in the days when Stevie Ray Vaughan, Jimmie Vaughan, and the Fabulous Thunderbirds were starting out.

A friend of Brick's comes onto the bus, and Brick keeps talking about the greatness of Albert Collins. They are interrupted by the unexpected arrival of Albert's nieces, Charlene and Darlene, who are the daughters of his sister in Fort Worth. Charlene and Darlene are twins, twenty-eight years old, and bubbling with exuberance. Albert hasn't seen them for more than two years and his gestures are excited, though he doesn't say much. Darlene, who works as a

kindergarten teacher, can't stop talking. Charlene is quiet and squeezes herself into a seat next to Brick with a smirk on her face.

A waitress comes to the door of the bus and asks if anyone wants a drink. Everyone orders a beer, except for Albert, who requests a tomato juice with lime. He stopped drinking four years ago and says that he feels better than ever.

" My mother was kin to all the Hopkins. Lightnin' Hopkins is my cousin. When I was a kid they had Saturday night fish fries out in the woods with kerosene lamps and lanterns. White folks used to think that when black people played that kind of music [blues] it was evil. I was born in Leona, Texas, about ninety miles out of Huntsville. It's twenty-three miles from Madisonville, Texas. But we didn't stay in Leona too long. I went to school there until I was about seven and then we left, went to another little town called Marquez, Texas. And when I was nine, we went to Houston, where I was raised up. I started playing guitar when I was twelve after hearing John Lee Hooker's "Boogie Chillen." The first guitar I had was acoustic, but soon after that I got an electric, an Epiphone. I played Epiphone all the way up to '52. That's when I got my first Fender.

I listened to T-Bone Walker, Guitar Slim, they were two of my favorites. Me and Johnny Guitar Watson and Johnny Copeland, we were raised up together in the Third Ward area. T-Bone was my favorite at that particular time, even before B.B., and another was Gatemouth Brown. I knew his family. Every little bit you hear helps.

I started playing the clubs in Houston in 1951, '52, signed with Buffalo Booking Agency and Evelyn Johnson got me bookings around, though I never recorded for Peacock or Duke. My first group was Albert Collins and the Rhythm Rockers. The problem with Houston was that if you played a white club, the minute we got off the bandstand we had to go to a little room, and we had to wait. Any time we wanted

Albert Collins with his niece, Charlene
Inside the tour bus
Dallas, 1987
Photograph by Alan Govenar

a drink, somebody would bring it in and give it to us. You couldn't leave that room. That was in the '50s, early '60s.

When we came along, I wanted to know about their race, you know, the other side. I wanted to express my feelings with somebody on how I felt, to which the usual reaction was, "Okay, we know how you felt, boy. Hey man, he's black and we don't worry about that." What I'm saying, I'm talking about heart to heart, like we were trying to have a heart-to-heart talk. But they'd sit down and have argument to argument. This is something I always wanted. If I could just express it in my fingers, let them know how I feel.

I did my first recording of "The Freeze" in Houston with Henry Hayes. Henry Hayes was my teacher. He encouraged me to play. He played jazz, anything. He taught me a lot when other guys wouldn't help me. He taught me about timing. That's the reason I always had horn players when I started out. I had nine pieces. He taught me to listen to the big band sound.

There was a time I was into piano. I took piano lessons as a kid. I always like piano. And I bought an organ one time, man, got ripped off when I was coming out of Port Arthur. I played down there a lot. I used to cut all of my records in Beaumont. There was Johnny Winter, Janis Joplin, we all hung out together for a long time. I was cuttin' for Big Bopper Enterprise. They named it after him after he got killed in the plane crash with Buddy Holly.

We cut a lot of stuff in Beaumont. Janis was with me when I cut "Frosty" in '62. She was just a kid. Janis didn't sing, she was just hangin' out. And I was with Johnny Winter, when Edgar Winter was a little baby. Johnny was very young, about eighteen or nineteen or so. In 1980 Johnny and I did an album together at the New Morning Festival near Geneva, Switzerland.

Albert Collins
Hard Rock Cafe, Dallas, 1987
Photograph by Alan Govenar

Albert Collins
North Sea Jazz Festival
The Hague, 1979
Photograph by Erik Lindahl
Courtesy Tommy Löfgren

I stayed in Houston until 1968, when I met up with Canned Heat. So they asked me about going to California. My first concert was at the Shrine Exposition in Los Angeles. They had me as a warm-up band. When I played the Fillmore West, Elvin Bishop helped me out with that. Buddy Miles, Elvin Bishop, B.B. King — we all did that show together. (Paul) Butterfield, Mike Bloomfield.

I did three albums with Imperial. And then I went with Tumbleweed Records out of Denver, Colorado, in 1972. I figured I was on the track again, and all of a sudden they went out of business, so ABC-Dunhill picked my stuff up. Then I free-lanced for four years, and a friend of mine, who I've known for several years, Dick Shurman, he introduced me to Alligator in 1978, and I've been with them since.

I really don't know what way my music's going to go now. The blues is really out here now, but I'm really afraid of what's going to happen. I just don't know. I've seen it happen, 1968, '69, '70 and first part of '72, it declined. See, what I'm trying to do now, I'm concentrating on music, but I'm studying to be in movies and to do commercials, trying to get something else to carry me along, just in case the blues get a little slow. I love playing. That's why I stopped drinking. I like my music so much that I get high off it.

The European festivals are great. They're more appreciative. They know every little detail about your career. They study it. They know blues players that I don't know. I like the North Sea Festival, I always like it best. It's more like the States. You don't feel like you're in Europe. There's so many people there from the United States, you feel closer to home. The food is the same as here, twenty-four-hour-a-day restaurants. When you go to Scandinavia, France, it's a lot different. That festival in Nice was beautiful. I'd rather play on a low stage, kind of even with the crowd.

Around 1953 I saw Jay McNeely, the saxophone player. He'd run out in the audience with his

Dancers at the Hard Rock Cafe
Dallas, 1987
Photograph by Alan Govenar

saxophone. So what I did, I said I can do this with the guitar, and I went out to Parker Music Company in Houston and said, "You all make me up a hundred-foot guitar cable." Everyone in the store looked at me and said this man has gone crazy. "What are you going to do with all this cord?" I say, "I'm going to play with it." So when I started doing that, it just caught on and I've been doing it since. It makes the crowd feel closer to you. They have more fun.

I usually am out on the road ten months out of the year, but I have to get away from it for a little bit. I'm taking it a little easier. I'm getting a driver for my bus. But I like driving, I'm used to it. I used to drive a truck, done a lot of driving over the years, but you can't keep doing it.

Blues is my music. I don't want to get away from that. I just want to update my style. That's what we're taking about now, what to to do with my next album. I used to listen to country music, jazz. There was a lot of jazz around Houston, Illinois Jacquet, Wynonie Harris. When I started out my playing was different. I played without a capo, but after four or five years I met up with Gatemouth Brown and that's what started me [using a capo]. Never did fool with a pick. When I started out guitar wasn't supposed to be played with a pick. I don't know where they got that from. I know they used thumb picks. Freddie King used to use a thumb pick. I could never use none of that. My fingers don't get sore until I'm off for a while, but it don't bother me. I pick with my thumb and first fingers, almost like playing a bass. I never did play many chords. I always wanted to be a lead player. I always had my own bands.

My style got the name of being "something cold" from a bass player who used to be with me, played upright bass. His name was Cooks, out of Houston, and I played in Corpus Christi, Texas, one night and we were on our way back to Houston and my windshield fogged up. He said, "Why don't you put your defrost on?" So I was just looking at the dashboard of the car, and later I cut me a tune called "Defrost." Down through the months, when I was cutting in Beaumont, they said, "Well, man that will be your trademark. Just like something in the icebox. That's how I got the name, something cold, and in 1978, a bass player I had said, "Why don't you call the band The Icebreakers?" And that's what I did.

My wife writes a lot of my songs, Gwendolyn Collins. She wrote "Master Charge," "Conversation With Collins," "Give Me My Blues Song," "Lights On, Nobody Home," "I Got That Feeling." We collaborate pretty good. It's hard for an entertainer, traveling all the time. I don't have any kids. But my wife and I have been together for twenty-one years. I think that's a lot for an entertainer. When I first met my wife, she didn't listen to blues. She used to like that song "Tremble" on the other side of "Frosty." That's what got her into my kind of music. She's a nurse, but she's going into computers now.

My songs usually come to me just by listening to people, just going down the highway, something come across my mind. Sometimes, I just write it down on a piece of paper so I don't forget it. Then when I have time to relax and be at home, I'll finish a few words to it, and then she'll look at it. She might add a few words. That's how we did "Conversation With Collins." We were just sitting there talking. We got dressed and we were ready to go out, but we just sat there talking from nine in the evening until four o'clock in the morning. We didn't go anywhere.

See, a lot of people misinterpret the blues. They feel it's depressing music. It's kind of hard for some people to relate when you say blues. Some people don't want to hear it, but it's reality. **"**

BEAUMONT, PORT ARTHUR, & ORANGE

The cities of Port Arthur, Beaumont, and Orange form what is called "The Golden Triangle" near the Gulf Coast of southeast Texas. It is an area of oil and sulphur production, as well as shipbuilding, rice farming, and shrimp fishing. It is also home to thousands of Cajuns and Creoles, descendents of the French-speaking Acadians who entered Louisiana after expulsion by the British in the period 1765 to 1800 from what is now Nova Scotia. Since the 1920s Cajuns and Creoles have migrated from southwestern Louisiana to The Golden Triangle in search of jobs and social freedom. Cajuns settled predominantly in the Port Arthur and Orange areas, while the greatest concentrations of Creoles went to Beaumont and Houston.

Today more than 50,000 people in Texas (with an estimated 30,000 of them in Houston) speak some form of French. Folklorist Nicholas Spitzer estimates that as many as 150,000 or more consider themselves Cajun or Creole culturally, although they do not speak the language. This population has been assimilated into the cultural mainstream of Texas, but has retained and modified aspects of the culture brought by their ancestors.

With the migration of Acadians to Louisiana and later to Texas, French music was preserved, but was modified by the different cultural contexts in which it was transplanted. For example, Allen Thibodeaux and the French Ramblers from Port Arthur added the pedal steel guitar to their otherwise traditional Cajun ensemble of guitar, accordion, fiddle, and triangle. In Houston, Cajun music was influenced by country and western; Creole music, by rhythm and blues. The trading of influences was an open exchange, however, and Cajun/Creole instrumentation is evident in the performance styles of both black and white musicians, such as Clarence Garlow, Pete Mayes, Janis Joplin, and Johnny Winter.

For musicians from The Golden Triangle, Houston was an important destination. It offered more opportunities to find industrial work, as well as to perform in clubs and to secure recording contracts. In Houston's Frenchtown the zydeco starts around 9 p.m. On Friday, Saturday and Sunday nights rooms fill with a pulsating enthusiasm that grows with the syncopated rhythms of accordion, electric guitars, drums, and rub board. The dance floors fill until the crowds are elbow to elbow, moving in a rough circular movement that changes with the tempo of fast two-steps, waltzes, and blues.

Zydeco fuses elements of traditional Cajun music with blues and Afro-Caribbean rhythms, but it is performed predominantly by Creoles. The term "zydeco" refers to the highly syncopated music and to the dance event itself. Zydeco translates from Creole French as "snap bean." Although some critics and performers themselves claim it comes from the line "Les Haricots Son Pas Sale," meaning, "the snap beans are not salty," others suggest the name derives from a common dance movement that involves holding closed wrists in front of the torso and then circling or flicking them in a motion that alludes to someone snapping beans.

The spelling of the word "zydeco" is also subject to some disagreement. In Houston the most common spellings on dance hall posters are "zydeco" and "zodico," although alternate spellings, such as "zoddico" or "zordico" are sometimes used.

In rural Louisiana, the music was usually performed on a one-row button accordion and accompanied by fiddle, angle iron triangle, or rub board. The rub board is strapped to the player's chest like armor and his two hands scrub the surface with "church keys."

With the migration of Creoles to urban areas, such as Lake Charles and Houston, the more versatile piano accordion replaced the one-row model. The rub board has been retained as a rhythm instrument, while the triangle and fiddle have been replaced by electric guitar, bass, drums, and some keyboards and horns.

In Houston, zydeco was first played at house dances. Since the early 1950s it has been performed in clubs, the oldest of which is the Continental Lounge on Collingsworth Avenue in the Fifth Ward. The most noted zydeco players of the day have appeared there. They have included Anderson Moss, L.C. Donatto, Lonnie Mitchell, Willie Green, and Clifton Chenier from Lake Charles, Louisiana, who is considered the patriarch of zydeco.

Today most Catholic churches in Houston with large Creole memberships hold zydeco dances. St. Francis of Assisi has the largest dances and attracts as many as 800 people, but zydeco is also sponsored in other parish halls. Clarence Gallien has organized church zydeco in Houston for more than twenty-five years. He says that he prefers to book Louisiana bands because they have a "truer French sound" than local groups, which are more influenced by rhythm and blues, an urban music of assimilation that has modified and utilized elements of the traditional zydeco sound.

Zydeco is welcomed by the Catholic churches not only because the dances are an important source of revenue, but they allow Creoles to preserve their heritage by meeting family and friends, eating Creole food, and listening and dancing to traditional music.

(At left) Pete Mayes (right), T-Bone Walker (center), Willard Mayes (left), Club Ravon, Beaumont, 1960
Courtesy Pete Mayes

Johnny Winter
Promotional photograph, 1987

142

JOHNNY WINTER

(1944–   )

66 There were great radio stations that you could pick up around Beaumont from everywhere. There was one in Del Rio, it was actually a Mexican station. Wolfman Jack had a blues show, and there was someone before him called Dr. Jazzmo. There was a station in Shreveport, KWKH. Frank Page, I think, was the disc jockey. He had a show from Stan's Record Shop. There were a couple of stations from Nashville. WLAC had two record shows, and there was Ernie's Record Shop. Ernie's had Excello Records. Later on that night there was Randy's Records. The good thing about those shows was that you could get the records if they weren't available where you lived. You could send in your five or six dollars around the South and get blues specials, great records even if you didn't know what you were doing. Literally, I bought every blues record that I could find. That's when I was still too young to go to the clubs myself and there wasn't anybody else that interested in that kind of thing that I knew of.

Later on there was a station in Beaumont, KJET, Clarence Garlow was a disc jockey and at night he'd play a lot of his own records. When I got old enough I'd go out to clubs and listen to him, but before that, through my teenage years, I just listened to radio.

After I started playing clubs I met Joey Long. I was sixteen or seventeen and started going to Houston, playing all over Texas and Louisiana. I got to meet people myself. There were never very many color lines among the musicians, though in clubs there were some problems mixing on stage. In the white clubs it was a little scarier than the black clubs, but nothing ever happened. We survived.

I don't know where Joey Long learned to play. He was about ten or fifteen years older. He had been doing it longer, but he was definitely the first white [part Mexican] guy that I was aware of that had been playing good blues. He opened for Fats Domino, B.B. King,

Johnny Winter
Promotional photograph
Circa 1976
Courtesy Barker Texas History Center

and a lot of people. They'd come through and he opened up for them. I think Huey Meaux managed him at that point, and he was bringing a lot of people in. He'd put Joey in with a lot of acts. Joey was really famous, we thought he was. In fact, I still go down and see Joey and he still plays practically the same way. He's kind of hard, it's just getting him in the right mood.

I've never really thought there really was much of a Texas style. If there is anything that really stands out, there are so many different influences in Texas guitar players. You just can't say they sound the same way. There's Lightnin' Hopkins, and how can you compare him with Blind Lemon Jefferson, or Hop Wilson? There's all that country and western and jazz influence. You can find so many different styles of music down there. In fact, it's just forced on you. You're exposed to a lot more varied styles.

Over the years I've learned more technically, what makes different things and where the influences come from, why people sound the way they do, but my actual enjoyment of the music hasn't changed at all. Emotionally I still feel the same way. At first, I didn't know exactly why I was doing it. If I liked them, I learned them. If I didn't, I ignored them, but I didn't really know why. I've tried to find out.

I bought every record I could get my hands on, but I never said, "This is what I want to sound like." The Chicago people, I guess, were the people who impressed me the most, like Muddy Waters, Little Walter. Those were the records that were coming out, that were new when I was first getting into it. Later on I heard the earlier stuff as it came out on reissues, then I heard the '20s and '30s music, but the Chicago '50s style, that and what was going on around Texas at that point — Bobby Bland, Junior Parker. Bobby Blue Bland had some great guitar players.

T-Bone Walker was probably my favorite of Texas people. Even though I don't sound a whole lot like him, I probably learned more from him than anybody. The way he would change the meter to different songs. Start out in one meter and switch back. He'd play that

big fat guitar with no feedback, so I don't have the same kind of tones that he did, the actual sound, but from his approach to playing I learned more than from just about anybody. He was very good at switching the meter around on things. That appealed to me. B.B. said that he learned a lot from T-Bone and most of the others I heard also listened to T-Bone. That's what I was trying to get to.

Then I heard Muddy Waters on the bottleneck style and there wasn't anybody around that played that kind of stuff that I was award of. I learned about that from records. I didn't have any idea of what that was at first. I thought it was steel guitar or something like that. I just learned it in little bits and pieces and finally I think there were a couple of articles out that mentioned how they were doing it. I tried cutting a test tube off and playing with the crystal on my watch, different things that took me a long time to develop because it wasn't really anything I did on the bandstand, something I just did for myself. I didn't start using that until the mid-to late 1960s.

I always thought that I always was more influenced by the music in Chicago and the Delta than the Texas music that was actually around me. Most of the records were from Chicago: electric versions of the Delta, Howlin' Wolf, Muddy Waters. It was always more primitive, more raw, I liked it a little better. It was something I had never heard. At the same time I started hearing rock 'n' roll, but blues was more of it and I couldn't understand why I was the only kid that felt that way. I didn't really think of myself as a Texas musician until later.

In the mid-1960s Roy Ames was doing some things with Don Robey and he had talked to Don Robey about me. Then Bill Hall came out of the woodwork and said that he had bought my contract from Ken Ritter and that scared Don Robey off. I only met Don Robey one time and talked to him for fifteen or twenty minutes. I recorded some stuff for Roy and Huey (Meaux) and both of them put out the same stuff at the same time. I was actually with Roy, but Roy was working with Huey and both of them got the tapes

from each other, and the music wasn't even well-produced. They might have been Roy's and he was just keeping them at Huey's.

I'm glad to be away from all of that. I had to move to New York to be closer to the management, the record companies, the booking agencies. Now, I suppose I could live anywhere, but I have kind of grown to like New York. I feel I've reached a point where I want to continue exactly what I'm doing and, if possible, put it into a little more commercial format. I've tried to do that, but it's always very hard to do, I've talked to the people who work with Robert Cray. The part that's hard for me is coming up with material. I'm not that great a songwriter myself. There's a lot I've thrown away. Once in a while I'll come up with something I like, but I can't depend on that to happen. Doing remakes of the old stuff is fun, but I'd like to come up with some original songs that I like. That's what I want to do. I've had the same band for the last eight or ten years — John Paris, the bass and harmonica player, and Tom Compton, the drummer, for three or four years. I really love having a trio. With a small group, you don't have to work things out. I think it's more exciting that way.

I'm still playing my Gibson Firebird for my slide, and I'm using a Lazer, designed by Mark [Erlewine] in Austin. I bought it because it was small and I thought it would be a nice guitar to just practice on

and I was playing it through an amp. I didn't even play it through an amp for a couple of months after I had gotten it. Then when I was doing "Guitar Slinger" I used it in the studio, and I've been using it since. It's a cheaply made guitar, but it sounds so good. I've been using the same one for three or four years now. I really bought it because I thought it would be easy to take on the plane. It's got a real nice sound. The thing I don't like about it is that it only has one pick-up. The one pick-up it's got is the one I generally don't use. For my next record, he'll have a new one made.

When I was younger I was afraid my blues would change. My brother, Edgar, would always try to get me to learn more chords. I was afraid that if I played the jazzy stuff he liked I wouldn't be able to play mine. At this point, I don't think it makes much difference. If you don't want to use it, you don't have to. But when I was thirteen or fourteen I wasn't real sure of that. I was afraid that if I learned too much I wouldn't like my playing. I tended to like the guys that played more primitively. If they got too good, I didn't like them too much. We used to have gigantic arguments about this stuff: music and what was good, and what wasn't good. Edgar would agree with me on Ray Charles and Bobby Bland, but he wasn't real sure if they were more primitive, or if they hit beats in the wrong places, like Lightnin' Hopkins, John Lee Hooker. He wasn't too sure about that kind of stuff at all. I was afraid I was going to learn too much. I love Edgar, I respect him, but our approaches are completely different. Now, I still have no interest to change my style all around. I just want to get better at what I do.

It's hard for me to say where blues stops and rock 'n' roll starts. I've always played both of them, and to me they're the same thing. The rhythm might be different. Writers have always wanted to put me in one particular category or another, and if you get out of that category, you're not real, things I never dreamed about and still don't make any sense to me. I missed that freedom to be able to do everything. I want every album to have a country song on it, a dance song, I like all that variety. I've done now about twenty-five albums, and they have their differences. But if you're going to have your audience out there, you can't confuse them with anything that's too weird. But if you're playing a good Texas bar, they want you to be able to play anything, a jazz song, you have to be able to play country, but you can slip in some rock 'n' roll here and there, blues. You can pretty much play all of it through the course of the night. Even Cajun music. That was an influence. Beaumont is so close to Louisiana.

Keith Ferguson was one of the first white guys I met who was into the blues, and he's been into all kinds of things. He loves the Mexican music. He understands what they're saying and I don't. It doesn't mean as much. But he still plays blues. In Texas even the Mexicans played blues, in San Antonio and Austin. They played in white bands [Doug Sahm] and they played in their own [Sunny and the Sunglows, Charlie and the Jives, and The Chili Peppers.] But where I lived you could hear Cajun, and you might never hear Mexican music.

I like traveling, hearing as much as I can, but if we did it all the time, I'd hate it. The way we do it, for about a month, is just right. At the first of the month, I can't wait to get out there, but at the end of the month I'm real ready to come home, then having a couple of weeks or maybe as much as a month to be at home and away from the road completely. I wouldn't go out on a six-month tour for anything in the world. I did that for years, and liked it, but now I couldn't live that way. I've been doing it this way for about the last fifteen years; keeps me healthier. When I'm off the road I like to hide and New York is a great place to hide. Living on the Upper East Side, it's quiet, a little neighborhood, peaceful. It's a lot easier than a small town, where everyone would know when I got back. I want some time to explore other areas.

My interest in tattoos doesn't relate much to blues. I was just wanting to try something new. I was thirty-nine, getting ready to turn forty. I had a lot of

friends in groups that had gotten tattoos (Stevie Ray Vaughan, Jimmie Vaughan, Preston Hubbard). I had gone to see Keith Ferguson and he was getting tattooed the next day from Spider Webb. I went to see what it looked like. The tattoos would look better on your skin. It's like the difference between drawing on tan paper and completely white paper. It would show up, and I said, well, at least I'm old enough now that I can't wake up when I'm middle-aged and say that I made the wrong decision. I figured if it didn't hurt too much I'd give it a try. I even had Spider to do a few cuts with no ink. He and my girlfriend played tick-tack-toe on my arm with no ink, so I could see if it was something I didn't want to get into. It really surprised me how little pain there was. The arm isn't a very painful spot, but when you get into your chest or legs, it can be real painful, but if you want it enough.... I'm still interested in getting tattoos from people I like. Ed Hardy does great work. Tattoos are a way of being different.

In that way, I suppose tattoos are like my blues. I still don't exactly know that my blues is any one thing. I used to feel bad about that, that there wasn't anything to fit into. Here I was from Texas, I was into the way people play in Chicago. The white players who have come along in the last twenty years from Texas probably have more in common than the people [black players] who have come before us. We all play the electric guitar and are maybe more influenced by the Chicago sound.

To me, blues is getting your feelings out. It's not a particularly fast thing, a lot of people think it's crying in your beer, let's all feel bad together, but it's really not that way at all. The blues has a lot of up songs, your experiences. Even if you're talking about the bad, you

Johnny Winter
Sweden, circa 1980s
Photograph by Hans Ekestang
Courtesy Tommy Löfgren

can feel better because you can relate to it. If it's done right, it should make you feel like you're sharing the experience. The music goes along with that, there's a lot of sevenths and ninths, I can play the bluesy notes, sliding up and down, but it's hard to put into words. Every time I do a song, I do it differently, according to the way I feel. With blues it's easy to communicate with other musicians that you've never played with.

You can usually play together and make it work out without pre-planning. There's a spontaneous part of it. It's a living music. It makes me feel good, whether I'm playing or listening to other people. That hasn't changed since the first day I heard it. One of the things that's fascinating to me is not quite understanding why I like it. It's mysterious, but whatever it is, it still works the same way on me. I don't feel good if I'm not playing, not hearing it, there's a real hole in my life. For me, blues is a necessity. **99**

Johnny Winter
Poster by Micael Priest; Austin, 1978
Courtesy Barker Texas History Center

Barbara Lynn
Promotional photograph, 1987

BARBARA LYNN
(1942–   )

❝ Elvis inspired me. I was playing piano then, I was a teenager. I started piano when I was in grade school, but I was getting tired of that. Then I heard Elvis and decided I wanted to do something odd. I thought it would be odd for a lady playing guitar. My first guitar was an Arthur Murray ukelele that my mother went out and bought me for nine-ninety-five. Then they saw that Barbara could really do something and they bought a solid-body guitar, and then one you could plug into an amplifier, a Gibson. Now I play the Fender Squirrel.

Huey Meaux heard about me, a girl playing left-handed guitar at a place called Lou Ann's. I had an all-girl group called Bobbie Lynn and the Idols, and we did a lot of the Elvis tunes, like "Jailhouse Rock," and I swung my instrument and we all wore pants. Joe Berry saw me sing and perform and went back and told him about me. Mr. Meaux came to my home and asked my parents' permission to record me.

We recorded a song out of Houston called, "Dina and Katrina." It didn't do very good until I recorded "If You Lose Me, You're Losin' a Good Thing." We recorded that in 1963 and that started it off. It took me to forty-some states; I've been overseas three or four times. I have really traveled with that one record. It was originally on the Starfire label, and then Jamie Records licensed it from Huey Meaux and thereafter it started blooming like a little flower, planted a little rose, and it kept going and going.

Around Beaumont and Houston there were lots of rhythm and blues singers — Gatemouth Brown, Guitar Slim, Ray Charles, Bobby Blue Bland, B.B. King, Junior Parker, O.V. Wright. I think my singing combines a lot of what I heard and brings together rhythm and blues with soul and a little pop now. I got ideas from other musicians. I observed and learned my own approach.

Some of the songs — "Until Then I'll Suffer," "You're Losin' Me," "Second Fiddle Girl," "Teenaged Blues" — I wrote these in the late 1950s, so by the time I got to perform them on stage, I was ready. My first LP was called "You'll Lose a Good Thing" in the late part of 1963, and then I had "This Is Barbara Lynn" on Atlantic in the early 1970s.

I got to be on Dick Clark twice. It was nice. Dick interviewed me, and I was finally looking at the blue-eyed man I had seen on TV for so long. This is when "American Bandstand" was in Philadelphia.

Then I got married, and that slowed me down a little, and in the 1970s not a whole lot happened. After the Atlantic release, it dropped off. I still had a band, and we played in Oklahoma, Louisiana, and Texas. After I got divorced I was able to pursue my music more. My former husband was interfering with my career and it was time to do something else. In 1978 I did my last record with Huey Meaux, "Movin' on a Groove," but it didn't go well. After that I slowed down, but have never stopped singing or writing, and am looking for new recording opportunities in Los Angeles. But I play sometimes at the Classic Club in Dallas, and at Antone's in Austin. Clifford says, "This is your club, baby," and whenever I'm there, I always feel at home. It's a warm feeling.

A lot of people say I started something because it's so odd for a woman to be playing a guitar. I use a thumb pick and I strum the strings with my first finger. I have a style all of my own. I can't play the way most guitarists do. If I get a title in mind, then I have to go right to my instrument and then I work out the lyrics on the guitar. I have faith, patience, and determination that it will break again. **"**

Barbara Lynn and Albert Collins
Austin, 1987
Photograph by Alan Govenar

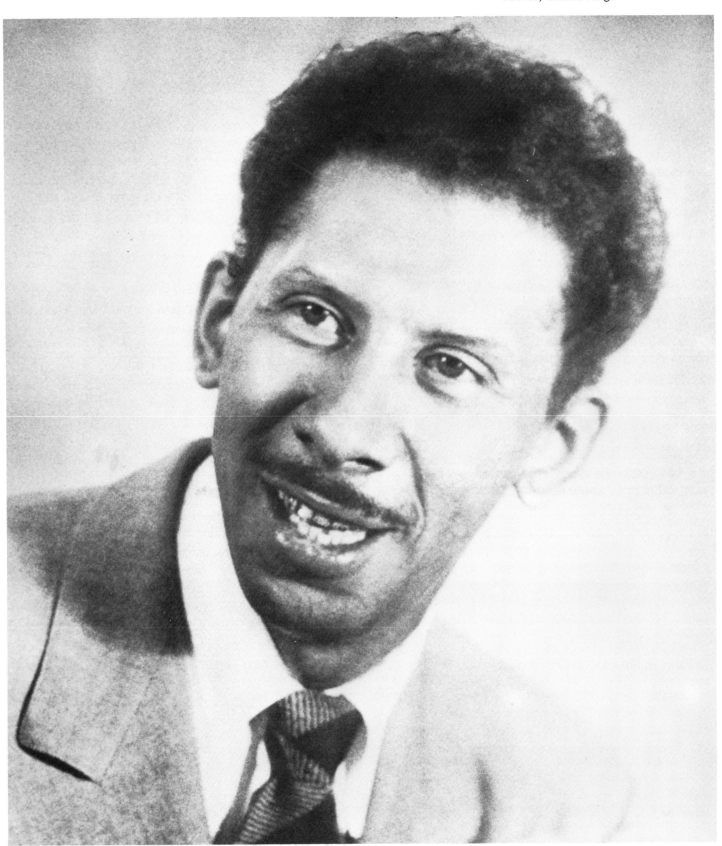

The Clarence Garlow Bon-Ton show on Beaumont's KJET radio that aired in the late 1950s and 1960s brought zydeco and rhythm and blues to a new audience. Among the audience was young Johnny Winter, who not only listened to the show, but sought out Garlow's band in local clubs.

Clarence Garlow was born in Welsh, Louisiana, in 1911. His family moved to Beaumont when he was five. His earliest musical instrument was his father's fiddle, which he started to play when he was eight. As Garlow got older, he began playing guitar and accordion and was influenced by English and Creole French music. But when he heard the "amplified sound" of T-Bone Walker, his attitude changed. He wanted to play electric guitar — and he wanted to meet T-Bone Walker. In an interview he recalled, "Sometimes I'd catch them at rehearsal, sit around and listen to them and get pointers from them. One time T-Bone came back through and said, 'Well, look old buddy, still got that mailbag on him instead of picking up a guitar! So I resigned my day job at the post office and picked up a guitar."

In 1949 Clarence Garlow formed his own band and went to Houston, where he played in local clubs. He was discovered by Macy Lela Henry, who decided to make him the first "race artist" of her newly formed Macy's record label. She took Garlow and his band to ACA Studio and there he cut his first six sides, which included "Bon Ton Roula" (the phonetic French that Macy's invented for "Let the good times roll"). In a relatively short time "Bon Ton Roula" became a small-scale nationwide hit, and Garlow continued to work steadily in southwestern Louisiana and around Texas.

His second recording session was in 1951 on Jay Miller's Feature label in Crowley, Louisiana. He then cut four sides for George Khoury's Lake Charles label, followed by sessions for Aladdin records in Los Angeles in 1953, for Flair in Culver City in 1954, and later for Eddie Shuler's Folk Star and Goldband labels, again in Lake Charles.

Over the years Clarence Garlow worked independently, negotiating his own business agreements, booking his own appearances, and refusing to sign binding contracts. For this reason his recording sessions were usually "one shot deals," which offered few residual benefits.

CLARENCE GALLIEN

❝ When I came to Houston thirty-three years ago, Lonnie Mitchell had already been playing for the Continental Lounge for five years. At that particular time the Continental Lounge was closed and was leased. So I approached the man who owned the building to start la la. He put me in touch with Lonnie Mitchell as reference for what kind of business he had. Lonnie Mitchell has played for at least thirty years at the Continental Lounge, but they didn't call it zydeco at that time, it was la la. They used to give different la la at the house or at a little cafe.

La la was a house dance when thirty, forty, fifty people get together and have a good time. The name changed from la la to zydeco when Clifton [Chenier] made the record *"Les Haricots Son Pas Sale"* ["The Snap Beans Are Not Salty"]. Clifton is the man who got credit for changing the name. When he made that record, people would ask him what *haricots* means and *haricots* is snap bean. And from then it was difficult to pronounce and spell the word, but now most around here spell it "zodico." He pointed to a flier. Clifton didn't really change the music that much, but any time anybody plays the accordion, we call it a la la, a country la la.

When I came to Houston I started a club, a country kind of club in the early 1940s. But Clifton wasn't playing at that time. The other musicians would charge me a base price for a night dance, and after that, Clifton liked the music so much that the guy who was playing gave Clifton an accordion. Well, Clifton was playing so good that for some reason the guy took his accordion back. So Clifton's uncle, Big Chenier, bought Clifton an accordion, and he went to playing. And before I knew it, he was number one in the zydeco business, and he's still number one. All the other guys that play, a lot of them copy Clifton's playing. But Clifton never played anybody else's records but his own.

Now zydeco is one of the most popular music styles in Louisiana and Texas. If a club give dance, or at a Catholic church, everybody will be at the zydeco. I

have been helping to put zydeco in the churches for twenty years, and over those years they never had a misunderstanding. The people are like brothers, sisters, or friends. They go out to zydeco to enjoy themselves and have a good time. We never have a problem.

When I first came to Houston I belonged to St. Nicholas Catholic Church in the Third Ward, and then I moved and we joined Our Mother of Mercy Church. But I was told to transfer my membership to St. Francis of Assisi. So I decided that I would transfer thirty years ago. It was a settlement of whites and I came over here and worked head and head with them in various bazaars. They used to tell me that "one of these days we're going to give it over to you." I said, "That's no problem." And when they finally did that, we had a $250,000 debt in this parish. My pastor, Father Cumming, needed some means of raising money. We were only collecting $36,000 a year and our expense was $52,000 a year because we had a school connected with the parish. So I told him that I wanted to give some entertainment, dance, zydeco, and he said, "Whatever you can do, please do it."

The first dance I had was a zydeco and we paid the band sixty-five dollars. Well, we had a full house and we made money. Then the next month I got Clifton Chenier to play. At that time he was charging one hundred and twenty-five dollars, and man, when he played there, everybody came of all walks of life, old people. Now it's kind of mixed up with young. But then all the old folks come because they wanted to dance the zydeco. Today, young folks participate in zydeco as much as the old.

The next band we got was a polka band, and I wasn't in favor of it. But they overruled me, and they went ahead and did it and came out eight dollars behind with the polka. From then on, we didn't substitute no other band but a zydeco band, and we've been successful. I go around and every place I help promote the dances, and the other churches saw how great we was doing and started zydeco — St. Nicholas, St. Francis of Xavier, Our Lady Star of the Sea, St. Peter the Apostle, St. Gregory the Great, St. Anne, and others. We now got about twelve or thirteen churches that are giving zydeco in rotation, once a month, all churches. Some churches take it every other month, so that there isn't competition.

I retired from promoting the dances, but I still go out and advertise for my churches. I emcee just about anywhere I go at churches in Houston. I start the dance off at ten, and then I emcee the whole dance.

The world is going for zydeco now, but it was never popularized on the radio until recently. We've been trying and I'm so glad that somebody woke up for creole cooking and zydeco. In San Antonio [at the Texas Folklife Festival] people were amazed. I love to cook. The ladies from the Altar Society make the gumbo at the dances. Of course, my wife is usually in there with them. I do the advertising and what I can to help out. I don't get paid anything. But I get a thrill out of this. I work with the senior citizens, I go and pick up bread for the needy. Whatever I do is no charge. I'm available. **99**

CLIFTON CHENIER

(1925–1987)

Clifton Chenier
New Orleans Jazz and Heritage Festival, 1975
Photograph by Michael P. Smith

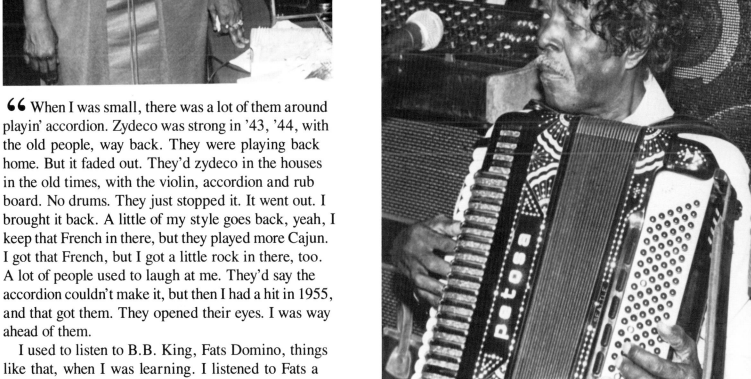

Mrs. Clifton Chenier
Photograph by Alan Govenar

Clifton Chenier
Photograph by Alan Govenar

66 When I was small, there was a lot of them around playin' accordion. Zydeco was strong in '43, '44, with the old people, way back. They were playing back home. But it faded out. They'd zydeco in the houses in the old times, with the violin, accordion and rub board. No drums. They just stopped it. It went out. I brought it back. A little of my style goes back, yeah, I keep that French in there, but they played more Cajun. I got that French, but I got a little rock in there, too. A lot of people used to laugh at me. They'd say the accordion couldn't make it, but then I had a hit in 1955, and that got them. They opened their eyes. I was way ahead of them.

I used to listen to B.B. King, Fats Domino, things like that, when I was learning. I listened to Fats a whole lot, and all those New Orleans piano players. Professor Longhair was one of 'em. Guys like that. The beat came from the religion people [clapping his hand in time, demonstrating the fast syncopated rhythm]. My daddy was a musician, so I guess it rubbed off. Even in the little clubs, it seemed like everybody was playing rock in those days. Something just came to me. I said to myself that I wanted to change from that and so I started playing rock with French music mixed in.

I learned to play in Lake Charles and in Texas, Houston mostly. My sister lives there. I never picked up an accordion until 1947, and after my uncle got me one, I kept it up and played around Lake Charles.

(*Left*) Clifton Chenier
Promotional photograph
Courtesy Charlie Lange

Cifton Chenier's Big Wheel Rolls To Eldorado

HOJSTON — Clifton Chenier's "Big Wheel" will roll into town Tuesday, June 16, and add to the reasons why our town is called "Feavenly Houston." Opening at the Eldorado Ballroom, the Argo records star who created and introduced a new sound in a style of music synonymous with blari-: saxophones and tinkling pianos, seems destined to break into the private echelon of big blues musicians with his magic accordion.

Backed by the big beat of his orchestra — organized with the aid and under the supervision of Dallas promoter Howard Lewis —

the a :ordionist weaves a spell with threads of silver sounding squeeze-box notes and broad bands of harmony.

The Port Arthur native has amazed name band leaders by moving in on their territory, turning the heads of enchanted fans, and leading them away with the magic ease of a world fa-mous musician — the Pied Piper. Though he discovered for him-self that the road to fame is paved with cocrete — stubborn promoters who didn't want to take a chance on an "unknown" — he has inched his way along and collected hordes of support-ers throughout the Southwest.

As a matter of fact, his first our through the South and South-west yielded such big results that he was immediately signed by Chess Records. Now he is rolling like "A Big Wheel" across the country.

BLUE STAR OINTMENT
FOR RELIEF OF
Itch, Eczema, Ringworm and other Skin disorders. There is nothing Retter than TIME TRIED GUAR-ANTEED.

155

Continental Lounge poster

Clifton Chenier and Lightnin' Hopkins
Photograph by Chris Strachwitz

I was working in the oil fields. When I was back on the farm, I wasn't playing at all. I remember when that song "The Honeydripper" came out. That was the first record I learned how to play. I started from "Honeydripper" to "Caldonia." I was in the clubs by this time. Then I learned how to play boogie on the accordion. People didn't understand how the accordion could make those sounds. What I did was my own thing. Nobody showed me.

That zydeco music, people who don't know how to dance, it still gets them up on the floor. They got to dance. That zydeco's got the beat, but it's a pure country sound. We was country boys, and you never lose that country feeling. **99**

Big Roger Collins birthday collection

Happy Birthday, King (cake)

John "Bones" Nobles
Beaumont, 1985
Photograph by Alan Govenar

JOHN H. NOBLES

(1902–   )

" I don't care how much rhythm we had. We didn't have no way to let it out. My dad was making fifty cents a day. Three dollars for six days. There wasn't no money to buy musical instruments. The only way for us to let our rhythm out was to find us some bones, but the fact is we didn't use bones at first. We cut our rulers at school at the six-inch mark and made us two little sticks to knock and that would give us our vent.

Well, after a while, some of them boys got a little combo going and I wanted to play with them. One boy had a jew's-harp, a rub board, and I was the bones player. See, I found this old cow and the buzzard done cleaned him up and the weather had done cleaned him up and had done them bones white. I went and got me a saw and sawed me off some bones. That put me above them boys who only had sticks. They kept asking me, "Johnny, where'd you get them bones?" And I'd say, "A man done come through here from up the country and gave them to me."

I went out there and cut me a bunch of bushes and covered up that old cow so that they couldn't find it, and I was kind of unique. So they had to use me in that band.

I process these bones. I put a salve in them. It takes about two months to get a set of bones where they'll give you the right sound.

This white girl from Lamar College once stopped me and said, "Look there, Mr. Bones."

I say, "What you see?"

"Why is this [bone] white and that one here black?"

I say, "Why are you white and I'm black?"

So, she say, "Go on with the show."

I didn't make them. That man put colors where he want them. These bones were white when I got them. These bones were black. So the good master put color where he want it. I ain't got nothing to do with that. But the white and black ones have a different pitch. The black ones have a sharper pitch, keener. I play them both. Black and white get along mighty fine when I play them together. You hear that [snaps the bones together]?

I can play myself or with a band. I played with Gatemouth Brown, Clifton Chenier, lots of bands. I like that zydeco beat. I always had a style of rhythm that was a little different from what they were puttin' down. You have to follow that beat.

I was a dancer, man. I could cut a rug, but arthritis took care of that. I can't do much dancin' now, but I got good rhythm in these bones. I'm eighty-five, born in a little place in Georgia in 1902, been in Beaumont since 1922. Back then when everybody was either choppin' cotton or hoein' corn. But when that dance time come you put the hoe down. You put your hoe down and everybody come to the dance. That's the way we had a lot of fun.

I learned to dance when I was shinin' shoes. It was a nickel for a shine, but it was two boys, one working against the other, one shining one shoe, the other shining the other, and the one that shined the best got the nickel. If he couldn't pop that rag and give you a hoodle-doodlely, well, he didn't get nothing. I was the one who was going to get that nickel. I'd pop that rag and sound like a buck dancer. **"**

(*Above*) Gatemouth Brown
Promotional photograph
Courtesy Barker Texas History Center

L.C. DONATTO

(1932–   )

(*Left*) Silver Slipper Club; Houston, 1986
Photograph by Alan Govenar

have no horns because it does not go well with zydeco. Today we don't have violins, but it still fits in the Cajun music, early zydeco, like Canray Fontenot. I knew Alphone Ardoin, and his son, Lawrence "Black" Ardoin. I was born in Opelousas in 1932, and I heard a lot of it when I was coming up, and I still love it. I love to look at the people having fun. I get a kick out of them dancing.

My wife only comes to listen to me if I'm playing at the Catholic hall, but she won't come to the cafes. When I'm not playing, I be working or I stay home and rest. I work a day job for the city of Houston. I do floor work, I'm figuring on retiring. I've done it for thirty-three years, but I'm continuing with my music, can't let that go by.

You can play blues on the accordion, but blues is blues and zydeco is zydeco. They think it's French if you play that accordion, but it's not, they're different. You have to play from your heart. And what makes it really good is when you get a full crowd of people. It makes you play better. I'm not a drinking man, can't be, especially if you're going to pull that accordion. It weighs thirty-five to thirty-eight pounds. I have a bigger one at home, that weighs forty-some pounds, but now that I'm getting a little older, I want to get me something a little lighter.

Clifton [Chenier] did his part. I'm related to Clifton on my mother's side and my wife's side. We're double kin. I play mostly in the style of Clifton and like Joseph Riley, who taught me to play button accordion.

Willie Green, he's dead now, and I were the first two blacks who played zydeco here. When I did start off, it was very hard to make a living in Opelousas. I was only getting but four dollars a week, but soon after that time I was able to get about eight dollars a night in Houston. I knew how to work. Well, when I got here, I went to a little cafe and Willie Green was playing and I stood over at the bandstand. He said, "You know anything about this?" And I said, "Oh, a little bit." He said, "I'm going to let you try," and I got on there. Everybody was surprised, I was a small

❝ Up from where I live is called Frenchtown, off Liberty Road, the Frenchmen everywhere now. In this part of town there is probably as many French Creole as Texas people. I moved to Houston in 1944, and brought the same zydeco I heard when I was coming up. When you talk about adding saxophones and horns like they do now, that really is not zydeco. The real zydeco was accordion, violin, rub board and an angle iron, a triangle. I've added a drum and guitar, but I

Zydeco Cha Cha Lounge
Houston, 1986
Photograph by Alan Govenar

L.C. DONATTO, JR.

boy. And then one time, we were driving around on Christmas morning in Sixth Ward, playing that accordion, and somebody on a front porch banging on a guitar stopped us and went in the house and asked his wife if we could play some of that, and she said, "I'd like to hear it myself." And before you knew it the yard was crowded. They stamped all the lady's flowers in the ground, but she didn't pay no attention to it. She said, "Forget about the flowers, you all." So, Miss Irene heard us and came around and seen all the people in the yard. She said, "Come on over to the cafe." And we did; we're the first two blacks to play zydeco in Sixth Ward. That's how we got started.

Now I play piano accordion, too, but I still play button accordion, single row French accordion, and a three row button accordion, organ and piano. My mother used to play the French accordion. My father couldn't play nothin' and he was real jealous that mama could play. So I learned, got it in my blood from mother and it's carried me a lot of places: Paris, France, Switzerland, El Paso, St. Louis, Chicago, Los Angeles. I have had a whole lot of fun. My mother and father never taught us how to talk French. The few words I do know I learned it by listening to the records. By me being French Creole, it's not hard for me to say it, but I can't hold a conversation talking French.

We can play zydeco, rock 'n' roll, blues, and French. Zydeco you sing in French. We mix it up. They really went for it here and they still do. There is lots of zydeco in Houston — Paul Richard, Jabo — but for the real zydeco you have to get with the old players like Lonnie Mitchell, Anderson Moss, Vincent Frank. Anderson Moss, he's seventy, I'm gonna bring him my accordion, so he can play. I'm fifty-five and I feel better than I did when I was young. I take better care of myself. I have fourteen living children and I've been married thirty-five years. I've been playing for a lot of years. Sunday evening at the Silver Slipper, you have to get there real early if you want a seat, or even a standing place. 99

66 I've been playing zydeco since I was twelve or thirteen. I play rub board. It takes a lot of work, yes, indeed. It keeps the rhythm and I'll be watching dad all the time, watch his feet, checking him out. I love zydeco. I love everything about it. It's beautiful music. When I get off into it, that's where my mind is deep into the music. I sing sometimes behind dad. Dad, mom, I love doing it for them. I like to see them enjoy the music. I'm thirty-three, thirty-four in May.

I have two brothers. They box. All of my brothers box, Daniel, Joey, and Otis.

It took a while to learn the rub board, you know, with both hands, but then once I got on to it, I tried to put on my own rhythm into it. I used forks; different people use different things — bottle openers — but I love to use the forks. A friend of daddy's made my rub board and he died, and dad let me have it. 99

ASHTON SAVOY

(1932–   )

" I've been playing since back in the forties. My daddy used to be a violin player and guitar player, and I just took it up from him. I'm from Sunset, Louisiana, and back in them times he'd play that Louisiana music, blues, country la la. My daddy could make that violin cry. My mama used to dance. They used to play it on the porch. I used to find that funny, but it was sounding good. My daddy started to teach me when I was seven or eight. He learned me a few chords on the guitar, but it wasn't really what I wanted to do. I was catching the blues on the radio, out of Nashville.

I started playing blues when I went on my own. I had an uncle in Chicago. He came out here one Christmas and the day after New Year's he went back to Chicago and he took me with him. I started at playing different places across the River where they had all them bands playing, Lil Son Jackson, Bo Diddley. Then I started liking the blues and I started playing blues.

My uncle had a club in Chicago, called the Palomino, with sixteen-, twenty-piece bands, that old jazz, back in the forties, '46, '47, Louis Jordan, the big bands. I was about fourteen years old. That's where I got interested in music, but what I heard my daddy playing, that violin and guitar, it was back when there was Blind Lemon Jefferson and all that back yonder. It come a little bit ahead of my time and I didn't like that kind of music. In Chicago, that music I really started liking. I bought me a little old guitar and amplifier. I started playing like that and catching on fast, T-Bone Walker, a little bit this and that. Lightnin' Hopkins, Jimmy Reed, I started playing their style.

I came to Texas in '62 and I'm not playing too much. It kind of got away from me for a little bit. I stopped playing for six, seven years, and then L.C. [Donatto] asked me if I wanted to get something together, me and him, and get some drummers and stuff like that. But when I first came to Houston I had a bad band, about an eight-piece band. We were really jumpin'. I was playing then, but now I done forget a lot of what I was doing. Now, I'm playing something I can hold on to, but I used to be way up there.

I did a little recording, for Goldband, Eddie Shuler in Lake Charles, and J.D. Miller out of Crowley. I did some recording, "Down Mexico Way," "You Upset Me, " and they said I sounded too much like Jimmy Reed and they didn't want to take too many chances. So I just quit recording then.

Zydeco in Texas is a little different than the way they play it in Louisiana. In Texas they're kind of mixing that zydeco up, but in Louisiana they play that natural zydeco — accordion, rub board, triangle — that's all they had back there, no drums, no bass, and they play on them wooden floors back out in the cottonfields, you hear that old accordion about five miles down the road. The accordion player and that rub board were over there in that corner just stomping the beat, pulling that 'cordion. And everybody started running trying to get there, walking, on horseback, in the wagon filled with about twenty people. They had some bad accordion players who would play until they fall out. And then they'd put that accordion in the sack and go back home, wringing wet across the field. They call them the good old days, but I think the days now are better then they used to be. The music is different now. When they started coming to Texas, they put horns in it. When Clifton [Chenier] first used to play in Houston, he just had accordion and rub board and then after that in the '50s he started getting him some horns, bass, drums.

T-Bone Walker
Guitarist with the Milton Larkin Orchestra
Rhumboogie Club, Chicago, 1942
Milton Larkin Collection
Courtesy Metropolitan Research Center
Houston Public Library

Janis Joplin
The Matrix
San Francisco, 1970
Photograph by Burton Wilson

I met L.C. in Texas and saw him playing around, and about five years ago he asked me if I wanted to play with him. I said, "Let me think about it," because I wasn't too familiar with that zydeco. So we had a little rehearsin' and we got together that little old group there. There's more blues in the zydeco now than what they had in Louisiana. The people today don't know how to dance that zydeco, they jumpin' that rock 'n' roll. With that zydeco you see a joker start in one corner and when you look again he's in the next corner, kicking that dust up. The woman and the man know how to zydeco. The young folks today, they're just rock 'n' rollin'. Back in them days they used to play them old waltzes and two steps. Today they're mixing it with blues. **99**

THE MOVE TO CALIFORNIA

The blues came to California via the thousands of blacks who migrated from such states as Texas, Louisiana, and Oklahoma. They were looking for work in the shipbuilding industry of Oakland and the oil refineries along the coasts of Longbeach, Bakersfield, and other California cities. Census figures reveal that in 1930, there were only 81,000 blacks in the entire state of California; by 1950 the number had increased to more than a half million. There were some blacks that settled in the San Fernando Valley to work on farms and seasonal harvests, but the overwhelming majority were concentrated in the urban centers and lived in segregated areas of Oakland, Richmond, and Los Angeles. With this migration came numerous blues and jazz musicians who sought greater opportunities in the recording industry after World War I.

Many of the musicians who migrated from Texas to California had been encouraged by the success of T-Bone Walker. Walker went to California for the first time in 1935. He had been playing with Les Hite and decided to go on the road with his own band, managed by baritone player Dick Jim Wynn. Though Walker had made his first recordings in Dallas in 1929 for Columbia, it was not until he went to California that he found his distinctive style. In Dallas, Walker had tried different instruments — guitar, piano, ukelele and banjo — but in California he devoted himself to the electric guitar. He developed advanced harmonic chordings and made inventive use of jazz-inflected arpeggios and fleet, single-string runs. In addition to introducing a new role for the electric guitar in rhythm and blues, he defined a performance style, playing the guitar as he held it behind his head or back and suggestively thrusting it through his legs.

The contemporaries of T-Bone Walker who moved to California were influenced by his playing and performance style, but they also brought together distinctive regional traditions. The music that grew out of the Texas-California migration fused current styles with other regional musical traditions that included country blues, boogie-woogie, and jazz. This fusion developed into what Arnold Shaw has characterized as the "murmuring, gentle ballad style" of blues piano players like Charles Brown, Ivory Joe Hunter, and Amos Milburn, and vocalists like Percy Mayfield. These musicians left Texas but maintained strong contacts there, especially in Houston.

Amos Milburn was from Houston; Percy Mayfield was from Minden, Louisiana, but spent time in Houston regularly, as did Charles Brown, from Texas City, and Ivory Joe Hunter, from Kirbyville. They combined the boogie-woogie blues piano and

big band swing sounds of Texas with the blues-ballad style of the popular singers of the day — Leroy Carr, Cecil Gant, the Ink Spots — and the crooning of Nat King Cole.

Lowell Fulson, Smokey Hogg, Pee Wee Crayton, and L.C. Robinson were guitarists who emulated the style of T-Bone Walker, using the electric guitar as a lead instrument in front of horns, piano, bass, and drums. But they added other dimensions to the eclectic California sound. Lowell Fulson, who had worked with country bluesman Texas Alexander for three years, developed a smooth, ballad sound. In 1942 he was drafted and stationed in California, where he settled after the war. There he met Bob Geddins, originally from Marlin, Texas, who had started a record label and cut two sides, "Come Back Baby" and "Three O'Clock Blues," both of which had success on the charts. This success sparked Fulson's career and launched Geddin's Big Town label. Geddins would become an important producer of the Texas style of rhythm and blues in California.

In contrast to Fulson's sound, Pee Wee Crayton, who went from Austin to San Francisco, had a style influenced by T-Bone Walker and by jazz guitarists John Collins and Kenny Burrell. Two lesser known musicians, but also popular in the black community, were Smokey Hogg, a country blues singer from rural Cushing, Texas, and L.C. Robinson from Brenham, whose sound incorporated the influences of country fiddling, blues, and western swing. Hogg and Robinson were not, however, as successful as Fulson and Crayton in developing a commercial California sound — their styles remained more purely Texas — and consequently, they were not recorded as often.

In California in the 1950s and '60s the Texas styles were reshaped by the recording companies: Aladdin, Modern, RPM, Imperial, Specialty, and numerous other independent labels. The California sound brought together black musicians and white producers who were committed to creating new music that was geared toward mass market distribution and radio. The success of Texas musicians in the Los Angeles and San Francisco areas spread nationally and had great impact on the development of rock 'n' roll and popular music in America.

Although many of the first generation of Texas-born, California-based blues performers have died in recent years, it is clear that their legacy has become the musical threshold of the next generation. Performers as varied as Sonny Rhodes, Frankie Lee, Dave Alexander, Roy Gaines, Cal Green, Johnny Guitar Watson, Floyd Dixon, Buddy Ace, and Katie Webster, while integrating various musical influences, all retain elements of the Texas heritage in their performance styles.

(Left) Big Jim Wynn and T-Bone Walker
Promotional advertisement
Courtesy Charlie Lange

Bob Geddins at his shop
Oakland, 1983
Photograph by Pat Monaco

BOB GEDDINS

(1913–   )

acetate and had it processed. You put it in a copper tank and copper would build up on them lines so thick that you could peel it off and have a plate. At that time I had to get them processed in Los Angeles and then later on we got our own processor. We were making 78s. You had to put them on a wheel and spin them, grind the edges.

I had a guy running the day shift, a guy running the midnight shift. We pressed twenty-four hours a day. The press in them days, you could only press one record at a time, take about a minute to make a record, so you know about how many we got in twenty-four hours.

I'd rehearse the bands for a week or two. Then I'd take them to the studio. I was using KSFO in San Francisco. I made my first big record over there with the Rising Star Gospel Singers and the song "If Jesus Had To Pray, What About Me?" Church records and blues records are similar. They'd have a moanful tone and sound. The same people [that bought the church records] got them blues, too.

I'd find the singers. I'd go to the clubs, the churches. I went to clubs in Richmond, all blues, Jimmy McCracklin, Lowell Fulson, Jimmy Wilson [who sang "Tin Pan Alley"]. All of the clubs wanted them. I put out the records and they were promoted on the radio. The record shops all around would call me up looking for the records, and there'd be a line waiting for those records to be pressed.

Scotty's Records in San Francisco. That was a big place, on Third Street. That's where all the black people went to get their music. Scotty was a white man, but he had all the records. Most of them sold for a dollar and eight cents with the tax. We'd sell them to the stores for about sixty cents apiece. I took them around myself in my car. I'd load about a thousand and go all over San Francisco and Oakland. On a weekend I'd take a trailer and go to Los Angeles. I'd sell all of them. I'd sell one distributor in Los Angeles about five thousand records.

There was a lot of blues around Oakland, Los

66 I started a record company in 1945. It was called Big Town Recordings at Eighth and Chestnut in Oakland, but it wasn't much more than a double garage. It was a nice lookin' building, and the building next door is where I put my first pressing company.

We didn't have a tape recorder. We had a disc machine, the needle cut the voice right into a acetate disc. You sang to a microphone and the needle would go around and make a groove. Then we took that

Bob Geddins
Oakland, 1987
Photograph by Pat Monaco

Angeles, and Richmond in those years, 1940s, '50s. It attracted the workin' people, who worked in the shipyards. A lot of them were like me, from Texas. They'd get together and dance in them little clubs, doin' "Walk the Dog," "The Chicken," all kinds of dances.

I remember them old (Texas) singers, like Peter Wheatstraw, Blind Lemon Jefferson, Texas Alexander. I've seen all those guys. They'd play in the little towns with that big old acoustic guitar. They came to town where I lived, Marlin, Texas. That's where I was born in Texas in 1913. They'd come up to the black part of town. All of them would come through, but I moved to California in 1933 and I've been here since.

I've worked in the recording business, and after the Rising Star Gospel singers' hit, I didn't have to advertise. If you're a company and you put out one good record everybody in the neighborhood is going to come to you. When I had my studio, people were coming all day long. I'd have to turn them down. They'd want me to listen to them. Some of them didn't have nothin' but some of them were pretty good. Sugar Pie De Santo, the first day he came to me we made a hit record, named "I Want to Know" [in 1960]. And there were others: "Tin Pan Alley" by Jimmy Wilson, "The Gamble" by Ray Agee, "The Thrill Is Gone" by Roy Hawkins, and songs by K.C. Douglas, Jimmy McCracklin, Juke Boy Bonner, and Lowell Fulson. Some of them were from Texas, Jimmy Wilson was from Dallas, Mercy Dee Walton from Waco, L.C. Robinson, and Juke Boy Bonner, he was from Texas. I recorded him first, and then I let Chris (Strachwitz) have him.

Blues has always been popular in the South. That's all they bought. That's what the jukebox played. And when these guys come out here they were lonesome for the blues. We had a record shop and they were coming asking for blues. "Got any blues?" "Got any blues?" And we were selling Cab Calloway and Louis Jordan. That's what gave me my idea. I had put the spiritual out, and I saw all them people there, and I

switched to the blues. Nobody else had that blues. So I got a record manufacturing plant, cost me about, at that time, ten thousand dollars. And my mother's husband and a preacher next door with the church and another boy had to give me about fifteen hundred dollars apiece. That preacher liked me. I was in the Baptist church. And I had a little money, too, that I saved from that religious record that tore up the country. So I got that record company and it took off from there, [With several labels — Big Town, Art-Tone, Cavatone, Down Town, Irma, Plaid, Rhythm — producing and leasing masters in the 1940s and '50s to the major West Coast labels: Aladdin, Swingtime, Modern, Specialty, Imperial, and Fantasy, as well as to Checker in Chicago].

I took those records once to Texas, stayed eleven months, selling records on the road. I carried samples, about two thousand records with me, different ones. I'd go to El Paso, stay about a week or two weeks, and I'd move from there — Big Spring two weeks, Austin, Texas, two weeks. I'd go to every record shop and jukebox and they would take all of them. I'd send the orders back to California and they'd ship them out. I'd got those records known all over Texas.

In the 1960s the blues started to go down, and I got into electronics, repairing radios, televisions, and car radiators part time. I had some big records, but the whole demand wasn't as great as it was. The radio stations was the fault. They wouldn't play the blues, but I stayed with it. **99**

Interview by Bob Geddins
Oakland, May 1987

LOWELL FULSON
(1921–   )

Lowell Fulson and wife
Oakland, 1982
Photograph by Pat Monaco

❝ My first singing was done in churches, for picnics and socials. I was brought up around Oklahoma, born in 1921. They had outdoor picnics. I'm part Indian, Choctaw. My grandfather was a good fiddler. My father used to play second for him on the guitar, but I lost my father when I was a small boy. One of my uncles played a guitar; another played mandolin. I started playing when I was very young. They didn't have anything more than guitars and violins, harmonica. In 1939 I worked in a string band for a while in Ada, Oklahoma — Dan Wright and his string band. I couldn't get the blues feel for the type of music they were playing. So, Texas Alexander came through there, and he wanted a guitar player. So he heard

Lowell Fulson
Sweden, 1980
Photograph by Erik Lindahl
Courtesy Tommy Löfgren

me. He started singing a few songs when I started plucking on the guitar behind him. And I went on a trip with him to Texas. First, we started out in Western Oklahoma and played Saturday night fish fries and whatever else they had going on. They'd cut the nickelodeon if they thought you sounded pretty good. They let you play there, and then they passed the hat around, take up a little collection. There were no nightclubs at that time to play this kind of music, but the people had fun. Sometimes there'd be an old beat-up piano and somebody would bang on that while we played. We'd sing and play, and people danced. Cats payed pretty much money to hear them old blues. We'd make ten or twelve dollars and split it up, and why, that was a week's work.

I moved on to Gainesville, Texas, in 1941, and got a job as a fry cook, still playing my guitar every Saturday night at the country ball. They wanted to hear something other than that nickelodeon, and a guy with a loud voice, that was good. They'd give me three or four dollars and all the tips I could make. I mostly did it for my recreation. Cat was going to pay me to play, I was going to play anyway. I made up my own blues. "West Texas Blues" was the first one I made up. "Sitting here wondering if a matchbox would hold my clothes." It was a bunch of verses added together. Some called it "West Texas Blues." Others called it "South Texas Blues." It depended on where you made it.

The blues is a song a guy made up to himself the way he was feeling at the time. He had the blues. So the song matched the feeling that he had.

In Texas the blues is different. It's in the fingering of the strings, the tones, the moans and the groans. Texas blues singers seem to hold notes longer than other singers. They've got more spiritual type delivery to the blues than they do in other parts of the country.

T-Bone Walker made the electric guitar popular with "Bobby Sox Baby" in 1943. He brought the guitar player into demand. I came to California the same year, but I was in uniform. I was in the service.

I saw T-Bone here. He was the first to really play electric guitar. I saw Charlie Christian back in Oklahoma, but he was more a jazz player and played what I called a modern blues, where T-Bone played swing blues. There was a difference. T-Bone made blues his style, and Charlie Christian went with Benny Goodman. T-Bone came to California.

In those years was when blues was big in Los Angeles, but now it's quieted down. It has a bigger audience in Europe. Next time I play is in Switzerland, and then in London. I've played in France and Spain, Germany, Belgium, several places, all over, full houses and enjoyable sets.

Blues you can play a lot of different ways. You can sing ballads, moanful, play it shoutin' it, play a kind of rock style, dancing type. So we play it all kind of ways in Europe and they find it entertaining. I go as a single and they furnish bands. I rehearse with the fellows, or I send them a tape and they get it down before I come over and get to work. I don't have a band anymore. I move around mostly by plane, and the dates are too far apart, and I don't have a hit record. But there's more audience in Europe than stateside. It's mostly a white audience. They've taken a liking to the music. A lot of blacks want to listen to something else and think maybe that they've heard the blues all their life, they want something new.

Personally, there's nothing I enjoy better than a good blues, if it's done right, tells a good story if the music is put with it properly. I've lost track of all the songs I've written, I think, close to one hundred. Some are about me, but a lot are about other folks. If they were all about me, I'd be in pretty bad shape. You see a lot of things in travel. You see what other people do, whether it's good or bad, joyful. I've seen guys sing blues and cry like they were singing a spiritual. The blues will touch the soul. You'll feel it. It's looking like your hair is going to stand up on your head. Then you're getting into the blues. **99**

THE PITTSBURGH COURIER   AUG. 11, 1956

8

THE BATTLE OF
the guitars

PEE-WEE CRAYTON

TEE-BONE WALKER

By CHESTER HIGGINS

"He may tell you," Pee Wee Crayton confided, "that he taught me how to play the guitar. But it ain't so."

Thus Crayton, a 42-year-old showman with only 10 years in the business, touched off what bids to be a feud in fact between himself and T-Bone Walker, a veteran of 32 years of entertaining.

The two were appearing at The Flame in Detroit in "The Battle of the Blues Guitar," and Crayton brought the battle off the stage out into the streets.

"I think I'm better than he is," Crayton told The Courier. "He can play with but three fingers. I use all mine. He may be a better showman — he does the splits and puts his guitar behind his head — but I can play better.

"Anyway," he continued, "when he puts the guitar behind his head he can't play anything. He may hit a few chords, but that's all.

"I can play my own chords when I sing. He can't. You'll notice he puts his guitar down at his side when he goes into a vocal number.

"A fellow named Eddie Young taught me to play. He may say so but he didn't," he added. "But he's my friend."

"I patterned after Charlie Christian. I liked his style," Crayton said. "I was past 30 and working in a shipyard when I decided to learn to play. Young helped me."

In a later interview, T-Bone snorted, "Pee Wee might say anything. I can take T-Bone Jr. here and run him off the stage. Pee Wee plays two or three pretty good numbers, but the rest of them he stole from me.

"He never even met Charlie Christian, because Charlie died while Pee Wee was still working in the shipyard. If he says he patterns after Charlie, I'd like to know why he has such a large stock of my records in his home. I taught him what strings to use to get the sounds."

Crayton said he wrote the 1949 "Blues After Hours," but T-Bone said "Uh, huh, I'll get the record and play them against the one I made in 1935 and recorded in 1939 and which Louis Jordan made a hit of in 1940, and you'll see nothing is changed but the name," T-Bone retorted.

T-Bone Jr. (his nephew whose name is R. S. Rankin, 23) and Sr. are making the joint jump during their two-week engagement at the popular night spot.

And this hot rivalry may spill over into hot news items throughout the country.

Easy, Sweets!— Guitar ace T-Bone Walker seems to be saying "This is how it's done, Son" as he demonstrates his technique.

Hey, Now!—Detroit's Ziggy Johnson looks on as T-Bone Walker and Pee Wee Crayton work together on their respective guitars. They appeared together in the Motor City.—All Photos by Johnson.

Let's Go!—In an effort to see who is the best guitarist Pee Wee Crayton and T-Bone Walker combine for a session on their strings.

Pee Wee Crayton
Circa 1940s
Courtesy Esther Crayton

PEE WEE CRAYTON
(1914–1985)

Pee Wee Crayton
Circa 1950s
Courtesy Esther Crayton

Pee Wee Crayton's long and vast influence on post-war blues guitar has been extensively documented, including a lengthy two-part feature in *Living Blues* #56 and #57. He recorded for around forty years, beginning with some obscure efforts as a band leader and as a sideman for Ivory Joe Hunter and Turner Willis in the Bay Area. He achieved his renown on the Bihari family's Los Angeles-based Modern Records, where he turned out classics like ''Blues After Hours'' and ''Texas Hop.'' Under the tutelage of T-Bone Walker and John Collins, and the spell of Charlie Christian's records, he developed a guitar style that mixed jazzy single-note lines, wide bends, fancy picking, and some of the biggest, prettiest chords ever waxed by a blues player. He readily admitted that in the early days his repertoire was very limited and his voice was light, but in his prime and right up to his death in 1985, he was a confident, accomplished musician and entertainer.

Within a decade of his success on Modern, he was starving in Detroit, where he managed to befriend and influence jazz great Kenny Burrell. When he made it back to L.A., he found work as a truck driver and stayed with it 'till his retirement around twenty years later. But he never left music behind.

Pee Wee left his mark on modern blues guitar, and he got to savor some acclaim. After being somewhat maligned by country and Delta blues lovers in 1960s blues journals, he made a notable 1970 appearance at Monterey with Johnny Otis that resulted in a Vanguard album. Besides making subsequent new recordings, he was able to see the bulk of his early work reissued in the United States, England, and Japan. He played as a sideman with Big Joe Turner, Sarah Vaughan, and Roy Brown. He was interviewed frequently, and his graciousness is partly shown in the never-ending stream of vintage photographs he provided to accompany the resulting articles. In general, he was able to spend his last years knowing that his family was fairly secure in their comfortable duplex, to work some pleasant musical engagements, and to play a lot of golf. When he and Eddie

Pee Wee Crayton
Promotional photograph,
Circa 1950s
Courtesy Esther Crayton

Cleanhead Vinson were waiting to do their show at the Chicago Blues Festival, they passed some of their time by taking a spectator's hole-by-hole tour of a Los Angeles public golf course.

There's much to be said in praise of Pee Wee's musical legacy. He left a substantial body of records behind and memories of a lot of exciting performances. He was a master of those haunting after-hours mood pieces, aggressive blues vocals like "The Telephone Is Ringing," rhythm and blues pieces like "Treat Her Right" or "Down Home Blues," and poignant blues ballads. Probably the best place to start in appreciating his available recordings would be the two reissues from England on Ace, which contain the bulk of the songs Crayton released on the Modern label.

Dick Shurman
Living Blues #67

❝ John Collins taught me to play with all four fingers. Before that I only played with three like T-Bone Walker. But John says, "Play with four fingers and you'll get prettier chords." So he showed me how with all four fingers. Many of my friends are jazz guitarists.

Kenny Burrell and I are very good friends. He's a jazz guitarist, but he has what you might call a bluesy sound. I do a couple of his tunes, but I'm not a jazz guitarist. I'm a blues singer.

I sang with a gospel quartet years ago when I was real, real young, but that didn't influence me to start to singing the blues. Lot of the blues singers [in Texas] said that they started singin' blues because they were singin' the gospel end of church. Well, some of it is true. Some of it is not. I think it's just making up something, if you're not doing it. I used to sing in the choir and I used to have a quartet, but that didn't influence me to singing the blues.

I don't think that a bluesman is like a preacher. Sometimes guys can relate to different things that they do and feel they can be a preacher. Some of the Baptist preachers years ago would put their hand up in the air, holler a holy tune. They said that was a way of preaching.

When I get ready to play, I can't plan out a show. I might play one song one way this time and the next time I play it, I play it altogether different. Every guitar player has got a trait, and mine is hitting the high notes, like this [picking up his guitar and gently plucking a high E], followed by some of mine. It's like my song "The Telephone Is Ringing." [He times out three chord changes with a quick single string run]. But if I wanted to sound like B.B., I would go like this [He demonstrates again]. It all depends on what you want to do, the audience, the groove that you're in at that time, how the band is sounding. That's the way my playing comes out.

If I'm doing a show, I get to walking through the audience. I pick up different ideas, vibes from different people. I'll be at one table and I'll feel like this way and I get to another table and something else will come to me. It just changes. I never try to outplay anybody just to make anybody look bad.

Some guitar players never talk about their influences, but me, I like them all — Albert King, Albert Collins, Muddy Waters and I were good friends. There's T-Bone, Lowell Fulson, B.B. King, Freddie King, Earl King, bunches of kings. There were a couple songs that Roy Brown did that I really liked. He had a real high voice. You know, the thing that he put out — "The cold ground is my home tonight," something like that, and "I heard you were at the good rockin' tonight" — Those are the kind of things that I like to do. He was a good showman. We worked together on several jobs, like Percy Mayfield. He and I were the very best of friends, just as close as T-Bone and I was. He wasn't a guitar player, but he was just a blues singer and we were very close. He had a nickname for everybody and he called me "Wee Wee," and called Lowell Fulson "Cherokee," but he was a wonderful person. I loved him.

I met Elvis Presley when he first started learning how to play guitar. He came to hear me play in Memphis, Tennessee. He was a little bitty boy. He said that I was one of his idols at that time. He came to hear me play and I talked to him. We were in the dressing room together, but then he skyrocketed to the top.

For a lot of musicians, there's professional jealousy, but for me, I'm not jealous of anybody. I love all the musicians, the singers, Wynonie Harris, Jimmy Witherspoon, Big Joe Turner, Arthur Prysock and his brother, Red, who used to play tenor in my band.

Kim Wilson, he's a harmonica player. He's with the Thunderbirds now in Austin. Well, he lived in California for a while. I used to play with him. I taught him how to sing the blues. There are lots of musicians, white boys, these days that are out of sight.

The blues reaches people in different ways. There's one song by Jackie Wilson, "Don't Keep Doggin' Me Around," well you know, some woman feels like she's mistreated, that's the blues. They [women] like the blues like that. And when you start doing them kind of songs and everybody is getting too carried away and getting happy about it, I'm ready to quit singing and go in the dressing room. There's probably going to be a fight. So I get away from that. I like to try to play, to set aside the crowd, keep them happy. I like to get the audience to be involved with my show, let them participate in it, too. It's better like that. You have more fun. When somebody else is helping you sing or applaud, keeping the beat for you, it's nice. It's just one of them things.

The blues will always be around. It will never die. It's something that will always be here. Blues is the basic foundation of the music. 99

PERCY MAYFIELD

(1920–1984)

Percy Mayfield was a distinctive vocalist and performer whose songs have been borrowed by people as diverse as Robert Nighthawk and Dale Evans, from Lovie Lee to Shirley Scott and Junior Parker. He was an exclusive songwriter for Ray Charles and B.B. King, and was a major rhythm and blues stylist, whose musical roots were in Texas.

In an interview in the book *Urban Blues*, B.B. King told Charles Keil that Percy Mayfield could "put a song over better than anybody." And though he doesn't have a wide vocal range, further affected by tonsil removal and his terrible 1952 car wreck, he makes effective low-keyed use of "growls," bent and choked notes and phrases, and nuances picked up mainly from the smooth big band singers he followed during his youth. His words are full of dryness (even the ones about liquor), irony, and earthly acceptance of man's condition. He's first and foremost a blues balladeer, and his songs are often 32 bars.

Physically slight, he was neither a producer nor an onstage instrumentalist. He's been described as "the poet laureate of the blues." His songs and positive messages have strong religious roots. A frequently mouthed credo during an interview in January 1980 (with Dick Shurman) was "acknowledge God in all thy doings," and he explained his role: "I'm a poet, and my gift is love."

Mayfield's parents had musical and performance inclinations, but he left early to hobo hustle and do odd jobs. He spent time in Houston regularly, beginning before his 1942 move to Los Angeles, and started a family in Texas. He spent most of his time between tours in Houston, L.A., Louisiana, or Chicago. He began his professional ambitions as a songwriter. But when he took "Two Years of Torture" to Supreme Records for Jimmy Witherspoon, he was induced to sing it himself and was backed with a superb studio group led by Maxwell Davis and veteran Texas/California guitarist Chuck Norris. The rights to the record were passed around, and John Dolphin pushed it successfully on the West Coast. His next session was for Specialty, in 1950, and it magnified his success on a national scale through "Please Send Me Someone To Love/Strange Things Happening." He rode the popularity of those and subsequent releases through most of the 1950s, though his auto accident disfigured him and set him back for a while. At the end of the decade, after a series of attempts to retain Specialty's momentum on other labels, he began a five-year contract as a private writer for Ray Charles.

A lull through the late 1960s in Chicago was punctuated by an obscure but excellent album on Brunswick, then a deal with Stroud Productions, which generated three RCA albums. Since the last was released in 1971, times have been too quiet for one of the great figures of popular music. He made an unplanned, un-

advertised appearance on one song of a live Bobby Womack LP. He paid for a session with instrumental and production help from Johnny Guitar Watson, which was sold to Atlantic, and did twelve more tracks out of his pocket in 1979. Not only has he had to pay for his own sessions the last ten years, but it's safe to say that today the best-known musical Mayfield is Curtis. Meanwhile, covers of Percy's songs continue from all sorts of expected and unexpected sources.

He divides his own recording into his "career" (sustained relationships with attention to quality and promotion) and "hustles." The former group includes the hit version of "Two Years of Torture," his long affiliation with Art Rupe and Specialty, which numbers thirty-four issued songs and a "Best Of" album, Tangerine (two albums, 23 songs released) and the trio of RCA LP's. The Brunswick deal put together by E. Rodney Jones is borderline ("fly-by-night"). The hustles include a session for GruVTone, which may be his first recording, one coupling each on Chess, Cash, 7 Arts and Atlantic, two on Imperial and a 78 of two early

(*Above*) Percy Mayfield with Bobby Murray
Sacramento Blues Festival, 1984
Photograph by Pat Monaco

(*Left*) Percy Mayfield
Promotional photograph; *Courtesy Charlie Lange*

Percy Mayfield
Los Angeles, 1943
Courtesy Tina Mayfield

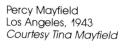

compositions on Selective by Dallas Red. His pre-Specialty blues and jump gave but little hint that a prayer in ballad form would top the charts for him next. Specialty also kept the blues mood going with songs like "Lost Love" (a.k.a. "Baby Please"), "Life Is Suicide," "River's Invitation," "Hopeless," "I Dare You Baby," "Lost Mind," "Bachelor Blues," "I Need Love So Bad," and "Memory Pain" (usually called "Serve Me Right to Suffer" when it's covered), and bittersweet offerings like "You Don't Exist No More." The Chess, Cash, and 7 Arts are worth finding but made little impact; nor did the Imperials, though they allow interesting comparison to B.B.'s first treatment of "My Reward." There was also some association with Don Robey in Houston, since Percy's first Tangerine recording, "Never No More," has some of the customary Duke credits. The Ray Charles tie-up yielded the classic "My Jug and I" album, a second compilation, "Brought Blues," and other excellent singles. Meanwhile, he was writing hits for Ray like "Hit the Road Jack/Danger Zone," "But on the Other Hand Baby"/"Hide nor Hair," "At the Club," and brilliant lesser-known releases like "Something's Wrong"/"My Baby Don't Dig Me." Ray's bluesy "Crying Time" LP deserves finding and/or dusting off to hear Percy's pennings "We Don't See Eye to Eye" and "You're in for a Big Surprise." Percy's Brunswick LP, "Walkin' on a Tightrope," contains the basic blues feel one would expect from a Chicago production with prominent guitar by Wayne Bennett. The songs and performances more than make up for murky sound. RCA put out mixed bags as blues, ballads, novelties, and inspirational messages attempted to keep up with tastes without much visible success. The Atlantic 45 lives on mostly through Watson's 1979 cover on his DJM LP "Love Jones."

The best Percy Mayfield compilations are on reissued albums now available: "My Heart Is Always Singing Sad Songs" (Ace), "The Voice Within" (Route 66), and "The Best of Percy Mayfield" (Specialty).

❝ Well, my native home was in Louisiana. I was born in Minden, Louisiana, August the twelfth, 1920. August twelfth right there in that hot sun. Leo. Now I got quite a bit of pride, you know. And there's nothing that I'm really tryin' to outdo nobody on, it's really just me, you know. Yeah, that's the way it is. You see, we had a big farm about seven miles out of town. And I came to California in '42. I was properly raised in Houston. See, I went everywhere. But I never did anything like show business around there before I came to L.A.

Tina Mayfield and Vida Lee Walker
Los Angeles, 1987
Photograph by Pat Monaco

I just wanted to be a songwriter. You see, I been singin' all my life, when I was a boy growin' up I was singin' in choirs and things like that, you know. And I never — when I came back to L.A. — after I came to L.A. to live, I just looked forward to just pennin' for artists in the background. I like to hunt and fish, and I just wanted to be in the background and be a starmaker. But the cat would only accept it if I would sing 'em, you know. And that's the reason I really got started. And after I got a taste of it, I loved it, 'cause I love the people.

I was supposed to be the co-writer for our recordin' company, for our talent club with singers and dancers and all those people. I was in the Al-Muzart Talent Club. I don't know what the name means; it already had the name when I came into the club. There was about twenty or thirty of us in it. Monroe Tucker was the biggest name and George Comeau, he was the trumpet player. And everybody was talented in it.

I couldn't refuse that cat [at Supreme Records] when he accepted mine 'cause it was a Mexican girl, Ida Bravo, was at our club, and she had a tune called "How Wrong Can a Good Man Be," and I just put a melody to that. I couldn't refuse because I'd be lettin' them down, see. So I recorded "Two Years of Torture/Half Awoke" [Supreme 1543, Swing Time 258], "How Wrong Can a Good Man Be," and another melody [Supreme 1549, Swing Time 262].

What a lot of people considered my style, which I got acquainted with now over the years — when it first started on me, they let me know they dug it. Actually, I'd be runnin' out of breath. There's that "Baby, pleeeese." You know what I'm sayin'? Then I'd sing, "Baby, please." Then I found out that was my style through the public. So I started bendin' most of my notes on the blues. And so it just comes out natural 'cause evidently it must have been my style, you know. But it was forced on me.

Tina Mayfield at Percy's piano
Los Angeles, 1987
Photograph by Pat Monaco

Percy Mayfield
Eli's Mile High Club
Oakland, 1984
Photograph by Pat Monaco

I just created it, tryin' to be a little bit different from anybody else. So I wouldn't have so many followers, you know what I'm tryin' to say. Now on ballads, I don't mind. But on the blues, you got so many blues singers out there that if you want to stand out, you got to be a little bit different. But what I mean by being myself, I laugh a lot. You know I grunt or bend notes or somethin' like that. But it's all comin' natural. If the band is kickin' then they can kick out a lot of new material on me. 'Cause I just create as I go along.

Well, it's courtin', man. Now if the melody comes first, you see, then I have to make the words marry it. And if the words — sometimes the words and melody come together.

Most of my style, and when I'm singin' sadness, started from pain, you know. But after I got set in my ways as to find out what my title or my talent was, I could sell more sadness than joy. You see, 'cause there's more sadness in the world than there is joy. However, that don't mean that I got to live as sad as I sell. You see, you got to have somethin' for that mass. Now, along about intermission, after intermission when the booze has started soakin' in, they want blues or sadness. Well, it can be a blues straight or a blues ballad, see, like that. But novelties like from the time you hit the bandstand till midnight like that [snaps fingers], jumpin', it ain't like that. So it's just a twin thing with me. I gotta do what I feel, you know. I gotta write it as I hear it and see it.

Oh, man, I just love the people and I love to travel. It's no particular one strong point. I mean it's universal. I just wanna tour one more time, but I could have me somethin' new. I don't. I wouldn't go out there now. They can't hardly pay me enough to make the tour 'cause I'd be second, or third, or be on a bill. So-and-so and such-and-such plus, or also Percy Mayfield. Well, I got too much pride. Maybe — it look like to me that I'm just being given a handout. I like to be featured, too, you know what I mean. So I'd have to have them somethin', I wanna have somethin' new out there for them, you see. That's the reason I don't cater to one particular incident. I cater to the universal. I don't know how else to put it, man. I just wanna go, go, go [snaps fingers]. I used to say in my slogans that "the world is my playground, I'm at home everywhere I go." Well, that because of what I believe in. It made me a poet, and my gift is love. And I love people and there ain't no two ways about that. And to travel across the country [snaps fingers], you know — to see the old faces and the old places that I ain't seen in a long time and sing to them, and then have something to offer. That's my highlight. **99**

Interview by Dick Shurman
Living Blues #50

CHARLES BROWN

(1920–   )

Charles Brown
Promotional photograph
Courtesy Tom Mazzolini

❝ Well, during my stay in Texas, my high school days, one of the teachers who taught chemistry and physics, Mr. James, had what you called little one-night stands out on the beach front there with these nice white clubs and this was just a little extra money to be made, and at that time I was a good reader in music because I was taking classical piano. He had a lot of guys who couldn't read, so he said, "Charles, I want you to come out here and learn this music that we play." And I went out on the beach with him and I was satisfied with what I was doing because I was making a little money, and at that time if you were making $18 a week you were making good money. That was when I was first introduced into this type of music, "Stardust," beautiful tunes like that, standard tunes, "Beer Barrel Polka." I stayed out there until I got the gist of the music, this was in, oh, I won't tell you when, it was a long time ago, but that was starting me into this music because my grandmother really didn't want me to play that type of music because I was playing in the church. She was a devout Christian woman. So, I went on and played.

At that time, a guy who sang so well, Pha Terrell with Andy Kirk, I was always enthused with his singing. I just thought he sang so lovely and so beautifully, and I just wanted to sing like that. Then here comes The Ink Spots with this high type of singing and everybody was trying to sing like that. Fats Waller with his kidding and things like that, we called it comedy singing, and we would try to pattern after those records, but I figured that wasn't my style, I liked the sweeter things like "No Greater Love," and "What I Feel for You," and I was influenced really by this Pha Terrell.

When I went to college after finishing high school I got into the college band. They asked me to sing only one number, "Big Fat Mama," which was a risque number, and they would go wild over that. That was the only type of singing I did at that time. After I finished school I got a job as a teacher there in Baytown, Texas.

[I attended] Prairie View State College, forty-five miles northwest of Houston. Majored in chemistry with a mathematics minor. In fact, I had two minors: math and education. Everybody ventured into teaching because that's all we knew at that time, but when you finish college you teach school. But, we did take chemistry because at that time the war was raging and they said chemistry and the chemical industry was very prosperous.

I taught school in Baytown. Mr. Archer, he was the principal, he wanted me to teach because he liked my personality. He said, "Charles, you'll do well with children because you have a beautiful personality." I went down there, but I didn't like it because we were paid $22 a week. You had to go to church, you had to pay your room rent out of that and when I got through I don't think I had five dollars left. So I had to find something else. I heard they had these jobs in chemistry and you could take a civil service examination. So I took this examination and made 96, which was a very high grade as a junior chemist. Washington, D.C., sent for me to come to one of the plants. I had a choice of Pine Bluff, Arkansas, Arsenal, or the one in Maryland. So I chose Pine Bluff because it was close to Texas, but I didn't want to go too far. I was a junior chemist there. I stayed there for six or seven months, then I wanted to transfer, but the war was raging and you had to go register for the service and they classified me 1-A. Then they asked me if I had asthma when I was young and they wouldn't let me go. After that I thought I'd go to California and make a new life.

Berkeley, California, they had a research laboratory there called Western Research. They transferred me there because I had asked for a civil service transfer. I don't know what happened but the job was taken and I got another job and registered at school there to get my master's degree. And I think I stayed there about three months when I said this wasn't it, because everybody wanted some piano players and I got a job working a little place there in the International House, that was out near Chinatown, playing the piano. I worked there as an added attraction.

That was 1943 and into '44, that was the year I went to Los Angeles. My uncle had a church there and he asked me to start playing for his church and he would give me money on Sunday. So, I started playing in church. I didn't like that too well because it wasn't enough money. Then I got a job with the Broadway Department Store as an elevator operator and I heard about an amateur showdown at the Lincoln Theater on Central Avenue, and on Thursday nights they were giving away twenty-five dollars for the first prize. At that time "Boogie Woogie on the St. Louis Blues" by Earl Hines was very popular, and I went down there and won first prize. When I played this number, they had a fit, then I turned around and played the "Warsaw Concerto" and they didn't expect that. You know, here's this guy from Texas, and they gave me a week's

work at the Lincoln Theater. So that was the start of Charles Brown, in the pit band at the Lincoln Theater.

Ivie Anderson, who used to sing with Duke Ellington, her husband came to the Broadway Department Store. I was working two jobs. He asked me to come over and work for him and I started playing for people as dinner music at Ivie's Chicken Shack. I stayed there until I made a lot of money, then she said she had to go to Mexico and I wasn't satisfied with forty-two dollars a week so I left and I didn't have any work at all. I quit the theater because they didn't pay enough money, but I had saved up my money and I went to Sugar Hill, which was in one of the most fabulous sections of Los Angeles. Ethel Waters lived there, Ben Carter, who was a great comedian, Man Tan Moreland was right around the corner. Nat King Cole, Noble Sissle, all of them living over there. When I moved up there Johnny Moore came looking for me, he had heard about this piano player that had won an amateur contest. He had lost his piano player and he come to me to replace him and he wanted to hear me play. I played for him and he said, "Well, you'll be the right thing for us. We have an audition out in Beverly Hills at the Talk of the Town. If we can make it we can use you. It pays $600 a week." I went with him and rehearsed. Our theme song was "Warsaw Concerto," trio playing these heavy classics, and "Holiday for Strings." So we practiced up. He said, "Do you sing?"

I said, "No, I don't sing."

He said, "Well, you got to sing."

So we practiced up for about two weeks before the audition, this was in 1944, and in September we went to the auditorium and they had about twenty trios and we figured we didn't have a chance at all. Then we came up there and these guys had done their stuff, and the guy was asking questions, "Can you play this type of number?" So when we got up there we had it together, when we opened with "Warsaw Concerto" and went into our theme the man said, "When could you open?" We said, "Next week," and we had the job. Jon Hall, the movie star, and Martha Raye would come out there every night, and Tommy Dorsey.

Martha Raye and Ben Blue wanted me to play for their parties up in Cold Water Canyon. So a guy called Johnny Shadrack and I, he'd sing, we did a duet, and they'd give us $300 for every party. So we had it made and all the movie stars just loved me. Then we started working out on Hollywood Boulevard, the Swing Club, which was one of the great clubs at that time. They had Eddie Heywood, Cee Pee Johnson, Harry "The Hipster" Gibson, and others. Frankie Laine, he was working out of Billy Berg's, and he started coming over. He said, "I want to sing like a spook; I'm trying to develop a style," and he was trying to sing like Nat King Cole, too. I was singing in an exaggerated style [sings], "To spend one night with you." That was my type of thing, and Frankie Laine took that type of style, but it didn't come out in him, so he had a style of his own.

We made our first recording [for Atlas Records] with Frankie Laine, called "Melancholy Madelaine." I was on one side with "Tell Me You'll Wait for Me," the same number Ray Charles did in his "Genius of Ray Charles" album, that I wrote with Oscar Moore. So then, Frankie Laine took this record out to Mercury Records and they signed him up. He was made after that.

After we made the first record with Frankie Laine, Johnny Moore was the type of guy who wanted to always see that his trio always got over, so he wanted to make some records of the trio. Well, we were singing this "Driftin' Blues" and all the people were going wild over "Driftin' Blues" during the war, but we had never made a recording of it.

We liked to go to the races and to the horses and Johnny said, "Look, I know Mother Davis over here on Forty-sixth Street. Let's go over and see her because she can give us some numbers to play at the races and they'll come in." When we went over there I told Johnny, "I don't believe in it," but I sat out in the car and she had a lot of people out there waiting for her.

Johnny went in there and she said, "Bring that fellow out in the car in here. I want to read him because I see something about him." So Johnny came out there and got me and brought me into this house. And she prayed this prayer, and I didn't want to go. It looked like the hair rose on my head and she said, "I see where you're going to sign a contract in twenty-four hours; it's going to take you across the country. And this fellow has a magnet, I'm going to tell you something, if you stay with me you will be successful. Listen to what I tell you." And we were listening, and she said, "I know you come here to play the horses and I'm going to give you a horse tomorrow." I think she said the fourth race, a horse named Lovely Millie. I'll never forget it, Number Seven. She said, "Don't ever come here with this gambling no more." Johnny was glad, he didn't want to hear no more. All he wanted was this horse.

We went out there with our little money, about eighteen dollars between us and put it on that horse and that horse came in and paid ninety-some dollars. We went back to work. We had a little job at the Copa Club, and clubs were going very late during the war, and about 2:45 a knock was on the door and we looked through the door and a guy had a satchel. It was Sammy Goldberg and Eddie Mesner, and Sammy said, "I want you to hear this "Driftin' Blues" that Johnny Moore's playing and Charles Brown is singing." He told us to play it and then asked us to sign a contract to make it for eight hundred dollars. So, John said, "Is that all you got?" He said, "Yeah, if the record does good I'll give you more. I'll give you a piece of the action in the company." It was the biggest mistake we ever made in our lives.

So when "Driftin' Blues" came out — we made it in '45 for Philo Records, which later became Aladdin — the other side was "Groovy," everything was cute then. And they put "Driftin' Blues" on the jukebox and we'd go from one jukebox to another to hear it because we wanted to know what we sounded like. And the jukebox operators in New York sent for us to come to New York. Then we had to get us an agent. So Johnny Moore went out to the William Morris Agency and they signed us up. Sammy Davis, Count Basie, and Pearl Bailey were the only black acts they had signed and we were the next one. They told us they could get us right into New York, but the Apollo Theater wouldn't take us because we weren't strong enough. So they booked us at the Renaissance Casino on a one-night stand with Luis Russell's band. Nat King Cole introduced us, lemme tell you. The Apollo Theater had Buddy Johnson and Ella Johnson in a showdown there. They had to call the fire department, this place was packed. You get on Seventh Avenue, and the Apollo didn't have nobody in it, we had all the people. So Schiffman came down, he was the big boss of the Apollo, he owned it. He talked to us at intermission and asked us if we'd be interested in working for him. He asked us, "Would you take twelve-hundred dollars for the first week?" He said, "If you do good that first week, the sky is the limit."

So when the Blazers opened the Apollo Theater, the band had to play a theme song, which was "Air Mail Special," that was our getting-on-stage number. And you had to run out there and get to the piano and get everything ready and boom. You had to be quick. People came up to the stage screamin' and hollerin' when we did "So Long" and "Moonrise." They'd be crying, "Don't sing it no more," "Do you love me? Do you love me?" Billy Eckstine came up there and Jackie "Moms" Mabley was on the bill, she was doing a single then, and we went over really terrific. And we had our own show and Johnny Moore hired Buddy Rich. We had Buddy Rich go to all the theaters with us.

We toured from '46 to '48, and when Oscar (Moore) left King Cole we added him, because Johnny (Moore) was very sick. So I had to go on as Johnny Moore because the people heard the singing, and they thought Johnny Moore was the singer. They didn't look on the corner of the record and see "Charles Brown, vocal." In those years the records said "Johnny Moore's Three Blazers." It was his trio,

but I was still the singer and the piano player. Then when we broke up in '48, there were a lot of misunderstandings about money.

So when I started on my own I quite naturally had to get a recording company and I got Aladdin back. When I left Johnny Moore we cut a first record, "Get Yourself Another Fool," and everybody thought I was telling Johnny Moore this (and) it made a big hit. I was getting big then. I was getting to be the number one rhythm and blues artist and I could hire anybody I wanted with the show. All the other acts that came into the office, like Ruth Brown, they would try to get them on the road with me, ask me if I'd take them, to introduce them at $50 per night. That's what she was getting, but when she made her first round she went up to $450 a night, she did so good. She had "Mama, He Treats Your Daughter So Mean."

Then I took the Dominoes, the Clovers, and Ray Charles. Ray Charles was working for me because I was the number one R&B artist. They booked him with my band and we made our rounds — Chicago; Lima, Ohio; Somerset, New Jersey; on around. We didn't go to New York. We went to little towns.

I had a good band. I took all the young guys that never had a chance: Boogie Daniels, Clifford Solomon, Walter Henry [who played with Johnny Otis]. And I had my cousin, who sings now. None of these people had played anywhere. I groomed them in how to play. Freddie Simon, of course, he's dead down, but all these people were just beginning. But now they all play with great bands. On guitar I had Wayne Bennett. He was with Amos [Milburn], but Wayne Bennett played with both of us. After him I had Jesse Ervin, who was my cousin who's in L.A. now. He made "Black Night" and all the best of them. I had about seven pieces and a manager.

When we would go out to play these places people would ask, "Why don't you sound like that in person?" See, now on the records, it really disgusts me because the records never show what I really could do. Because when you heard the records you heard a little plink-plink piano, a very simple guitar, a simple bass, plain singing. We didn't venture out. We had a style and that's what people knew us by. I didn't venture out to take a lot of solos, just enough to make the record. The people would say, "Charles, why don't you play more? Why don't you sing more to show yourself?" I said, "No, I'm satisfied." Then when we went in person with the band we sounded ten times better than the records. We even tried to get Eddie Mesner to record us like we sounded [live], but he said, "No, since you made money with a trio the way you sound, that's the way we want it, because that's what the people buy."

I stayed with Aladdin until 1952. Then we had a big run-in about royalties. I never got any royalty checks. They wanted to buy you Cadillacs but never give you royalty checks. I wanted an accounting of my royalties and what I had accumulated, and because I asked for an accounting they tried to put me in jail. I sued them, but I only got $8,000, but I could have got $100,000. Then for suing them they put me on the shelf and I couldn't sign with nobody for about a year or two. I figure [I did] two hundred sides at least for Aladdin, and they have some stuff they never released. Beautiful numbers. Aladdin had a fire before they sold out to United Artists and it burned up a lot of those masters.

I didn't sign with nobody after I got released from Aladdin. I just free-lanced. I went back to Exclusive Records. We had a short-term contract before Aladdin Records. We did "New Orleans Blues," "Merry Christmas Baby," "Lost in the Night," "My Silent Love," "You Are My First Love." **99**

Interview by Tom Mazzolini
Living Blues #27

Charles Brown
Oakland, 1987
Photograph by Pat Monaco

DON WILKERSON

66 As a kid I liked the blues. My mother was a piano player and I would hear her playing different tunes, and I'd hear different songs on the radio. My first knowledge of the blues was when Uncle Sammy's Grab Bag was on the radio in Houston. I'd listen to Basie, Jimmie Rushing, Joe Turner. They had all the blues artists on the program, and I would wait for that program every day. And as I grew older, I had the feeling for it and I started doing it professionally. The first time I ever performed was at the Eldorado

Ballroom with Milton Larkin, one of the greatest band leaders. I played alto, and then I worked different clubs around Houston, the Paradise Club for four years. Then a booking agent gave me forty-five one-nighters with Joe Turner.

Later T-Bone came through and heard how we youngsters were doing and we did thirty-one dates with T-Bone. I cried when he passed. I used to go by his convalescent home once a week, in Vernon, not too far from here. Bone was a hell of an inspiration for all the musicians. I consider him the genius of the blues guitar. Charlie Christian was a good jazz guitarist, but he just didn't have the blues feeling that T-Bone had. Everything was mellow. He could stand there at the mike and it would flow out with perfect delivery. No changes you called T-Bone couldn't play.

After playing with T-Bone my reputation continued to grow, and I've worked all over the country. I moved to California in about 1960, but I still love Texas and I go back every year. And when I go back to Houston, I play with La La Wilson, Lester Williams, get in on whatever sessions come along. I play both jazz and blues. There isn't much difference for me. It's in the arrangements and the singing. If a musician cannot play blues, they can't play jazz. You have to have that feeling.

I wrote several blues, "My Baby Hiding From Me," "Low Down Dirty Shame, Parts 1 & 2," a shuffle blues with a backbeat. The blues is an expression of feeling. The meter is important, lyrics. It takes a lot of different things, you got eight bar blues, twelve bar blues, sixteen bar blues, big band arrangements, ballads. When it comes down to it, blues is what matters most to me. Last week, I was playing behind Z.Z. Hill and he did "Down Home Blues" and it hit me so. I wasn't really supposed to take a solo on it, but I got up and I blew and that moved me. I thought this was the living end. Some kind of blues, it will make you do things you had no idea you could do on that horn. 99

(*Left*) Don Wilkerson; Los Angeles, 1984

LITTLE FRANKIE LEE
(1941–   )

❝ My full name by birth is Frankie Lee Jones. I also go by the name of Little Frankie Lee, my stage name. I was born in Mart, Texas, eighteen miles east of Waco, Texas, and I'm forty-three years of age, raised up in St. Mary's Baptist Church, and graduated from Anderson High School. I've been in California since 1968, the Oakland bay area since 1973. The whole while I've been out here, I've been in the music field, blues, what we call soul-gospel blues.

I sung gospel for a while back in Texas, at home. After I did my first recording on the Duke-Peacock label in 1963, then I stopped singing gospel and started doing R&B, and I've been doing it ever since. I have a new LP on the Hightone label, premiering it at the Monterey Jazz Festival, and hopefully, we'll take off from there.

I don't know how I got started singing blues. I was singing gospel in the church, and one day I found myself singing blues. I always loved blues, but I wasn't allowed to sing blues in my home because in the church, as I was raised up, the blues was devil music. During that time blues was down music, and if you grew up in the church, the only time a person would let the pressure release of blues come out was when they were drunk. And all the people in the church could hear down the street was B.B. King, Jimmy Reed, Howlin' Wolf, or Muddy Waters, every record

(*Above*) Frankie Lee; Oakland, 1982
Photograph by Pat Monaco

they were playing. After I found out years later that blues was an upper for me, my attitude changed.

I don't play an instrument. I was more influenced by singers: Reverend C.L. Franklin, Sam Cooke, Little Willie John, Bobby Bland, Ted Taylor. I'm not a writer, so I have to depend on others. I have Miles Grayson, Jimmie Lewis, and Dennis Walker. I don't know if they're from Texas, but they have the Texas influence. They wrote songs for Ray Charles, Z.Z. Hill, Little Johnny Taylor.

There were so many different blues artists we had to listen to in the late 1940s and '50s. I dug all of it, country-western, gospel. I just found myself singing blues. In 1963 I made my first record, as I said, on the Duke-Peacock label, "Full-time Love," which was the answer to Little Johnny Taylor's "Part-time Love." And the song took off and I got deep into it. Then we had a follow-up, "Taxi Blues," on the same label. I was around all the people I admired, the people I wanted to be with and see perform. I was in the middle of them. It was like a dream come true. There were Big Mama Thornton, Johnny Ace, Bobby Bland, Ted Taylor, Al Braggs, Gatemouth Brown, Little Junior Parker, O.V. Wright, James Davis, Joe Hinton. At the time I came along, Peacock was the gospel label and Duke was R&B. There were only two blues acts on Peacock, Al Braggs and myself, and then they started branching out with Songbird, BackBeat and SureShot labels.

I left Texas in 1965 with Albert Collins and we stayed on the road touring for five or six years. I made one other record on the Peacock label, which was "Hello, Mr. Blues," because by this time the relationship between Frankie Lee and Duke-Peacock had kind of turned sour. Mr. Robey had no plans of renewing my contract by releasing another record. Just before Mr. Robey died, they sold everything to ABC

and then MCA bought it from ABC. So I kind of drifted around for a while. Then in 1974 or '75 my cousin Johnny Guitar Watson and I were company shopping, and I landed a contract with Elko records. Johnny Watson produced the session for me and we did a few things together. Now I'm on the Hightone label.

I love the blues. It lifts me up. When I have the blues, and I have the blues every day, I can talk about it or I can sing and release this pressure and I feel like a brand new person. Nowadays, people are starting to get more into blues. It used to be a few years ago, my kids wouldn't listen to blues. It was all about disco, rock, or whatever, but now it's blues. This makes me know that the younger generation is getting more into blues then they have been. They're beginning to feel that the blues can lift them up, rather than keep them down.

Blues and gospel have so much in common. If you were to listen to a gospel record and just take the lyrics away, you might have a blues instrumental. The main difference is the change in the lyrics. They both come up together, and they both send a message. The blues is a way of talking about problems, just like gospel. The blues is a religion. Once you have been spiritualized, you feel better. When the blues is delivered from the stage, you've touched someone out there because you're talking about everyday life. By the end of the evening, if someone tells you that they understand, that they've relieved that pressure, then you've accomplished what you set out to do.

Every day that you wake up, you have the blues for some reason or another. It's not all the time that you have marital problems, but have got to wake up and go to work. So you put yourself in the frame of mind that this is what you got to deal with today. This is reality and blues is reality. It's something you got to tackle. It's life and success. **"**

Frankie Lee
Houston, circa 1960s
Photograph by Benny Joseph

KATIE WEBSTER

(1939-   )

66 I'm from a state where they have many great musicians, Texas. I mix it. I have a little bit of everything in my style. I don't just do blues. I do country and western, gospel. My dad was a minister and my mother was a missionary and classically trained pianist. We had a piano, but my mother said we couldn't play any blues, R&B, R&R, or jazz on that piano. It was gospel in the mornin', gospel in the evenin', gospel at supper time.

My father was from Chicago. When he was a little boy he heard sidewalk musicians and hung around the clubs. I'm excited to come to Chicago to be near where he played in the speak-easies when his father would go out and gamble and stuff. And my grandmother would send my dad with my grandfather to keep him from doing wrong. My father was maybe ten, eleven, twelve years old and playing the blues in these places. They would get dimes and nickels in this little cup, like a spittoon or something for him. He played ragtime piano. Later he went into the ministry. That was one reason I really wanted to come here, [to Chicago] because my father was raised in this area.

Amos Milburn and Little Willie Littlefield were friends of my family. Most of the guys I knew were guitar players. Like Juke Boy Bonner, I played a lot on his records. I created my own style. The only person I ever copied in my life was my father. I copied his left hand. He had a very dominant left hand on the piano. If I could play heavy like my father with my left hand, then I could always improvise with my right hand. So I kind of created my own style.

I loved Dinah Washington, Ella Fitzgerald, Sarah Vaughan. I heard Sippie Wallace and Helen Humes sing, but the piano players that were really my favorites — Hazel Scott, Dorothy Donegan — I liked their styles, but I put what I felt with what I heard from my father and came up with my own style.

At age fifteen I knew seven hundred and fifty songs. Now I know over three thousand. I'm forty-seven. I haven't changed my style, but my repertoire is broader. I did more ballads when I was younger because I was

just getting into the field. I was into the soul music scene more. I toured with Sam and Dave, and Otis Redding, and James Brown. So I was more into the soul thing than the blues. I always loved them blues. In the late 1950s I played with Ashton Savoy and Lazy Lester at Goldband records. Then I recorded with Juke Boy Bonner and other people, and slowly I got away from blues, but in the last twelve years I've gotten back into it.

There's a demand for the blues because so many blues artists have passed away. The younger people don't want to be classified as blues artists, or even affiliated with the blues. They just want to be known as rock singers. I'm just classified as a versatile artist because I do everything — pop, R&B, soul, gospel, country and western. I love country and western because it's closely related in theory to the blues.

I live in Oakland, California, now. But I'm in Europe nine months a year, touring, I'm going to

Katie Webster
New Orleans Jazz and Heritage Festival, 1984
Photograph by Michael P. Smith

Floyd Dixon
Promotional photograph. *Courtesy Hans Kramer*

Japan in July. I'm going to Montreux in Switzerland, Antibes in France. In Europe, they know if they don't get there at a particular time, they won't get another chance. They really love the music in Europe. And they know more about you than you know yourself. The day you were born, your grandparents' names, how many records you've played on. I don't know about some of this, you know! Storms don't keep them away. They sit out with their umbrellas. They really appreciate the music. They're so happy that you're there!

I play for my audience, for their feelings. As long as they're enjoying themselves, time doesn't bother me. You know, like some people watch their watches to see how long they've been on stage. I could never do this. My manager has to wave a flag, say, "Hey, it's time to come off," and I ignore him and keep playing [laughs]. Once I'm into it, I'm into it. **99**

(*Above*) Katie Webster; Montreux International Jazz Festival, 1987
Photograph by Edouard Curchod

Floyd Dixon began his recording career as a pure bluesman, then made a series of attempts throughout the late 1950s and early '60s to keep up with trends. Generally his Modern, Supreme, Aladdin, and Specialty sessions are the best, but later sessions for Chess/Checker, Dodge ("Opportunity Blues"), and Chattahoochee ("Don't Leave Me") show that throughout the years of ballads and rock 'n' roll, the blues touch was still there.

Floyd was successful early in his career. After "Dallas Blues," his first big hit was "Broken Hearted" on Supreme, authored by Mark Hurley and bluesman Smokey Hogg. Billboard's September 1949 review of "Broken Hearted" said: "Dixon warbles a strong blues, ably backed by the combo, setting a warming after-hours mood that should snare heavy attention." Like others of his Supreme sides, this record was issued under the name Eddie Williams, bassist for Floyd and earlier for the Three Blazers. Floyd's two other commercial triumphs were both on Aladdin: "Telephone Blues" stayed on the charts for six weeks in early 1951 and climbed to No. 5, and "Call Operator 210" reached No. 4 during an eleven-week stay in mid-1952. Initially, Aladdin thought enough of Floyd to sign him to a long-term contract, but none of Floyd's other records ever made Billboard's national charts, and despite his claims, he never had a No. 1 record in Billboard.

Floyd Dixon showed impeccable piano technique, fabulous timing (especially on slow blues), and a voice like a foghorn — a surprise for one associated with such

FLOYD DIXON

(1929–   )

a supposedly subdued style of blues singing. Like so many Texas bluesmen, his non-conformist style was never fully accepted by the West Coast recording establishment and he never won the recognition accorded to other West Coast pianists, such as Roy Hawkins, Little Willie Littlefield, and Amos Milburn. Dave Alexander (from Marshall, Texas) was right when he told Floyd, "People don't usually sit in here, but I got to let you — you're one of the great cats."

Dick Shurman and Jim O'Neal
Living Blues #23

❝ I got into music when I came to Los Angeles. I heard a record by Amos Milburn, "Money Hustlin' Woman," and a record by Charles Brown, and I decided I want to sing. But Louis Jordan was my favorite artist at the time, you know "G.I. Jive," "Choo, Choo, Ch'boogie" and all that kinda stuff. So I started playing the piano — I didn't have one but would go to school and kinda practice and learned how to play and studied a little harmony. I went to an amateur hour and I won first prize at the Million Dollar Theater when Johnny Moore and the Three Blazers was there. And I left there and went to the Barrelhouse and won first prize there. Johnny Otis was co-owner there. He thought I sounded very good and told me I ought to start recording. So then I went out to the Bihari Brothers, and I didn't intend to record, but a guitar player named Tiny Webb was there and a bass player, and I asked them if they would run over a couple with me. I brought a tune called "Dallas Blues" and I didn't know they was recording it in the back and so they said, "Listen to it back." So when Jules Bihari and Saul played it back for me they said, "We would like to put it out." And I was shocked! They wrote me out a check for just doing those couple of tunes and asked me if I was in the union and I said no, and they gave me the money to go join that day.

Those were on Modern. They were put out in three weeks, and in about six weeks, "Dallas Blues" was number two in *Billboard*. Well, I didn't know anything about *Billboard* and Cashbox, and he said it'll be number one in a couple of more weeks, and that surprised me because I didn't think it was nowhere but in California. But then I got letters from my home and Dallas and Shreveport and different places, saying I heard your record and wonderin' if you's the same one, because everybody called me "Skeet," a lot of people didn't know my name was Floyd. And that was a thrill to me.

I was seventeen, well right at eighteen, because it was a month before I be eighteen. This was in 1948, right at 1949. I was born in Marshall, Texas, February 8, 1929.

I would play whenever I could. I took one music lesson from a fellow named Julius Hayward, but he beat my hands so much with a ruler that I didn't care to take no more lessons. So I stopped at one lesson there. ❞

Interview by Tom Mazzolini
March 22 and May 17, 1975
Living Blues #23

(*Above*) Amos Milburn: Promotional photograph
Courtesy Hans Kramer

L.C. "GOOD ROCKIN' " ROBINSON

(1915–1976)

L.C. "Good Rockin' " Robinson was one of the most dynamic artists to emerge from the San Francisco/Oakland blues scene. An energetic performer who earned his nickname from his rocking music and showmanship, Robinson entertained Bay Area audiences for over three decades.

In 1940 he arrived in San Francisco from Texas. An older brother, A.C. Robinson, was already in San Francisco, and the two joined forces as they had years earlier in Texas and formed the first of many Robinson groups on the West Coast.

Louis Charles Robinson was deeply influenced by the western swing bands that had emerged in Texas by the 1930s. Consequently his style of blues offered a unique combination of violin, Hawaiian steel and guitar. A.C. was adept at the harmonica and bass, often playing both instruments simultaneously, and the Robinson brothers were backed from the beginning by drummer Teddy Winston, a veteran of numerous big bands of the late '20s and '30s.

Although the 1940s and early 1950s would prove to be prolific years for the recording of modern blues, they were essentially empty years for Robinson. For the most part, record companies on the West Coast were focusing their attention on such stylists as Amos Milburn, Floyd Dixon, and Lowell Fulson, thus limiting the rough-edged blues of L.C. to just a few recordings.

In 1957 A.C. Robinson quit the blues to devote his activities to the church and its music. He joined the Pentecostal Temple Church of Christ in San Francisco. Aided by his wife on piano, Robinson recorded a few gospel sides for Golden Soul Records, performing in a blues harmonica style. His voice was similar to Clifton Chenier's.

During his active blues days, however, A.C. played alongside such West Coast notables as Louis Jordan, Ivory Joe Hunter, T-Bone Walker, and Jimmy Witherspoon. He claimed his harmonica style was different from most. "I can play with anybody," he said, "Take Sonny Boy Williamson, for instance, he always needed a piano, but I can play with anything, even a 20-piece orchestra."

❝ I was born the 15th of May, 1915, in Brenham, Texas; that's sixty miles outside of Austin. I was born on a farm and we used to give country dances. Quite naturally, we was small, my brother and I, and my daddy hired two brothers to play out in the country there, one played guitar and the other played violin. And I noticed the one playing guitar and I told my brother, I said, "I can play like him!" He said, "Why don't you try then?" Well, we didn't have a guitar. My sister went to a country fair and she won one — that's the old hollow body with the hole in the middle — and she brought it back and gave it to us. And in about a week my brother was playing the harmonica, and he said, "I thought you could play like that fellow was playing the other night." And it come up to me how he made a G-chord, "Blues in the Bottom," and "Hold That Tiger."

Then I had a brother-in-law played bottleneck guitar. He was Blind Willie Johnson. He used to come stay with us two, three nights, and he'd sit there and play that guitar, religious songs, and I was watching him with that bottle on there and started out playing like that, too. But I was playing blues. Yes, some of Lonnie Johnson blues, you know, and I would play with the bottle on there. I used to keep a turpentine bottle in my pocket, they was smaller, and I would play like that. And finally I got up in age and we went to playing different places, my brother and I. We got a little better and better every time we played and so we decided to move to Temple, Texas, in 1934. That was near Brenham, ninety-five miles from there. My brother was there first and he came back and got me out there with him. I was quite young, and got around there and got to playin'. We hooked up with the Three Hot Brown Boys at that time and went on the air. We just about had the town sewed up. At 4:15 in the evening people would beat it home to hear that

(*Left*) A.C. Robinson
1976
Photograph by Paul Kohl
Courtesy Tom Mazzolini

(*Far left*) L.C. Robinson
Promotional photograph
Courtesy Tom Mazzolini

program on KTEM, Temple. We stayed on the air three or maybe two and a half, three years broadcasting.

We played every evening, but on weekends we'd play dances out in the country somewhere, in town; we always had somewhere to play. On Saturday evening we'd play at an ice cream parlor called Marshall's, out in the front. That's when I met Clyde Barrow and Bonnie. They drove up in a green '38 Ford. I had one just like it. He called me to the car and asked me, "Can you all play 'Sittin' on Top of the World?' "

I said, "Oh, sure," and he gave me twenty-five silver dollars, playing with them in his hand. He handed them to me. "Tell him to play it!" And my brother really blowed that harp because twenty-five dollars in them days was a lot of money. And he sat in the car, he and Miss Parker, and Barrow had on this big white hat, and she was bare-headed. Her hair was cut real short, dark like yours. Finally, she put her hat on and he beg for me to come back to the car again. He gave me twenty dollars and said, "Wait a minute." I looked around at him, he said, "You know who I am?" I said, "No, sir." I just thought he was just an ordinary cowboy because where we was playin' they showed nothing but western pictures there. I said, "No, I don't." He said, "My name is Clyde Barrow and this is Bonnie Parker." I thought she was another man the way she had her hair cut, and she had a machine gun laying across her lap. They both had on two pistols. He said to me, "Where's the police around here?" I

said, "I don't know." Finally, he gave us twenty more dollars and took off and went due South, and brother, he left there in a hurry, too. And about twenty minutes the police came around, looking at my car and saying, "Did you see a car like that?" I said, "Yeah, he just went over the hill," and they took off. They didn't want to see them.

I learned [to play guitar] by watching. When I was in Temple I came into contact with a lot of western music, which I used to play a lot. Such as Bob Wills, Milton Brown, which was a great favorite of mine. The Brownies. Jay Maynard, Bill Monroe, Joe and Bob Calahan, the Sunshine Boys. I knew all of them boys. I picked up the steel mostly from seeing Leon McAuliffe. He was with Bob Wills. I learned lots from him. He played my style. He was a good steel man.

And I liked Bob's style of playing the violin. He was a good blues violin player in his way. He had another lead violin with him. I don't know what became of him. His name was Louie Turner. He was the best in the business on the violin. But for blues I would take Milton Brown. He got killed in a car wreck. I liked the set-up he had, you know, and he had a terrific piano player they called Papa Calhoun and I loved the way they played. My brother and I, we used to play a lot of western music, and I didn't change until I got to California. And for a long time I played western music on Howard Street here in San Francisco.

Nineteen-Forty, I come here. My brother was already here [in California]. He sent for me to come out here. I hitchhiked into Abilene around 1933, and the only thing I had was a fiddle. I worked there in a cleaners until I bought me a guitar. I left there and come here in 1940 and stayed in San Francisco for twenty-some years. I finally organized me a band here called the Three Hot Brown Boys, and then I changed the name to The Combo Boys, and so now I've changed the name to the California Blues Band. **"**

Interview by Tom Mazzolini
San Francisco, February, 1975
Living Blues #22

Ivory Joe Hunter (b. 1911) was originally from Kirbyville, Texas, about 135 miles northeast of Houston. His most vivid memories of his childhood concerned his mother, who sang spirituals and organized her family of eleven boys and four girls into a choir. The family moved to Port Arthur, where Hunter quit school after the eighth grade to begin working as a professional musician. As a teenager he had his own radio show on KFDM in Beaumont and became known as "Rambling Fingers" because of his abilities on the piano. In 1936 he settled in Houston, but left in the early '40s to pursue opportunities in California.

In 1945 Hunter launched Ivory Records in Oakland, but this venture was short-lived due to wartime restrictions on shellac. He did, however, produce one successful record, a Leroy Carr ballad, "Blues at Sunrise," that he later recorded on Dot. Johnny Moore and the Three Blazers were the session band on Hunter's early recordings. Through his association with Moore, he met and worked with Charles Brown, whose vocal and piano style shaped his own.

On stage Ivory Joe Hunter fronted a basic rhythm and blues band: piano, bass, drums, and tenor saxophone. In his recordings he combined blues and boogie with pop-ballad orientation. After his Ivory label folded he started Pacific Records and issued "Grieving Blues," "Heavy Hearted Blues," and jump tunes like "Boogie in the Basement." In addition, he recorded for Excelsior, 4 Star, and King labels, but did not attain widescale success until he signed with MGM Records in 1949. His two original ballads, "I Need You So" and "I Almost Lost My Mind," ranked high on the Billboard charts.

In 1956 Hunter moved to the Atlantic label and achieved gold record status with "Since I Met You, Baby," and later had a hit with another of his songs, "Empty Arms." These songs were released at a time when young white rock musicians were "covering" black records and the music was receiving greater exposure and popularity. In order to make the most of this crossover audience, Ivory Joe Hunter began performing not only blues, but country songs, spirituals, and pop ballads. Prior to his death in 1975 he was honored with a program of his songs at the Grand Ole Opry in Nashville.

Ivory Joe Hunter
Promotional photograph
Courtesy Hans Kramer

Lloyd Glen
Promotional photograph

Lloyd Glenn and Dave Alexander
Sacramento Blues Festival, 1983
Photograph by Pat Monaco

Lloyd Glenn (b. 1909) had a style shaped by the sounds he heard early in his San Antonio childhood from his father and friends, and the early boogie-woogie kings like Pinetop Smith, Meade Lux Lewis, and their cohorts. Jimmy Yancey's influence is strongly felt on Glenn's best-known record, "Old Time Shuffle." Lloyd was self-effacing about the development of his characteristic harmonies and block chords; he said he worked them out because he "didn't have the reach." Instead of just playing rolling or boogie-type bass lines, which he left to a bassist, he liked to use his left hand more rhythmically and play frequent octaves. He also liked to play guitar-style intervals and use the volume pedal to make the piano ring like a guitar.

In 1928 Lloyd began working with Territory bands including those of trumpeter T. Holder, with whom Lloyd first visited California in 1931, and Boots (Douglas) & His Buddies. In 1942, he moved to Los Angeles because his wife's parents were in California. He felt that whatever "West Coast blues style" existed, it existed because "migration brought the blues here." While working as a packer and a lifter in an aircraft plant during World War II, he began playing piano around town, and things began falling into place during a twin piano engagement with Walter Johnson on Western Avenue.

Lloyd's recording career began as a sideman on the records of T-Bone Walker (including his original "Stormy Monday"), Lowell Fulson, and B.B. King. He became one of the most sought-after pianists at that time and recorded with Gene Phillips, Jesse Thomas, Harmonica Slim, Big Joe Turner, and Gatemouth Brown, among others. His own releases, usually on Aladdin, Imperial, or Jack Lauderdale's Swing Time and associated labels, were widely popular and influential, and have been internationally reissued on Stockholm (along with new recordings), Polydor, and Oldie Blues. In the last decade of his life he made albums in France for Black and Blue, including one co-billed with Gatemouth Brown and one of Tiny Grimes' finest. He also appeared at the 1982 San Francisco Blues Festival and toured with Big Joe Turner. Glenn put a strong stamp on many of B.B. King's Kent and ABC records, was reunited on record with T-Bone Walker, and became, along with Charles Brown, one of the top pacesetters of West Coast blues piano.

With all of Lloyd's experience and versatility, he observed, "I've been playing music for a pretty good while, and I found out blues will move you faster than anything else. I don't care what kind of blues — somebody will listen." He helped the artists he worked with make some of their very best records; his influence on the playing of countless piano players is incalculable.

Dick Shurman
Living Blues #68

Buddy Ace was born in 1936 in Jasper, Texas. He spent his childhood in Baytown and then moved to Houston at age fourteen. He was part of a gospel singing family and was influenced by his father, Johnny Ace, who performed as a singer and guitarist. Buddy started singing in public at age four and retained an interest in gospel throughout his life.

In high school he sang in a gospel quartet with Joe Tex but in time he developed an interest in Ivory Joe Hunter, Big Joe Turner, and B.B. King. Buddy Ace began to sing rhythm and blues and earned a reputation by winning talent shows. In 1955, after the death of his father, he signed a contract with Don Robey to record on the Duke label and to replace Johnny Ace in the Blues Consolidated Revue packaged by the Buffalo Booking Agency.

Buddy Ace's first single was "Angel Boy" and his most successful was "Nothing but This World Can Hurt Me," his only hit in fifteen years on the Duke label. In addition to Duke, he has also recorded for Jewel and Sunny and Specialty. The self-proclaimed "Silver Fox of the Blues," he is known primarily as a singer of ballads.

(*Above*) Buddy Ace
Oakland, 1983
Photograph by Pat Monaco

SONNY RHODES

(1940–   )

Ladies night at Eli's Mile High Club in Oakland starts up slowly. There is a small sign at the door that says "Wednesday Night, Ladies Free," but the ladies don't show up until after 9:30. The audience is a mix of blacks and whites. By 10:00 Sonny Rhodes and the Texas Twisters take the stage. Sonny Rhodes wears his trademark turban, wrapped tightly around his head and pinned by a large costume gem. He sits in front of the band, his cherry-red lap steel guitar stretched across his thighs, and above the twanging sounds, he wails, "I loved a woman, but she got cancer from smoking cigarettes. I tried to discourage her, but she never heard a word I said. She woke up coughin'. She thought she had a cold, but after years of smokin' cigarettes, her lungs were about to fold."

The crowd is sparse, but the enthusiasm grows with the intensity of the music. On any given night, the stars of Bay Area blues can be found at Eli's in the audience or performing on stage — Frankie Lee, Buddy Ace, Maxine Howard. There is an earnestness in the voice of Sonny Rhodes when he says, "The blues have haunted me. The blues have comforted me. It makes me feel good. The blues is just like a religion. It's something you can take out and preach to someone. Just like a preacher prepares for his Sunday sermon, I prepare for my nightly sermon that I have to go out and play for the people who come in."

❝ "I'm Clarence Edward Smith, also known as Sonny Rhodes, the disciple of the blues, guitar player, singer, songwriter from Smithville, Texas, born in 1940. I've been living in California since 1963. I've been playing since I been out here. Course I haven't had that many jobs, but in the back of my mind, playing the blues is my first priority that I went out and went for.

I play a 1954 Music Master. It is probably one of the best guitars. I have three, a Gibson ES325, a rare one. I also have a thirty-year-old Hawaiian steel guitar that was made, of all places, in Japan.

In Texas there was this guy that played with Jimmy Heath and the Melody Masters; he had a slide guitar. He was probably a little more modern than mine. The instrument sounded so beautiful. I didn't know who I could take that instrument to and ask them to show me how to play it. Living in racist Texas, you couldn't go up and ask no white how to play nothing. You asked yourself. So I just concentrated on playing the guitar and bass, and when I got to California, there was a man I met [several] years ago. His name was L.C. "Good Rockin'" Robinson. He was an old Texan, and he was playing the Hawaiian lap steel. And I played with him and was able to observe what he was doing.

I finally got myself a Hawaiian lap steel about eleven years ago and I've been playing ever since. It has become standard procedure with the Sonny Rhodes performance to see the electric guitar and the Hawaiian lap steel.

L.C. Robinson, when he was living in Texas, before he moved to California, he was playing the lap steel. He was from East Texas. Also, there was an old man in Houston. They called him Hop Wilson. He was a nice slide player. He just died in 1980. When we were down in Houston, he played quite a bit of slide. I guess, along with myself and Freddy Roulette, we are

Sonny Rhodes
Eli's Mile High Club
Oakland, 1984
Photograph by Alan Govenar

the only slide players that play the blues here in California. I'm probably playing the most blues on the slide guitar. I adapted the Elmore James style, and I adapted the way of individual picking the strings. Mine is tuned to an open E chord, striking it from the E first to the E sixth when you got a complete chord. I use a Steven's bar, which I grab and use to make and change

my chords, and take out and play a solo I want to play while I'm singing.

It wasn't until I came to Austin, from Smithville, as a youngster that I really got to listen and understand the blues. Only the fortunate ones had radios, and enough money to put in the nickelodeon to listen to the blues. At this point in the late 1940s and early 1950s I wasn't able to go out to the nightclubs, I was too young. Only thing I could do was partially hear something from behind the tin walls of the beer joints and beer halls.

In Austin, the woman who raised me — my mom and dad died at an early age — this lady had a machine, they called it a Victrola, it was a record player, but it was before electricity. It was something that you wound up and you put the record on and you had this horn and it would play. So when my mom had company, I was the one who would sit near the Victrola. My job was to keep the Victrola from winding down. It kept the party happy, kept everything live, and I got to listen to a lot of records by T-Bone Walker, Blind Lemon Jefferson, Memphis Minnie, Bessie Smith, a whole bunch of people I listened to.

And finally I got to the point, by playing all these records, that I could duplicate the sounds that I heard. That put me into a vast identification with the blues. Everything else I heard didn't move me like the blues did.

I continued to sing and play this way until I got good at it, and I said, "This is what I'm going to do. I'm going to be a guitar player or blues singer." I went out and tried very hard to do that. I can look over my life and see some of the things I did right and some that I did wrong. If I were to do it all over again, I don't see one thing I would change because it's given me the momentum of the blues. Sometimes you have to work at things a little harder, if you don't have things to begin with. I'm still working at it and I'll continue to work at it.

When I first started out the critics compared my singing to T-Bone Walker, Junior Parker, and Percy Mayfield, but as the blues evolved in me, I became my own style, what is truly me.

(*Above*) My Club
Oakland, 1982
Photograph by Pat Monaco

Sonny Rhodes and Frankie Lee
Oakland, 1983
Photograph by Pat Monaco

I came to California because I thought there were better opportunities for black bluesmen. I had a hard time in Austin. The biggest outlet for blues in Texas was the Houston-based Duke records. They always had such an abundance of artists that I found it difficult at the time to try to crack that barrier. So I had to change environments and get into a new place, and continue to keep my cultural province within me. I had to get out where somebody else could hear me. So I came to California, and I guess I kicked it around for about a year and a half before I was able to get my first 45 out on a label that was a subsidiary of Fantasy at the time. I put a record out called "Forever and a Day." From that record, it got into the audition hands of the people of Fantasy/Galaxy in San Francisco. They sent out contracts for me to do another recording for the Galaxy people. That was in 1965. I did another recording, but economically it wasn't feasible. I look back at it as an experience. I was just a young blues artist. I figure whatever was took from me, I could regain it, if I had enough longevity to hack it.

There were several Texas bluesmen in California: Johnny Guitar Watson, Lowell Fulson, Phillip Walker, who was originally from Louisiana, but was raised in Texas. I'd say there were probably at least thirty or forty blues musicians from Texas out here. My drummer, trumpet player, and my bass player are from Texas. I have one guitar player from London, but I tell everyone he's from London, Texas.

For me, T-Bone Walker was the ultimate, as far as guitar playing was concerned. He could make the strings say exactly what he just got through singing in lyrics. I found that he was able to answer himself. That's a characteristic of just about all Texas guitar players. Whatever they said lyrically, they could come back and say it instrumentally. It might not be in the same tone, but you can find a direct link to what they just got through singing.

The style of Texas blues depends on the region and culture from which the musicians came. You take an Otis Rush up against a T-Bone Walker. They're both

excellent guitar players, but it wouldn't sound the same. There is a distinct characterization of Texas guitar, having the ability to repeat the lyric with your fingers on the guitar.

Blues is truth. Blues is about something that actually happened, in other words, being able to see why things exist, being able to look at someone and turn your head away and say, why not. The blues is a state of mind that is brought about by an unfortunate situation that could arise from self-pity or shame, or heartache.

My audience in California is mainly the young intellectual, hippie white kids that come out and like to hear it because they can understand it. We have people come in that are black who are over thirty-five. I find them very receptive to what we're doing. Younger blacks tend to be more into the commercial music, but I think that in time this so-called fad music dissipates, people will come back to the music of truth and start all over again.

Both blues and the spiritual have soul. One calls on the good Lord to help them find a way, and they do this with abundance, and the black blues music don't always call on the Lord. They will tell you about the situation and speak optimistically that it will get better. For me, the blues is a religion. It makes me feel good. It makes me happy to sing blues and look up at an audience that is responsive. If it's enlightening you, then it's enlightening them, too. I feel like a preacher. Any time you take a message to someone, that's the primary goal. My audience is my congregation. My guitar is my pulpit, and my heart and my mind are my vows. Somewhere in the Bible, it says praise him with singing, dancing and instruments. So I look at all of that. The blues and the spiritual has the ability to penetrate the mind and the heart, because the person who wrote it has had the experience. When I sing, I think I talk. There's a message in the music and in your voice. **"**

T-Bone Walker
Circa 1940s
Courtesy Institute of Jazz Studies

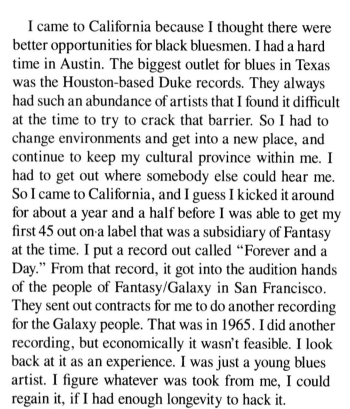

Eli's Mile High Club
Oakland, 1982
Photograph by Pat Monaco

Dooley Jordan Orchestra with Claytie Polk
San Antonio, circa 1930s
Courtesy Mariellen Shepherd

SAN ANTONIO, CORPUS CHRISTI, & THE RIO GRANDE VALLEY

n the 1970s the music of the Texas-Mexico border region began to attract both critical and popular acclaim. This music, which is usually called Tex-Mex or Chicano, is unique in that it brings together Mexican *norteno* music and American country and western, blues, rhythm and blues, and rock 'n' roll. The increasing popularity of this music is due in part to the recent upsurge in ethnic pride among Mexican-Americans, but it also builds on a long musical history. Adrian Trevino, a classically trained musician from Corpus Christi who performed with Sunny and the Sunliners in the 1960s, says that there were isolated Mexican-American groups playing blues and jazz in Texas as early as the 1930s. Knocky Parker, piano player with the Light Crust Doughboys, described western swing as a mixture of "Mexican mariachi music from the south with jazz and country strains coming in from the east."

In the 1940s and 1950s interest in country and blues, and rhythm and blues grew significantly among Mexican-Americans in San Antonio and the Rio Grande Valley. Sunny and the Sunglows (formerly the Sunliners), Vincent Cantu and the Rockin' Dominoes, The Chili Peppers, and Charlie and the Jives were among the most popular Tex-Mex groups of the day.

In the late 1940s Arnaldo Ramirez established Falcon Records in McAllen and introduced Alegres de Teran and Freddy Fender. The success of Falcon Records sparked the formation of other small Texas independent labels: Corona in San Antonio; Ideal and Norco in San Benito; Duncan and Talent Scout in Harlingen, El Pato and Bego in McAllen. In Dallas Johnny Gonzales started Elzarape Music and promoted Little Joe (Hernandez) and his Latinaires.

During this period musicians of Mexican ancestry integrated traditional music with music that was not specifically Mexican. Vikki Carr and Freddy Fender dropped their family names so as not to be stereotyped as "Mexican" in the U.S. market. Vikki Carr sang pop ballads, while Freddy Fender recorded blues, country, rhythm and blues, and rock.

Freddy Fender's real name is Baldermar Huerta. He was born in 1936 in San Benito, the birthplace of the legendary accordionist Narciso Martinez. The musical interests he formed during his teenage years were, however, influenced more by popular radio than by *norteno* and Tex-Mex music. He listened to the Nashville stations and followed the country singers and steel guitar players. In the field camps of black farm workers, he heard records by Muddy Waters, Elmore James, and T-Bone Walker, and then later while in the Marines he learned about the music of Elvis Presley and the rhythm and blues of Fats Domino and Bobby Blue Bland.

Cora Estell Woods
San Antonio, circa 1940s
Courtesy Mariellen Shepherd

ADRIAN TREVINO

(1943–   )

The hard-won success of Freddy Fender exemplifies the aspirations and the struggles of so many Mexican-Americans of his generation. For more than fifteen years he searched for the right sound and recorded for numerous small Texas labels and for national labels, such as Imperial and Argo, a subsidiary of Chess. With his rhythm and blues-styled song, "Wasted Days and Wasted Nights," Freddy Fender gained some national attention in 1959, but in 1960 he was arrested in Louisiana and convicted of marijuana possession. He spent two years in Angola prison and when he was released, worked five days each week as a farm worker and performed only on weekends. It was not until 1974, when Fender met Houston producer Huey Meaux, that his musical career began to take shape. In 1975 Meaux persuaded Fender to release the song, "Before the Next Teardrop Falls," which quickly became an enormous success on both pop and country charts and established Freddy Fender as a singer of national stature.

Huey Meaux has worked as a producer and promoter for more than two decades and has recorded a varied group of Texas and Louisiana musicians on his own labels (currently Starflite and Crazy Cajun). In addition to his success with Freddy Fender, Meaux has been instrumental in helping Doug Sahm and other Texas musicians achieve national prominence.

Doug Sahm grew up in San Antonio, where he absorbed many of the same musical influences as Freddy Fender in San Benito. As a teenager Sahm put together the first white rhythm and blues band in San Antonio and featured West Side tenor saxman Eracleo "Rocky" Morales. Sahm recorded for small San Antonio labels (Harlem and Renner) from 1958 to 1964, when he signed with Huey Meaux's Tribe label. Meaux transformed the image of Doug Sahm and promoted him nationally as part of a British-styled group called The Sir Douglas Quintet.

In the 1970s Doug Sahm returned to Texas and resumed playing a Mexican-influenced sound, working with border musicians, such as keyboard player Augie Meyer, drummer John Perez, saxman Rocky Morales, and accordionist Flaco Jimenez. The blending of musical influences in Sahm's performance style reflects the cultural diversity of Texas and the important interplay of Mexican music with country, rock, and rhythm and blues. Contemporary Mexican-American music combines these influences to create a distinctive sound that in the 1980s has been popularized by Esteban Jordan and Los Lobos, and has gained an international audience.

(*Left*) Freddy Fender
San Antonio, circa 1960
Courtesy Huey P. Meaux

66 I came at rhythm and blues music in a way by fault. In 1964 I joined a group called the Rockin' Ravens in Corpus Christi, Texas. I was going to Delmar College to get a degree in music. I had heard *conjunto norteno* music in my background when I was growing up in the Valley in a little town, eight miles northeast of Harlingen, six miles north of San Benito, and thirty miles northwest of Brownsville. I'm forty-four now and I heard a lot of *norteno* with accordion, or with a violin, guitar, and *bajo sexto*. But in 1964 I was coming in at the tail end of the Chicano combo type of thing: rhythm, bass, lead guitar and drummer. Those types of groups were fading and the groups that were coming in were rhythm guitar, bass guitar, lead guitar and drums, plus one or two saxophones. Previously, we were imitating bands like Chuck Berry. Whatever was happening in the Anglo market in the East we were imitating because we were having problems with identity, even me. We had a kind of follow-the-leader syndrome. If the top Chicano band does it, then every other Chicano band does it, too.

When the Chicano bands started to add saxophones and organs, that's what we did in The Rockin' Ravens. We had one tenor and one alto. I was playing electric bass. We would go to high school sock hops and play entirely in English. We did some B.B. King, and others by Bobby Blue Bland when he recorded in Houston, Texas. We heard the Duke and Peacock recordings, but we did it our way. Put yourself in a high school hop and you don't do anything else but English, the blues, the top hits, rock 'n' roll, doo-wop music and the whole works. The ironic thing about it was that once an Anglo came up and said, "Can you play a polka?" We said, "We only know one or two," and he said, "That's okay. That'll do." Usually, a polka was a "Rancho Grande" or "Jalisco" and that was it.

There have always been Chicano bands doing other kinds of music. These are the unknown heroes. I wish I had the money and time to go interview some of them, like Beto Garcia. He was a jazz performer, he played saxophone.

Henry Cuesta, one of the top saxophone and clarinet players of the 1950s, you're not going to believe this, but he's with Lawrence Welk. He's from Corpus Christi. One time when I interviewed him, I asked why such a great musician that you are, why are you playing Lawrence Welk and those simple tunes? And he said, "Well, they pay you ten grand a week to play these tunes. Yes, I would, and I signed up."

The biggest Chicano R&B band was Sunny and the Sunglows. The first album that they did all of the musicians were on the front cover, and somewhere along the line Sunny [Ozuna] thought, "It's my thing, not your thing." That's why none of the musicians have been given enough credit. And we kind of feel bad about that, but what the heck, he was paying us one hundred and fifty dollars a week. Anyway, Sunny felt that the musicians are there and you're getting paid to do a job, rehearse in the morning, and then again in the afternoon. In the morning we went over the music and in the afternoon we practiced dance steps. So everything we went up there and played, we did synchronized movements to the music. We all had tuxedos.

I started playing with Sunny in 1965, but it only lasted a month and a half [laughs]. I couldn't take it anymore. The musicians were workers. Sunny is still around today, but he's lost his voice. He can only talk to you in a whisper. He never really had a band. Sunny hired musicians and told you what to do. That's what he did. He gave us the charts and we memorized them. Or sometimes we listened to the records of Bobby Blue Bland or Junior Parker and we imitated that.

We were doing a second job of rhythm and blues, but we were playing it pretty well. We played high school dances, community dances. Of course, the saxophone had also been used in *orquesta* music at the turn of the century. The Union Pacific Railroad Company had a band, and all the Mexicans played trumpets, saxophones, trombones, and what not. There were also community bands that had *profesores* who had come from Mexico and set up shop. They taught people how to read and write, and talk music. The *profesores* would teach you to play an instrument and read music. They were jacks-of-all-trades, very well educated and held in very high esteem. There wasn't much money that circulated around South Texas, but the *profesores* were provided for. So from the late 1800s on there have been Mexican and Chicano bands with horns in them, even if sometimes they were just pick-up bands that played for a special occasion, eight or ten or twenty musicians. They were all Hispanics.

There weren't any mixed bands until the 1950s. There were record companies, Falcon Records, which had been started in the late 1940s in McAllen. And there were others in San Antonio: TNT, Harlem, Ebony, Cobra, Renner. There were Johnny Olen, Rickie Aguary, Mando and the Chili Peppers [Charlie Alvarado, Vince Cantu, Little Jesse, Sonny Ace]. Then some of the bands had Anglos — the Lyrics, and Denny Ezba's Goldens, who later were called B.F.B.S.A. [Best Fucking Band in San Antonio. Mike Nesmith and Augie Meyer came from this band; they later played with Doug Sahm and The Sir Douglas Quintet, which featured the saxophone of Rocky Morales.]

Aside from these bands, a lot of *conjunto norteno* bands played some blues, but if the audience doesn't like it, the music doesn't survive. Some of the low-riders were into R&B and early rock 'n' roll and they still are. Some of the low-rider musicians who I have interviewed say, *"Conjunto norteno* is my dance music, my mom's music, but R&B is the cruising music." The slower tunes were for cruising — your music follows your heartbeat, which I think is about seventy-two beats per minute. So R&B is perfect when it's about sixty beats per minute, because the motors often go at sixty cycles. It all fits together.

To me, the blues meant you had a black vocalist and a good band backing it up. The blues was a way to transcend the [cultural] barrier. The R&B music that I came closest to was in the 1950s. I was a low-rider, had a 1947 Mercury. R&B was the music of civil rights, and we listened to it on the radio. It was hard for us to pick up blues. Bobby Bland's "Love and affection, a heart so true, I'm yours for the asking" was one of our favorites. The radio stations played it over and over. Sometimes we bought the records. We liked the sound, the rhythm and tempo. The lead guitar players wanted to learn those riffs, to be another B.B. King. My friend Phillipe Garza was one of those rare guitar players. He moved to Corpus Christi and joined a black band called Boo and the Trojans. He played with them because he wanted to learn it. For the first month or so, he said, "They were telling me the chords over and over," and he got it down. He was fantastic. In a way it was easier for the lead guitar player. For the singer it was harder. But there are still Chicano bands playing rhythm and blues. It's a way to experiment, to improve technique. **99**

Doug Sahm
Los Angeles, circa 1973
Photograph by Eric Wehner

Juneteenth; Austin, 1900; *Courtesy Tary Owens and Austin History Center*

AUSTIN

ustin was slower to develop as a recording center than Dallas or Houston, although there is a long history of blues in Central Texas. The relatively small black population of Austin made it unappealing for record producers, who auditioned blues musicians in Dallas and Houston. It was not until the 1960s that a recording industry began to develop in Austin, although what became known as the Austin Sound was progressive country music and redneck rock, which incorporated elements of blues, but was itself a hybrid.

The Austin Sound began to change in the 1970s because of the influx of musicians from other areas, such as Jimmie Vaughan, Stevie Ray Vaughan, Joe Ely, Angela Strehli, and Kim Wilson. These white musicians brought enthusiasm for the blues to a predominantly white college audience, and generated new exposure for black musicians from the Austin area.

In Austin today commercial and cultural appreciations of the blues co-exist. The Sound Archives coordinated by John Wheat at the Barker Texas History Center has the largest collection in the state of vintage recordings and documents on blues history. Tary Owens has been researching and recording blues in the Austin area since the 1960s, when he was a student in the folklore program at the University of Texas and began going to black clubs on East Eleventh Street.

Owens suggests that the country fiddle may have had is strongest influence in the Austin area. In oral accounts and in music he collected in the mid-1960s there is evidence that there were black fiddlers in Central Texas as early as the mid-19th century. His field recordings of Teodar Jackson (Austin), Tommy Wright (Luling), and the Nelson Brothers (Cameron) display a distinctive blues sound in the bending and slurring of notes, while integrating white country tunes and fiddle styles.

According to jazz guitarist Eddie Durham, whose father was a fiddler in San Marcos, south of Austin, there were "a lot of black fiddlers who played at dances, for both blacks and whites. The audience was, of course, segregated, but the music overlapped." Mance Lipscomb (Navasota), and T.D. Bell (Austin) substantiate this with their own experiences in Texas, growing up with fathers who were fiddlers and played blues, country, and whatever else was called for. Essentially, black fiddlers were part of the eclectic songster tradition, which was also prominent among guitarists and is evident in the variable dance rhythms in the performance styles of Mance Lipscomb and Hosea Hargrove.

In addition to guitar and fiddle, it is clear that the piano was also popular as a blues instrument. It offered different stylistic possibilities and integrated the influences of ragtime, boogie, and stride. By the end of the 1930s there were many itinerant black piano players in Texas. Actively performing in the central area of the state were Roosevelt Thomas Williams and Charlie Dillard (Bastrop), Johnny Simmons (Hempstead), Mercy Dee Walton (Waco), and Robert Shaw and Lavada Durst (Austin). Although available recordings of these musicians are limited, oral accounts attest to the stylistic variations among them.

The performance style of Mercy Dee Walton derived more from the boogie-woogie techniques that he learned from Son Brewster and Pinetop Shorty in Waco. Walton moved to California in the 1940s and performed in the jump band of Big Jay McNeely. Robert Shaw and Durst stayed in Austin and remained solo players. Shaw was part of Houston's Santa Fe Group, who played their fast, syncopated piano blues in the juke joints and barrelhouses along the Santa Fe railroad line. He settled in Austin in the 1930s. It was there that he met Durst and taught him to play piano blues.

In the late 1940s Durst became the first black DJ in Austin on KVET radio and was known as Dr. Hepcat. He spoke in jive talk on the air, and his show, which continued into the 1960s, featured big band jazz and blues and promoted regional performers on Texas-based recording labels, such as Duke/Peacock, Freedom, and Macy's from Houston, and TNT, Harlem, Cobra, and Renner from San Antonio.

KVET radio provided airtime for Austin's black musicians as well as those of San Antonio, which at that time did not have its own black radio. Band leader Dooley Jordan says the blues and jazz in San Antonio "paralleled what went on in Austin, but was also affected by Mexican music and the Houston big band sound." Jordan formed his first group in the 1930s and continued to play through the 1940s and '50s at the Avalon Grill, where he featured vocalists Claytie Polk and Cora Woods, and T-Bone Walker when he was in the area.

T-Bone Walker made numerous tours around Texas and became an important influence to those he met and with whom he performed as a guest soloist. In the Austin and San Antonio area of Central Texas, Walker had great influence on musicians, including Dooley Jordan, Jewell Simmons, and T.D. Bell. Of these, Bell earned the most renown as a guitar stylist.

Bell was an important influence on black musicians, among them Herbert "Blues Boy" Hubbard, whom he met near Hubbard's hometown of Rockdale, Texas. Hubbard was playing in a small band and living in a rooming house. Bell remembers, "He was using a clamp (a capo); and I taught him to play without it. He listened to my playing and I helped him."

In addition, Bell had a great influence on W.C. Clark's career.

In 1955 he was introduced to Clark in a talent show at the Victory Grill on East Eleventh Street. W.C. Clark played electric bass but switched to lead guitar with Bell's encouragement and

Blues Boy Hubbard
Austin, circa 1950s
Courtesy Tary Owens and H.L. Hubbard

went on to become a prominent Texas bluesman. He was also an inspiration to early white players, such as Bill Campbell. Despite the far-reaching importance of T.D. Bell in the development of Austin blues, did not achieve commercial success. In the 1960s Bell stopped performing to work full time building a trucking business, which he has operated since. In recent years, with the growing interest in the history of rhythm and blues, Bell is re-emerging as a performer. In 1987 he participated in the Texas Blues Reunion, organized by Tary Owens, with help from Clifford Antone, Johnny Holmes, and W.C. Clark.

W.C. Clark has been active as a bluesman since the 1960s and has performed with his own group and in bands with Angela Strehli and with Stevie Ray Vaughan. In the 1970s, disco super-seded rhythm and blues in the black communities of East Austin, but was revived by a white audience at the Armadillo World Headquarters, Vulcan Gas Company, Soap Creek Saloon, and Antone's.

Over the last decade Antone's has become the preeminent Austin blues club, and has featured an impressive array of blues artists, including Muddy Waters, Howlin' Wolf, Eddie Taylor, Hubert Sumlin, Jimmy Rogers, James Cotton, B.B. King, Bobby Bland, Barbara Lynn, Albert Collins, Pee Wee Crayton, Johnny Copeland, Pinetop Perkins, Grey Ghost, T.D. Bell, W.C. Clark, Angela Stehli, Stevie Ray Vaughan, Jimmie Vaughan, Kim Wilson, The Fabulous Thunderbirds, and Omar and the Howlers. During his twelve years as owner and proprietor, Clifford Antone has worked to created an environment where there are vital inter-actions among musicians and their audience. As Paul Ray points out, "Antone's has been more than a club, it's been a home to the blues, where white and black performers could jam and learn from each other."

In the last two years, Clifford Antone has expanded his opera-tion to include a record store across from the club on Guadalupe Street. In addition, he has started his own blues record label, which has released a tenth anniversary anthology album and albums by Angela Stehli, Ronnie Earl, Memphis Slim/Matt Murphy, and Eddie Taylor.

Although Austin blues has clearly shifted to a predominantly white audience, there is evidence of renewed interest in the black community. Efforts are underway to restore the Victory Grill and a block of East Eleventh Street. Dr. Hepcat, Lavada Durst, says that the perception of blues in the black community is different today. Bluesmen are no longer the fringe elements within the community. They are very often its standing members — and they are helping to bring back the blues to a black audience. Robert Shaw was a deacon of his church before he died, and Durst is now assistant pastor at his. "I don't play where people are smoking or drinking," he says, "but I do like educational programs at schools, colleges, and community programs. It's not the music of the devil if it's not doing any harm."

Freddie King/Mance Lipscomb
Poster by Jim Franklin
Austin, 1970
Courtesy Barker Texas History Center

ROBERT SHAW

(1908–1985)

❝ I've been playing the blues all my life. Sometimes I forget it. Sometimes it be six months before I remember a song. My mama bought a piano when I was a little boy. She got a baby grand, Steinway printed on the bottom. That's the real thing.

In the early 1930s I was around Kansas City and Oklahoma City. I hardly fooled with bands. There was too much static with that money. With some people alcohol gets the best of them. I don't know why. I always thought I could take care of myself better than anybody. There's one piano player, he could have two or three drinks of liquor and he'd misuse everybody, himself too. He just couldn't stand that whiskey. I found that in the black and the white some people can't handle the alcohol.

Blues is history and your actions down through life. It tells a story and it tell it like it is and that gets an individual. There's going to be something in this song that's going to run his mind back. Some of them can't stand it. Music is a fun and enjoyment type of thing and some people can't stand fun. They get out of line, and there are a lot of people that enjoy music to the highest.

A whole lot of sacred music is timed on jazzy timing now. Because of blues all of them sing the blues, they're changing the sacred style. It's according to what the individual thinks. I sing in church. I go to the Ebenezer Baptist down here. They have sacred music in all kind of ways.

You know, at one time street people used to pattern after the society people and now it's been changed around. The society people pattern after the street people. Some people make harm out of nothing. You use a person to the extent, you don't like it.

I've written several tunes, and six or eight or ten blues. You got to get it timed so it will work. You can't put too many words in a verse that you run out of time on nine or seven. You may be short, six and eight and

Robert Shaw
Austin
Courtesy Barker Texas History Center

2/4 timing. When you write the words it has to be right. It's just like we talkin', but you got to know how to time it. Now, we can run out of time on a subject, but you can't have too many words in the next sentence. [Begins playing and then sings]

I'm gonna get me another woman
Who's going to be nice and kind.
I'm gonna get me another woman
Who's going to be nice and kind to me.
Lord, I'm going and I'm going back
To my old time used to be.

I'm gonna get drunk, baby,
And I ain't goin' to drink no more.
I'm gonna get drunk, baby,
And I ain't goin' to drink no more.

I can't love you, baby.
You don't treat me good no more.
I can't love you, baby.
You don't treat me good no more.

I wrote that in the late 1920s. I used to play at house parties. Another song was called "Santa Fe." I played on the Santa Fe line, it sounds like this:

I ain't goin' to tell nobody
What the Santa Fe done to me.
Carried away my good girl,
Come back and got my old time used to be.

My way of seeing it. My music really hasn't changed. I can go to a music festival where they got twenty-five hundred, three thousand people, I get my part from the people. I played in Berlin, Rotterdam, I was in Europe in '71 and about a year and a half ago [1982].

The blues makes you get your mind to think about both ways, for and against. What I mean, if I have a friend, it'll make me think if I mistreated him or mistreated myself. That's the way those things work. The blues is a two-way proposition. It will either make you think that you were wrong or your friend did something to you that wasn't right, or he was right. You get yourself hung up if you don't watch yourself. You sometimes wrong. You can't be right all the time. That's what the blues do to you.

There are a lot less piano players around these days. They're gone, the ones where I'm from in Houston and Fort Bend counties. There was one boy, Harold Holiday, but they call him "Shine," and he was something else. Peg Leg was a piano player, but he liked to shoot dice. In the '30s they had places outside the city limits called roadhouses. Women would get mad because their husbands would go down there. Friday and Saturday nights they were something else, depending on what kind of place it was would [affect] what kind of music was played. We were youngsters in those days. There were piano players like myself and others. There'd be a lot of musicians. People came from Houston, Galveston, Bay City, Richmond, Sugar Land, all of them surrounding cities, that's not half of them. People would come and do their sportin' work, dancin', and women made up.

Some people like emotions in music. Them that drink heavy, they like it slow. The blues is a hard music to play. There's so many frictions to it. **"**

T.D. Bell
Austin, 1953
*Courtesy Tary Owens and
Tyler Bell*

Johnny Holmes
Victory Grill
Austin, 1987
Photograph by Alan Govenar

T.D. Bell was born in 1923 in the Belltown community of Lee County, Texas. His grandfather played mandolin, and his uncle, guitar, but as a boy of seven or eight, Bell played banjo, which he "put down" at eleven or twelve. Later, as a soldier, he was inspired by the music of T-Bone Walker, and when he was discharged bought an acoustic guitar, which he soon traded in for an "electric with a small amplifier." In a recent interview he recalled, "After I heard T-Bone live in Temple (Texas) I had to get it. I'd stay up late at night practicing, keeping the neighbors and family awake. Then in 1949 Johnny Holmes asked me if I wanted to come to Austin to play in his club, the Victory Grill, which he had opened on V-E Day, 1945. And I agreed."

At the Victory Grill, T.D. Bell and the Cadillacs became the house band, playing T-Bone Walker hits like "Bobby Sox Baby" and other popular tunes. T.D. Bell and the Cadillacs were the opening act for B.B. King, Big Mama Thornton, and Bobby Blue Bland, who got his start at the Victory Grill by winning talent contests that Holmes held there.

LAVADA DURST

(1913–   )

I recorded one of my first records on Peacock. That was "Hattie Green." That was a blues, while I was a DJ. And I wrote a spiritual song, "Let's Talk About Jesus," and it sold over a million copies and I didn't get a dime. It was recorded by a group of Austin singers, the Bells of Joy. I gave them that name and they practiced over at my house. One of the fellas won't say that I wrote the song because I was in the blues business and people might not like it. So I didn't get any royalty from the lyrics, anything. That's it. I don't think I've lost anything.

There's a man in my soul
That keeps me free from sin.
My whole life had been changed
Since Jesus moved in.

Some of the fellas who say they wrote the song are still around here today. I've written a lot of other songs, "Hepcat's Boogie," "I Cried All Night." The tunes kind of slip me because "I Cried All Night" was put on the label here in Austin, called Uptown, and I got screwed out of that because I was just a goody-goody, but I haven't lost a thing about it. I'm still in possession of my faculties and still can maneuver my fingers and I still can sing good and I still got a chance.

I can improvise and I can write blues. I sing some traditional blues, like "Piggly Wiggly Blues." You know there used to be a grocery store back there. "My name is Piggly Wiggly, I got groceries on my shelf." That's a traditional blues. Robert Shaw used to sing that blues a lot. I've got several blues that I do. I'm the master of "Hattie Green," "How Long," "Black Gal," a number of those blues tunes. Recently I've written "Blues in Trouble" and "I Need My Baby," "I Got Something to Tell You," and one or two more I can't recall on the spur of the moment.

66 I worked as a disc jockey for about fifteen years, from the middle of the forties to the late fifties. I can't recall exactly. I was the first black DJ in Texas and in a lot of states. If you were black you had to get back. The radio station was the white man's property only. If you deliver mail you had to deliver it at the back door, but I broke that color line due to the fact that there were some powerful white men in that day. They owned that station, KVET, John Connally, that bunch. Connally was the one who spearheaded it. Of course, his political career was on the line, letting the black on the radio station. But I think they hit a gold mine, because the station became very popular, one of the most listened-to stations in this area. To stay on the air, they had to be different than the other boys, that's why I let them know the black jive talk that we were talking on the East Side, the youngsters at that time. That's the reason they call me "Dr. Hepcat."

I played rhythm and blues, down-home blues, upstate rhythms, T-Bone Walker. I used Duke Ellington's "Things Ain't What They Used To Be" as the theme song and I went out with blues. I played Lionel Hampton and those Duke and Peacock records. Big Mama Thornton, Gatemouth Brown.

(*Above*) Lavada Durst; Austin, 1986; *Photograph by Alan Govenar*

The Grey Ghost
R.T. Williams
Austin, 1987
Photograph by Gibbs Milliken
Courtesy Tary Owens

My thoughts are traditional. My music didn't pick up that modern beat. My songs are traditional blues, born of the fact of black communities that had names like Froggy Bottom, Stick Town, Guy Town, Buttermilk Flats, Sugar Hill — different black communities with their peculiar lifestyles, their loves, their dislikes, their differences, their songs, and what not. When you're in the middle of that environment, you had to sing the blues. You couldn't get no jobs. If

THE JIVES OF

DR. HEPCAT

1300 KVET 1300
Austin, Texas

The Jives of Dr. Hepcat; Austin, 1953; *Courtesy Lavada Durst*

you went to town to get a job, the law had a way of picking you up and saying you were a vagrant. They didn't want you to work on the county road. So when that situation exists, what else could you do. Play your piano or your guitar and sing the blues, but things always work out in due time. Sing where I want, go to eat where I want to, drink where I want to, no more shoes with holes in the bottom of them. I feel like I'm braggin' because I'm wearing Florsheims and suits and things with no patches in them. When you look back, I think we've come a mighty long ways.

The music hasn't changed. It's blues with that Texas boogie beat. A Texas piano player has got a beat that's different than other piano players. We have a boogie beat and it just has a riff. Other blues players play the blues, don't get me wrong, but you can tell a Texas piano player whenever you hear him [begins to play].

The blues is a way of expressing your feelings about the hard times and the troubles. A lot of blues songs, especially those down here in the South, if you listen real close, you find out a lot about the black experience [sings].

I'm just sitting here wondering,
Lord, what's going to become of me?
I'm just sitting here wondering
What's going to become of me?
I've been a bad man,
Lord, I intend to be.
My baby left me;
She did not say one word.
My baby left me;
She did not say one word.
Ain't nothing I done,
Something the poor girl heard.

That's all right, baby.
That's all right for you.
All right, baby.
That's all right for you.
Some day I going to be lucky,

Big Tex Gospel Records
East Austin, 1985
Photograph by Alan Govenar

Angela Strehli at Antone's
Austin, 1984
Photograph by Susan Antone

ANGELA STREHLI

(1947–   )

66 Curiosity led me down the path to the blues. I heard blues on the radio to begin with and didn't know how to find it or what to call it or anything like that. Then I began the long process of educating myself. There weren't that many people to talk to. I'd hear some Shreveport station, something like that, late at night. I had to find out what was going on.

I went to Chicago in 1966. I had been in college at Carleton College in Minnesota, but I just went crazy because there were no black people at all, and I realized that I was in the wrong environment. I worked that summer as a YWCA worker in San Antonio's West Side, and used to go to black churches. I loved the gospel music and different cultures of San Antonio. My father was a professor of Spanish at Texas Tech and was invited to teach in Argentina for the summer when I was sixteen. Well, we all went and it was there that I first heard *Musica folklorica.* In San Antonio these interests combined with what I wanted and liked about black music. But I also listened to *corridos, rancheras,* and *musica tropical.*

While I was working for the YWCA I got a chance to go to Chicago for a conference and wanted to hear some blues. I knew people who would not take me to clubs I wanted to go to. They thought I was crazy. I said, "Okay, I don't care." So I went alone to see some of the people I had only heard on records. In the three days I was there I listened to blues all over Chicago's South and West sides. I saw Howlin' Wolf on New Year's Eve at his club, Silvio's. I saw Buddy Guy, Muddy Waters, who at that time had Otis Spann playing the piano in his band. Muddy Waters was actually kind of hard up and he asked me if he could borrow some money. All he knew was that I was some little white girl from Texas who loved blues. So he said, "Well, have you got about three hundred dollars you can loan me?" He was very serious.

At that time I wasn't playing anything, just piddling around with a harmonica. Then I wanted to play bass. I never wanted to be a singer. But people made me start singing.

I grew up in Lubbock. There was a lot of good music there at different times [Joe Ely, Butch Hancock, Jimmie Gilmore, Terry Allen, Delbert McClinton]. You sort of had to make your own entertainment. In high school there was a folk music club, and Jimmie, Butch Hancock. John Denver wasn't from Lubbock, but he was there at that time.

I left Lubbock in '64, as soon as I was out of high school. I'm forty-one and I feel good. When I got into blues, the old blues was dying down, and rock music was bringin' rhythm and blues back in. Anyway, after I went to Chicago I became more interested in playing music myself. The following summer I went to San

(Above) Storm
Lewis Cowdrey (harmonica, vocals), Jimmie Vaughan (guitar), Freddie Walden (drums), Mike Kindred (piano), Paul Ray (bass)
Austin, 1972
Courtesy Paul and Diana Ray

Antone's club portrait
Austin, circa late 1970s
Photograph by Greg Stephens
Courtesy Paul and Diana Ray

Angela Strehli
Austin, 1985
Photograph by Susan Antone

Lewis. My side was "Do Something for Yourself" and Lewis's was "My Backscratcher." California got to be too much. It was '68 or '69, and we came back to Austin. I got a chance to be in a twelve-piece soul band with James Polk, who now plays organ with Ray Charles. This was a great experience to have. For most of the time, it was all black, except me. It made me really shape up and see if I was really a singer. There were some tough audiences, but it lasted a couple of years.

After that I had a good band with Denny Freeman and W.C. Clark, called Southern Feeling, and we traveled around and that carried me to 1975, when I felt I was kind of in a rut. I had done all my homework. I had my experience performing for a wide variety of audiences. I felt it was time to start writing and contributing something back to the idiom. I wanted to do something with some of my other influences in Latin music and Mexican, gospel.

My influences as a singer have been Tina Turner, her energy, but mainly I liked the low-down blues guys that didn't have beautiful voices: J.B. Hutto, Frankie Lee Sims, Dr. Ross, Etta James, Big Mama Thornton, who I got to know a little bit out on the West Coast. Magic Sam was a real favorite of mine. I still cry for him.

In 1975 was when Antone's was starting up on Sixth Street and I gave up having a band. I worked at Antone's doing the sound, being a kind of stage manager, and I had the opportunity to sing with everybody who came through. I didn't always get on stage, but I knew I could if I wanted to. I did get out on the road a little bit, with the Cobras, who needed a singer to take Paul Ray's place. Paul was having problems with his throat.

The band I have was started in 1981, '82, after Antone's moved from Sixth Street to North Austin. I had a little time to go into the studio and finally decided to get serious. Our newest member is Mark Kazanoff, who was touring with Marcia Ball. I had two guitar players, David Murray and Denny

Francisco with a band from Austin called Lord Greystoke and the Southern Fliers. We rehearsed a couple of times, but never played a gig. So I got a job in a black record store on Divisadero Street. Then, at the end of the summer I moved back to Austin to finish college in psychology and sociology.

In Austin I met Lewis Cowdrey and we started up a little band called the Fabulous Rockets, an integrated band, mixed blacks and whites. Then we had a band called Sunnyland Special. In the late '60s there wasn't much blues here, so we moved out to Southern California. We came back and cut my first record with

W.C. Clark Blues Review
Poster by Dale Wilkins
Austin, 1979
Courtesy Barker Texas History Center

Marcia Ball (left) and Angela Strehli (right)
Houston, 1986
Photograph by Tracy Hart/Heights Gallery

Freeman, and when Marcia started her new band she needed a guitar player. So she got David and I got Kaz. He kind of brings together both the Texas and Chicago sounds, playing both tenor saxophone and harmonica. The sax and other instruments are a real inspiration to my singing. My vocals often follow the saxophone and interact with the guitar.

Over the last three years we've gotten very tight. Derek O'Brien has been in and out of so many of my bands, but technically he's not in it now. Denny Freeman is the lead guitar, but he left for a while to work with Lou Ann Barton. The other members of my band are Pat Whitefield on bass and George Rains on drums and percussion.

We do some of the obscure music we've always loved, like Etta James' "I'd Rather Go Blind." To be able to sing like that is a kind of goal. A lot of the kids that come out to hear us never heard the older stuff, and it's new music for them. Otherwise, original material is where it's at. Some of my original songs are blues, but some don't come out that way. Songs like "Your Sweetness" and "Take It From Me" obviously have other strong influences, Latin things, country and western.

Being from Texas there's so much to be proud of. You have to be good because look at who you're following. All of the great bands — western swing, jazz, blues, Mexican music — there's so much to live up to, and I think that's why the musicianship in Texas

is what it has been. Musicians have always gotten along, but the society has been slow to catch up. It's a little discouraging. Ironically, black people have been cut off from their musical heritage, or have cut themselves off. Radio plays a big part in that. The social strides of the 1960s made blacks look in another direction. Blues was being dropped by a lot of blacks when white kids were getting into it. I don't completely know why. Maybe if I could fully understand it, it wouldn't be so appealing. To me, there's a sound in blues that goes beyond anything you can explain in words. It's something so deep inside that you have to be drawn to it. It's a pure feeling. All it takes is one note, one sound and that's it. That's the intensity that I strive for in my style. Straightforwardness. I like a wide-open uncomplicated sound. The fun part is the story, the expression, the poetry. Blues has its own language. It's not like everyday speech, but it's about everyday life. **99**

Jimmie Vaughan
Houston, 1983
Photograph by Tracy Hart/Heights Gallery

THE FABULOUS THUNDERBIRDS

❝ I just like that old Thunderbird rhythm myself. You can dance to it. It's got a good beat. It doesn't sound like a bunch of bees in a jug. You know what I mean?

Of course, I didn't know one rock 'n' roller from another until my daughter, Connie, started running around with Jimmie and the Thunderbirds. Then the more I was around them, the better I liked them.

We always liked Jimmie. But we've known Stevie longer than Jimmie. Stevie used to come to the house all the time. We had a little party room upstairs and Stevie would come up there and play his guitar. Someone else would bring an electric organ, another would have drums, and they'd have a little party up there. **❞**

John Crouch
Jimmie Vaughan's
father-in-law

❝ A friend and co-worker of their dad's gave Jimmie an old guitar, which I believe had three strings on it. And they were working out of town. So the next weekend when they came home, Jim picked out a couple of songs, and he said, "Well, that's pretty good. I'll just take it and get it fixed for you." It had holes in it. It was all beat up. So we took it and got it fixed for him, got it strung and that was it. It was just like he had played all of his life. He picked it up and started playing.

Well, we were so busy watching Jim that little brother, Stevie, got pushed aside sometimes, but I do remember him getting a Sears & Roebuck guitar for Christmas. We didn't pay much attention to him and then all of a sudden he was playing, too. I can remember him practicing a lot in his bedroom. No one was home but me and I could hear him singing. He was working on it as often as he could.

I always like their music. So it was never very hard to support what they were doing. Before Big Jim got sick, we used to dance to it. It was something we could dance to.

Jimmie Vaughan (left), Kim Wilson (right)
Houston, 1982
Photograph by Tracy Hart/Heights Gallery

Freddie King/Freda and the Firedogs
Poster by Jim Franklin
Austin, 1972
Courtesy Barker Texas History Center

When I hear them play, I'll say, "I believe I like this one best." Then another song will come on the record and I say, "I like that best." I like them all. **99**

Martha Vaughan

66 When I first moved to Austin, I was about nineteen. I was working construction with this guy. He was the construction boss; he was the foreman, and me and Denny Freeman were working for him. And he said, "Hey," when he found out we could play. "I'm going to get you all some gigs." In small towns, Bastrop, little places I don't even remember the names. And we would go and play these little bitty places that you didn't know they existed. And they would say, "Here comes Little Freddie King" and I'd play Freddie King instrumentals. It was a lot of fun, but a little scary, too.

When I lived in Dallas the blues scene happened at the Empire Room, the Forest Avenue Club. I saw Freddie King, Lowell Fulson, T-Bone Walker, Little Milton, B.B. King, Albert Collins. Two people I really wished I had gotten to see, if I had known better when I was fifteen or sixteen, are Lil Son Jackson and Frankie Lee Sims. I met him [Sims] one time when I was playing in Freddie King's band in Houston. And he started singing, "Lucy Mae."

Dallas might have been segregated, but I didn't think about that. I just wanted to hear the music. They didn't say anything about me.

I love blues the best, rock 'n' roll, rhythm and blues, country and western. I like good music, comes in a lot of shapes and sizes. I like music with feeling, with soul, it doesn't matter what it is. I really like the songs of Mercy Baby, he was the drummer with Frankie Lee Sims. We did one of his songs, "Marked Deck," on our first album.

I like to think that when I play the guitar it sounds like Dallas. That's where I learned everything, and all of the people I saw were playing here. I suppose it's a

Jimmie Vaughan (left), Stevie Ray Vaughan (right)
Backstage, Austin Opera House, 1984
Photograph by Tracy Hart/Heights Gallery

Kim Wilson (left) and Jimmie Vaughan (right)
Houston, 1982
Photograph by Tracy Hart/Heights Gallery

crazy way of putting it. I heard everyone that influenced me, either live or on the radio, KNOK or "Cat's Caravan" on WRR. However, Stevie and I grew up all over the South. I went to first grade in Jackson, Mississippi. Then we moved to Shreveport, Spring Hill, Baton Rouge, Arkansas. When we were kids, blues was on the music everywhere. On both sides of our family, folks played guitars, but never really did anything. We sort of liked Dallas, but I couldn't get a gig. So I went to Austin with my friends. We knew about a bunch of hippie joints where I knew we could get a job playing blues.

In my style I borrowed a lot of things: Freddie King, B.B. King, Lightnin' Hopkins, T-Bone Walker. I may have my own approach, but it's a Texas guitar sound. If I can make people aware of them, it's only a small part of what they've done for me. If it wasn't for them, there wouldn't be me. It's a black music. I think what really helped us go over was that we're a blues band that plays rock 'n' roll. We've always tried to play the fun part up and make the people like it. There have always been a lot of white bands doing this with blues, around Dallas, Houston, Austin. Joey Long is one of my heroes. He's an expert. Keith Ferguson, who used to be our bass player, was from Houston, he knew all about Joey Long. He's now with the Tailgators. Another white blues band I used to like around Dallas were the Nightcaps. They had a regional hit, which was actually a Lil Son Jackson song. The white crossover happened a lot earlier than when these English guys, like the Rolling Stones, got into blues. Of course, they turned it around, but there were white bands back in the 1930s, '40s, '50s that were playing blues, but not too many people thought about it like that. 99

Jimmie Vaughan

66 I started into blues kind of late, seventeen or eighteen years old. Some friends of mine in school turned me on to this kind of music. I played the horn when I was a young kid, about eight years old. There was a time in the middle there that I didn't want to practice. So I kind of quit it. Then these people turned me on to this blues stuff, and I picked up a harmonica and that was it. I was in a band a month later and have been in bands ever since then. I was born in Detroit, but musically I grew up in California, moved there in 1960, and then via other places, I moved to Texas in late 1974. I moved to Austin and I've been there ever since.

In California I played with Lowell Fulson and Lowell had this guy guitar player named Mark Pollack. He was from Texas and he told me about Austin. I was playing with all these greats in California — Pee Wee Crayton, Lowell Fulson, Luther Tucker, John Lee Hooker — and I was only making ten or fifteen dollars a night. I called to Austin and they said nothing was really happening. So I moved to

Lowell Fulson
Armadillo World Headquarters
Austin, 1972
Photograph by Burton Wilson
Courtesy Burton Wilson

me out. Then there was James Cotton, Little Walter, of course. I would play and I'd say, "Is that right?" and they'd go, "Yeah." I learned a lot of lessons from guitar players, like Lowell Fulson, who'd tell me I was overplaying, don't play all the time, very choice information. My playing improved real fast. I was a singer first, but I learned to play harmonica quickly. I would say there weren't too many white people that influenced me — my dad did, he was a singer on the radio, with Danny Thomas for a little bit.

When I first started singing blues, I liked Otis Rush. A lot of people requested Otis Rush, and then Bobby Bland. People compared my style to his. I don't see how, but they do. Also, I got into people like Junior Parker, singers. I was better with vibrato, and after that I kind of developed my own style. The doctor said I may get better, but I'll never get well [laughs].

We do our music our way. We're not forsaking any of our teachers. You got to resign yourself to the fact that you can't do like anybody else but you and that's it. Why try? I'd say we're going more toward songs than solos. It's not that we don't solo on harmonica and guitar. We think more about singles. We're doing more ballads. There's more balance, a little bit of everything we have. We re-made "How Do You Spell Love" because the audience reaction was so good. With Dave Edmunds as producer, he's making us sound more like us.

Up on stage we're on our own. We try to have a pure sound. We have the instruments we want, and we've learned how to play to the back row, to reach everyone in the audience. **99**

Kim Wilson

Minneapolis and then about a year later Mark's friend, Shirley, called and said she wanted me to work in some kind of music business. Well, I got a round-trip ticket to Austin and met Jimmie. I met him at a place called Alexander's. It was kind of a rib joint and it was a Sunday matinee. Jimmie was playing in a band called Storm, and Stevie asked if I could sit in and they said, "No." So Stevie, Doyle and I got up during the break and played and the crowd went crazy over it. I went up and shook Jimmie's hand and about a month later I got a call from Jimmie and he offered me a job. About a month or two later I gave notice and moved to Austin.

Nobody really taught me anything. I played a lot with George Smith in California, and he really helped

Jimmie Vaughan and Stevie Ray Vaughan
Austin, 1985
Photograph by Andrew Lang
Courtesy Barker Texas History Center

Stevie Ray Vaughan
Houston, 1983
Photograph by Tracy Hart/Heights Gallery

STEVIE RAY VAUGHAN

(1954–   )

Stevie Ray Vaughan has a new profile. He's calmer, more self-assured with his status as one of the reigning masters of blues/rock guitar. His single-string runs are as graceful as T-Bone Walker's, or as biting as Jimi Hendrix's. He pulls out every sound he can find, bending the strings, twisting the guitar behind his back, showing every note in the gestures of his tightly drawn face. His performance is neater, perhaps slicker in the shuffles; faster, playing the distortion into music with piercing notes. The counterpoint of tones is more subtle in his playing.

After a year of divorce, drug problems, and the death of his father, Stevie Ray Vaughan has adjusted to a new way of life.

“ I don't think that my attitude [toward blues] has changed that much, only in the sense that I've got more knowledge of what I've been listening to all along. That really hasn't changed a lot. I've always really liked the music for what it is and just try to grow with what I do with it.

Rhythm and blues and rock 'n' roll were my first interests. Before I got to playing when I was seven or eight years old, you might pick out songs on the radio that aren't too hip. My brother, Jimmie, was bringing home records — Muddy Waters, B.B. King, T-Bone Walker, Buddy Guy, Howlin' Wolf — and at the same time bringing home British blues boom records — Rolling Stones, Bluesbreakers, groups like that, and of course, the Beatles stuff started hittin' it. I was real fortunate because I was able to hear both sides of it, the originals and the re-makes. It was a lot of fun. That's the influence. All of the people I was getting to listen to as the originals were the same people that the Stones, Clapton and others were listening to. That's the way I heard it, with less restrictions about being a purist [bringing the Chicago small band approach together with the Texas guitar sound].

That Texas guitar sound is a good thing. I've never known what that means other than in some ways it's a little rougher and sometimes a little smooth, kind of mish-mash. It's a big place. As far as I know there's a kind of hard line, an attitude about it, more than anything. I guess that's one thing about all the players I listened to. It was all kinds of not necessarily this is the only way to do it. But this is how it's done. There wasn't any joking around about it. They might be funny songs, but the approach to the playing, it was right to the point.

I never saw T-Bone Walker live, but lots of times on record. But my biggest influence has been my brother, Jimmie, because of probably all the other influences he made it possible for me to have. Those people included Freddie King, B.B. King, Albert King, Lonnie Mack. The first record I ever bought was Lonnie Mack's “Wham,” the first one I ever bought for myself. But there was Freddie, B.B., and Albert, Buddy Guy, Hubert Sumlin. Hubert is still one of the wildest guitar players I ever heard, without a doubt. Of course, from Hendrix I heard all these different influences that I couldn't put a finger on. Bo Diddley, Albert Collins. This is 1966 or '67 that Jimmie first brought home a Hendrix record. After I heard that, then as I went along, I'd hear all these other people. I could pick this piece out of Hendrix's sound, and say this must have come . . . and go on and look at it from there.

Sometimes it's just the way I heard it. All these different people that I heard at different periods of time and they all seem to fit together to me. So whatever comes to mind, whatever style, whether I'm in tune or not, sometimes. Most of the time it's just putting everything into play. You know, there's all sorts of things that go on at different times. Believe me, my thoughts are a lot more in a flow these days than they were a year ago or more. A year ago or so, it was everything flying around at once. I couldn't grab ahold of anything, but some good music came out when I took the time to slow down enough to see it.

Stevie Ray Vaughan
Houston, 1987
Photograph by Tracy Hart/Heights Gallery

It can get a little strange without having a new record out. To be out on the road, promoting a live record, we're expected to play these same songs. It's gotten to the point where if we don't play "Cold Shot," or this one or that one, there's invariably somebody saying, "God damn, I came to see you, mainly to play that song." So I can't really win for losin' in that respect. If there's a time limit, we play as many songs as we can and try to have fun with it. We never have a song list when we go on stage. It's pretty much what comes to mind, and there's some nights we play more off-the-wall things than others. Sometimes it just seems that the right thing to do is to play familiar songs, but we're less and less doing that. We're trying to take the pressure out of the situation. Beside all the original stuff we plan to work on, and the stuff we're working on anyway, we're just thinking about in the mean time working a bunch of songs we always wanted to play, and go play some clubs, just have fun. To hell with all the pressure, and just try them out and see what happens. Out of what comes from just having fun, whether it's our new songs and songs we've always liked, is going to come a lot of new original stuff just from the excitement of playing new things. I've realized that any time that there is a block to write, any time there is anything that blocks that fun out of it, you need to just go back to square one, start off like a bunch of guys that want to get together and play some music that we like, and go from there.

Lately I've gotten my record player back, some of my records. I listen to KKDA a lot. I listen to old Bobby Bland, Albert Collins, Johnny Guitar Watson. I've been listening to a lot of Buddy Guy, B.B., the same people I've always listened to. It's like I've just found them, a newborn kid, remembering all these feelings I used to have. Now that I'm sober, it's all something just vague in the past. Oh, that's where I came from.

We're planning to co-produce our new record with someone who will be a kind of backboard for us, someone to bounce things off of. When they see us

going in a direction, going in and making it easy for us to do that, by pulling it out a little bit, by pulling out stops that we might not think of. When we go in, we want to know exactly what we want to do, which might mean finishing a couple of songs in the studio, which is what we do anyway.

I had a lot of fun working with John Hammond. It may not have been as much fun for the engineer. A lot of times the engineer is only involved in the technical end of recording and they really don't understand old school, where the performance is the most important thing, what clicks while you're playing. If there's some rough spots those can be worked out if you want to go out doing it that way. However, a lot of times an engineer-type producer or someone who is an engineer and wants to be a producer, becomes a lot more difficult to work with. John Hammond was mainly — all the knowledge he had, all the things he'd seen made you want to play from your heart, and just play good music. John Hammond wasn't there for the session for "Texas Flood" but we had him in mind. My thoughts during each track was that if this is the last record, I want to make the best I can do. And we only had a day and a half to do the tracks. "Texas Flood" was the last song we did, and they said, "That's all the time you got." But we had ten songs and that's what we needed.

John Hammond came to the sessions for "Couldn't Stand the Weather." He was there for that. For me, he was easy to work with, for the band, everyone as far as I know. It was the engineer that had some difficulty with John. We would leave the track alone as much as possible and rework it.

On "Soul to Soul" I played drums. So that was done quite a bit differently. The engineers did not want us to play the song at that speed. So he didn't want to turn on the recorder or anything. What ended up happening, we waited until he took a nap and we had his assistant run the recorder for us. Tommy [Shannon] played bass and I played drums, and we just did a long deal. I kind of mouthed the words at

him, so we would know where we were. We actually played it slower, and on record we sped the tape up, from C to D. The whole thing was fun to do. Even though it wasn't an actual live performance, it had that vitality. Then I went back and put a guitar part on it. Then the keyboard player did it, and I sang it. That was really the only stacked one we did, but it doesn't sound stacked at all. The beat is like an old Duke shuffle, kind of a backward shuffle, when the drums were used backwards. The actual rhythm of it is backwards.

I really liked Fenton Robinson's guitar on the Duke recordings, especially with Larry Davis. And the guitar on the Bobby Bland, they were heavily produced, but there's something that sticks up in your face, even though it's smooth. There's a lot of deep friendship in the music, a lot of people just coming together and making some good records. It's the kind

of thing we had at Antone's. Clifford got the idea to start the club, and everybody wanted to be the house band there. Everyone was claiming to be the house band that week, but we were all friends. You see, everybody was changing bands every three to six months. Every time anybody felt stale, they'd go hook up with somebody else. It kept us real fresh, and then when everybody found a good solid combination, musicians stayed together two or three years, and then they would shift it a little more. Well, the Thunderbirds have had the same musicians for eight years. Now it's twelve or thirteen years since they started, and I think they have really found a combination they like. It's the same with us [Double Trouble], we stayed together. I got back together with Tommy. Tommy and I have played together on and off since 1969. I met him in Dallas, the night he quit Johnny Winter. He was on his way to California to play with another band, called Crackerjack. And they came by The Fog on Lemmon Avenue [in Dallas], and it was the time of year that he had met Johnny at the same place, almost to the day, three years earlier. The night he quit. I was at The Fog. I was fourteen, and Tommy was the only guy in the band that would talk to me. Everybody else was too hip, I don't know. I was a fourteen-year-old fart. That was the second part of my first club gig. We had an eleven-horn band. We were doing some things off the radio and some things we had heard on record. We sort of had a big band. Put it this way, we had a lot of people in the band.

I like to play in a lot of different ways. With just a drummer, you don't have to worry about changes. I like to play with a trio, and trade with a keyboard player, and use a big horn section as well, two drummers sometimes, if they can work together. Joe Sublett played saxes on "Little Sister" and "Looking Out the Window," and another horn player on "Stang's Swang" on "Couldn't Stand the Weather." Other than that there isn't much horn playing on there, though I'd like to do a record with a big horn section, four or five or six horns. I love to dodge horns. I like to stand in the middle of a semicircle and play. I follow the horns

and they follow me. I love to play solos with the horns blasting and play in between them.

My phone message is a bad recording of "Soul Stretch," the Bobby Bland instrumental. It's that Duke big band blues sound. And I like the drums, not necessarily how they're done in the mix, but how they sounded, just the drums themselves on the record. It was bright, and didn't sound like they were playing loud. It was just there, not like the New Orleans backbeat sound, but I like that, too.

The blues doesn't have to be three chords, or two or one. It doesn't have to be a lot of passing changes. It can be any of those combinations, or notes. I don't think I'll be writing any "Everybody Go Out and Get High" songs in the future. The blues is just it in the first place, whether it does it by getting you mad in the first place, and then you get over it, or if it's relating to somebody else's story that's the same as yours, or worse than yours so that you don't feel so bad. Or it's a happy song. It doesn't matter. It's all soothing anyway. It's to help somebody's emotions. That's what it is. I hope I'm helping other people with my music. It helps me, makes me feel better. The blues gets me going. I have to wind back down.

My brother's guitar style is more poised than mine. I play like I'm breaking out of jail. I get excited and I can't stop. I don't really know how long my solos are going to be, but I try to bring them to a point without being redundant. When it stops being fun, it's time to do something else. Sometimes when you do something over and over, the meaner it gets.

One of the most memorable performances was Carnegie Hall. We had Jimmie and I on guitar, George Rains, and Chris Layton on drums, Tommy Shannon playing bass, Roomful of Blues horn section. Angela Strehli was there. It was the day after my birthday, October 4. There are so many that were a lot of fun. That's the main reason for doing it. If it's really just a job, then what are we doing?

I want to do an album with Jimmie. It's not too often that we get to play together. Usually if we do I'm sitting in with his band, or he's sitting in with mine. We are

Stevie Ray Vaughan
Houston, 1983
Photograph by Tracy Hart
Heights Gallery

Steve Ray Vaughan
Antone's poster, 1982
Courtesy Barker Texas History Center

all supportive of each other. I'm very fortunate that way. It's something that I missed for a long time, because I was runnin' from everything. It takes a person a long time to get out of old habits. The rehabilitation program made me realize a lot of things, about people and places and things. The main thing I found out was the problem, low self-esteem and a huge ego at the same time. No middle ground. That's what happens when someone is insecure, unless you can get by feeling sorry for yourself. Sometimes that works, too. When you find yourself in a place that you can't stop drinking and you can't keep going either, that's a pretty rough place to be. That's where I was, and at the same time, things I care about were quickly going out the window — those cares, not necessarily just material things. I was in a position where I could have hired somebody to babysit me, and buy the drugs, and buy me this and buy me that. Have them carry it for me, and if they got busted, "Ooops!" I could have done that, but I chose not to do that. Both Tommy and I went into the treatment program. Now the whole band is clean. Reese and Chris aren't alcoholics, though us alcoholics sometimes resent the fact that other people can drink [laughs], but that's the trap. You have to deal with those feelings.

I think my playing makes more sense. I listen to old live performances; we record every night. There are a lot of new things I really like. A lot of tones that I had no idea how I got. A lot of things connected. Fortunately, my addiction to alcohol and drugs hadn't taken away everything that I cared about, but it was fast becoming where those things were dying, because I was dying inside. Now, I can choose to live.

I'm just trying to take it as it comes along. All four of my records have gone gold in the last year. The next one, we just have to take our time and not try to top the other ones, but to make the best record we can. It's a matter of not paying attention to the other pressure. It's there, but what good does it do? We're planning to do club dates, maybe not advertise for a while.

Now, it's okay when there's blank spots. You know, I used to be scared to death of blank spots, and sometimes they still scare me. Sometimes you have to clean out the refrigerator before you put some food inside. **99**

SELECTED DISCOGRAPHY

The two standard discographies that cover the history of blues recordings are *Recording the Blues* by Robert Dixon and John Godrich and *Blues Records: 1943-1970* by Mike Leadbitter and Neil Slaven. More current releases and reissues by British, Dutch, German, Japanese, French, and Scandanavian labels are reviewed regularly in *Living Blues* (United States), *Juke Blues, Blues and Rhythm* (England), *Jefferson* (Sweden), *BN* (Finland), *Blues Life* (Germany), *Block* (Holland), and *IL Blues* (Italy). The following discography is a selected listing of Texas blues artists and recommended recordings.

JOHNNY ACE

"Johnny Ace Memorial Album," MCA 27014

"A Memorial to Johnny Ace," Ace CH 40

DAVE ALEXANDER

"The Rattler," Arhoolie 1067

"Dirt on the Ground," Arhoolie 1071

TEXAS ALEXANDER

"Texas Troublesome Blues," Agram 2009

"Texas Alexander, Vols. 1, 2, 3," Matchbox 206, 214, 220

BLACK ACE

"Black Ace," Arhoolie 1003

BOBBIE BLUE BLAND

"Woke Up Screaming," Ace CH 41

"Blues in the Night," Ace CH 132

"Foolin' with the Blues," Charly CRB 1049

LITTLE JOE BLUE

"Blue's Blues," Charly CRB 1150

JUKE BOY BONNER

"I'm Goin' Back to the Country," Arhoolie 1036

"The Struggle," Arhoolie 1045

"The One Man Trio," Flyright 548

CHARLES BROWN

"Drifting Blues," Pathe 154 661-1

"Race Track Blues," Route 66 KIX 17

"Sunny Road," Route 66 KIX 5

"One More For The Road," Blue Side 60007

CLARENCE "GATEMOUTH" BROWN

"The Duke-Peacock Story, Vol. 1," Ace CHD 161

"Pressure Cooker," Alligator 4745

"Atomic Energy," Blues Boy 305

"San Antonio Ballbuster," Red Lightin' 0010

"Alright Again," Rounder 2028

"The Original Peacock Recordings," Rounder 2039

"One More Mile," Rounder 2034

"Real Life," Rounder 2054

GOREE CARTER

"Rock Awhile," Blues Boy 306

CLIFTON CHENIER

"Classic Clifton," Arhoolie 1082

"Black Snake Blues," Arhoolie 1038

"Bogalusa Boogie," Arhoolie 1076

WILFRED CHEVIS AND HIS TEXAS ZYDECO BAND

"Foot Stompin' Zydeco," Maison De Soul 1013

ALBERT COLLINS

"Ice Pickin'," Alligator 4713

"Frozen Alive," Alligator 4725

"Don't Lose Your Cool," Alligator 4730

"Live in Japan," Alligator 4733

"Cold Snap," Alligator 4752

"Ice Cold Blues," Charly CRB 1119

"The Cool Sound," Crosscut 1011

ALBERT COLLINS, JOHNNY COPELAND, ROBERT CRAY

"Showdown," Alligator 4743

JOHNNY COPELAND

"Dedicated to the Greatest," Kent 067

"I'll Be Around," Mr. R&B 1001

"Down On Bending Knees," Mr. R&B 1002

"Copeland Special," Rounder 2025

"Make My Home Where I Hang My Hat," Rounder 2030

"Texas Twister," Rounder 2040

"Bringing It All Back Home," Rounder 2050

"The Johnny Copeland Collection, Vol. 1," Homecooking HCS-107

PEE WEE CRAYTON

"Rocking Down On Central Avenue," Ace CHA 61

"Memorial Album," Ace CHD 177

"Blues Before Dawn," Pathe 156 634-1

KING CURTIS

"That's Alright," Red Lightnin' 0042

"King Curtis & The Kingpins," WEA P8619

MERCY DEE

"Mercy Dee," Arhoolie 1007

"G.I. Fever," Crown Prince 49-55

FLOYD DIXON

"Opportunity Blues," Route 66 KIX 1

"Houston," Route 66 KIX 11

"Empty Stocking Blues," Route 66 KIX 27

ROBERT EALEY WITH THE JUKE JUMPERS

"Bluebird Open," Amazing AM 1004

FABULOUS THUNDERBIRDS

"Girls Go Wild," Takoma 7068

"The Fabulous Thunderbirds," Chrysalis PV 41250

"What's the Word," Chrysalis PV 41287

"Butt Rockin'," Chrysalis PV 41319

"Tuff Enuff," CBS BFZ 40304

LOWELL FULSON

"Blue Days, Black Nights," Ace CH 184

"Lowell Fulsom," Arhoolie 2003

"Lovemaker," Big Town 1008

"Lowell Fulsom," Blues Boy 302

ANSON FUNDERBURGH AND THE ROCKETS

"Talk to You by Hand," Black Top 1001

"She Knocks Me Out," Black Top 1022

"My Love is Here to Stay," Black Top 1032

"Sins," Black Top 1039

CLARENCE GARLOW

"Clarence Garlow, 1951-1958," Flyright 586

LLOYD GLENN

"Old Time Shuffle," Black & Blue 33.077

"After Hours," Oldie Blues 8002

"Blue Ivories," Stockholm RJ 203

"Texas Man," Jukebox Lil 698

CLARENCE "CANDY" GREEN

"Lady in Red," JSP 1022

R.L. GRIFFIN

"There is Something on Your Mind," Classic 0002

PEPPERMINT HARRIS

"I Got Loaded," Route 66 KIX 23

Z.Z. HILL

"Dues Paid in Full," Kent 018

"Z.Z. Hill," Malaco 7402

"Down Home," Malaco 7406

"The Rhythm and the Blues," Malaco 7411

"I'm a Bluesman," Malaco 7415

"Bluesmaster," Malaco 7420

"In Memoriam, 1953-84," Malaco 7426

SMOKEY HOGG

"Goin' Back Home," Krazy Kat 7421

SAM LIGHTNIN' HOPKINS

"Lightnin' Sam Hopkins," Arhoolie 1011

"Early Recordings," Arhoolie 2007

"Early Recordings," Vol. 2," Arhoolie 2010

"Houston's King of the Blues," Blues Classics 30

"Lightnin' in New York," Candid 9010

"Flash Lightnin'," Diving Duck 4307

"Lightnin' Hopkins," Diving Duck 4308

"The Blues," Mainstream 311

"Dirty Blues," Mainstream 326

BEE HOUSTON

"Bee Houston," Arhoolie 1050

JOE HOUSTON

"Rockin' at the Drive In," Ace CH 120.

"Kicking Back," Big Town 1004

"Earthquake," Pathe 156 138-1

JOE HUGHES

"Texas Guitar Master," Double Trouble TX 3012

IVORY JOE HUNTER

"Seventh Street Boogie," Route 66 KIX 4

"Jumping at the Dew Drop," Route 66 KIX 15

"I Had a Girl," Route 66 KIX 25

LONG JOHN HUNTER

"Texas Border Town Blues," Double Trouble TX 3011

"Smooth Magic," Boss LJ 001

LIL SON JACKSON

"Lil Son Jackson," Arhoolie 1004

"Rockin' and Rollin'" Pathe 154 667-1

BLIND LEMON JEFFERSON

"King of Country Blues," Yazoo 1069

"Blind Lemon Jefferson," Collectors Classics 22

"The Remaining Titles," Matchbox 1001

"Blind Lemon Jefferson," Milestone 47022

BLIND WILLIE JOHNSON

"Praise God I'm Satisfied," Yazoo 1058

"Blind Willie Johnson," Folkways 3585

COLEY JONES

"Coley Jones & The Dallas String Band," Matchbox 208

JUKE JUMPERS

"Border Radio," Amazing 1001

"The Joint's Jumpin'" Amazing 1005

"Jumper Cables," Varrick 016

B.B. KING

"One Nighter Blues," Ace CHD 201

"The Best of B.B. King," Ace CHD 198, 199, 201.

"The Rarest King," Blues Boy 301

"Live at the Regal," MCA 27006

FREDDIE KING

"Takin' Care of Business," Charly CRB 1099

"Rockin' the Blues," Crosscut 1005

"Gives You a Bonanza of Instrumentals," Crosscut 1010

"Hideaway," Gusto 5033X

"17 Original Hits," King 5012

"The Best of Freddie King," MCA 690

"Just Pickin'" Modern Blues MB2LP-721

MILTON LARKIN

"Down Home Saturday Night," Copasetic 933

HUDDIE "LEADBELLY" LEDBETTER

"Leadbelly," Archive of Folk FS 202

"Good Morning Blues," Biograph 12013

"Leadbelly," Columbia PC 30035

"Leadbelly Legacy, Vols. 3, 4," Folkways 2024, 2034

"Leadbelly's Last Sessions, Vols. 1, 2," Folkways 2941, 2942

"Leadbelly," Pathe 2c068-80701

FRANKIE LEE

"The Ladies and the Babies," Hightone 8004

MANCE LIPSCOMB

"Texas Songster & Sharecropper," Arhoolie 1001

"Texas Songster, Vols. 2, 3, 6," Arhoolie 1023, 1026, 1069

"You'll Never Find Another Man Like Mance," Arhoolie 1077

LITTLE WILLIE LITTLEFIELD

"Happy Pay Day," Ace CH 150

"Jump With Little Willie Littlefield," Ace CHD 114

"K.C. Loving," KC 101

"House Party," Oldie Blues 8003

"It's Midnight," Route 66 KIX 10

JOEY LONG

"The Rains Came," Crazy Cajun 1027

"Flying High," Crazy Cajun 1049

BARBARA LYNN

"We Got A Good Thing Goin'" Dead Ball DB2-2506

"You'll Lose a Good Thing," Jamie 3023

PETE MAYES

"I'm Ready," Double Trouble TX 3013

PERCY MAYFIELD

"My Heart is Always Singing Sad Songs," Ace CHD 153

"The Voice Within," Route 66 KIX 22

"The Best of Percy Mayfield," Specialty 2126

DELBERT McCLINTON

"Sometimes Country, Sometimes Blue," Quicksilver QSV 1004

JOE MEDWICK

"Joe Medwick," Crazy Cajun 1085

AMOS MILBURN

"Great R&B Oldies," Blues Spectrum 110

"Unreleased Masters," Pathe 154 670-1

"Let's Have a Party," Pathe 154 671-1

"Vicious Vicious Vodka," Pathe 154 140-1

"Chicken Shack Boogie," Pathe 156 141-1

"Rare Masters," Pathe 156-638-1

"Amos Milburn and His Chicken Shackers," Route 66 KIX 7

"Rock, Rock, Rock," Route 66 KIX 21

"Let's Rock a While," Route 66 KIX 28

ALEX MOORE

"Alex Moore," Arhoolie 1008

"Alex Moore in Europe," Arhoolie 1048

BILL NEELY

"Blackland Farm Boy," Arhoolie 5014

JIMMY NELSON

"Watch That Action," Ace CHD 228

SUNNY OZUNA

"Sunny and The Sunliners," Crazy Cajun 1017

JUNIOR PARKER

"Junior Parker & Billy Love," Charly CR 30135

"Blues Consolidated," MCA 27037

"Driving Wheel," MCA 27039

"The Best of Little Junior Parker," MCA 27046

ESTHER PHILLIPS

"Bad Bad Girl," Charly CRB 1100.

SAMMY PRICE

"Rockin' Boogie," Black & Blue 33.560

"Singing with Sammy," Blue Time 2002

"Rib Joint," Savoy 2240

"Play It Again, Sam," Whiskey, Women, And KM 702

"Do You Dig My Jive," Whiskey, Women, And KM 704

SONNY RHODES

"In Europe," Appaloosa 023

"Just Blues," Rhodeway 4501

L.C. "GOOD ROCKIN' " ROBINSON

"Ups and Downs," Arhoolie 1062

DOUG SAHM

"Doug Sahm and Freddy Fender Reunion," Crazy Cajun 1013

"The Best of Sir Douglas Quintet," Crazy Cajun 1003

"Texas Road Runner, The Renner Sides," Moonshine BLP 701

RAY SHARPE

"Texas Boogie Blues," Flying High 6502

"Live at the Bluebird," Flying High 6507

ROBERT SHAW

"Texas Barrelhouse Piano," Arhoolie 1010

THOMAS SHAW

"Do Lord Remember," Blues Beacon 63100

FRANKIE LEE SIMS

"Walkin' With Frankie," Krazy Kat 7428

J.T. "FUNNY PAPA" SMITH

"The Original Howling Wolf," Yazoo 1031

VICTORIA SPIVEY

"The Blues is Life," Folkways 3541

"Victoria and Her Blues," Spivey 1002

"The Queen and Her Knights," Spivey 1006

"Recorded Legacy of the Blues," Spivey 2001

ANGELA STREHLI

"Stranger Blues," Antone's ANT 0001

"Soul Shake," Antone's ANT 0006

HENRY "RAGTIME TEXAS" THOMAS

"Ragtime Texas," Herwin 209

WILLARD "RAMBLIN' " THOMAS

"Ramblin' Thomas," Matchbox 215

WILLIE MAE "BIG MAMA" THORNTON

"Quit Snoopin' Round My Door," Ace CH 170

"In Europe," Arhoolie 1028

"Big Mama with the Chicago Blues Band," Arhoolie 1032

WILLIE MAE THORNTON AND CLIFTON CHENIER

"Live Together," Crazy Cajun 1104

STEVIE RAY VAUGHAN

"Couldn't Stand the Weather," Epic FE 39304

"Soul to Soul," Epic FE 40036

"Texas Flood," Epic PE-38734

EDDIE "CLEANHEAD" VINSON

"Kidney Stew," Black and Blue 33.543

"Back in Town," Charly CRB 1046

"Eddie 'Cleanhead' Vinson," Delmark 631

"Cherry Red Blues," Gusto 5035x

"The Clean Machine," Muse 5282

"Mr. Cleanhead Steps Out," Saxonograph BP 507

AARON "T-BONE' WALKER

"Feeling the Blues," Black and Blue 33.552

"The Inventor of the Electric Guitar," Blues Boy 304

"T-Bone Jumps Again," Charly CRB 1019

"Plain Ole Blues," Charly CRB 1037

"The Natural Blues," Charly CRB 1057

"Singing the Blues," Pathe 154 675-1

"T-Bone Walker," Pathe 2C068-86523

"I Get So Weary," Pathe 156 144-1

BEULAH "SIPPIE" WALLACE

"Sippie Wallace," Atlantic SD 19350

"Sippie Wallace Sings the Blues," Storyville 4017

JOHNNY "GUITAR" WATSON

"Hit the Highway," Ace CH 70

KATIE WEBSTER

"You Know That's Right," Arhoolie 1095

"Pounds of Blues," Charly CRB 1087

"Whooee Sweet Daddy," Flyright 530

"Has the Blues," Goldband GRLP-7780

HOP WILSON

"Hop Wilson and His Buddies," Ace CHD 240

JOHNNY WINTER

"Guitar Slinger," Alligator 4735

"Serious Business," Alligator 4742

"Third Degree," Alligator 4748

"Early Johnny Winter," Crazy Cajun 1009

TEXAS BLUES COLLECTIONS

PRE-WAR BLUES:
"Texas Blues: Dallas, 1928," Fountain FB 305
"Jack of Diamonds," Herwin 211
"Tex-Arkana-Louisiana Country," Yazoo 1004
"Blues from the Western States," Yazoo 1032
"When Women Sang the Blues," Blues Classics 26

POST-WAR BLUES:

"Texas Rhythm and Blues," Ace CH 29
"Lyons Avenue Jive," Ace CHD 171
"Texas Blues," Arhoolie 2006
"Texas Blues, Vol. 2," Arhoolie 1017
"Honkers: An R&B Saxophone Anthology," Atlantic 81666
"Texas Blues," Blues Classics 16
"Houston Jump," Krazy Kat 7407
"Down in the Groovy," Krazy Kat 7418
"Houston Shuffle," Krazy Kat 7425
"Fort Worth Shuffle," Krazy Kat 7426
"Texas Country Blues, 1948-53," Krazy Kat 7434
"Guitar In My Hands," Moonshine 104
"Guitar In My Hands, Vol. 2," Moonshine 110
"Down Behind the Rise, 1947-1953," Nighthawk 106
"Angels in Houston," Rounder 2031
"From San Antonio to the Gulf of Mexico," Moonshine BLP 702
"Border Town Jive," Krazy Kat 7436
"Strutting at the Bronze Peacock," Ace CHD 223
"Chess Blues, Vol. 2, Texas/West Coast," Chess (Japan) PLP 6064

BIBLIOGRAPHY

CHRIS ALBERTSON, *Bessie* (Stein & Day, 1982).
SUSAN ANTONE, *The First Ten Years* (Antone's, 1985), *Picture the Blues* (Antone's, 1986).
HOUSTON A. BAKER, *Blues, Ideology and Afro-American Literature* (Univ. of Chicago Press, 1985).
BRUCE BASTIN, *Red River Blues* (Univ. of Illinois Press, 1986).
JOHN BROVEN, *South to Louisiana* (Pelican, 1983).
SAMUEL CHARTERS, *Country Blues* (Da Capo, 1975).
HELEN O. DANCE, *Stormy Monday: The T-Bone Walker Story* (Louisiana State Univ. Press, 1987).
ROBERT DIXON and **JOHN GODRICH,** *Recording the Blues, 1902-1943* (Stein & Day, 1970).
DAVID EVANS, *Big Road Blues* (Univ. of California Press, 1981).
WILLIAM FERRIS and **MARY HART,** ed., *Folk Music and the Modern Sound* (Univ. Press of Mississippi, 1981).
PAUL GARON, *Blues and the Poetic Spirit* (Da Capo, 1978).
BOB GROOM, *The Blues Revival* (Studio Vista, 1971).
PETER GURALNICK, *Lost Highway* (Vintage Books, 1982), *Sweet Soul Music* (Harrow, 1986).
SHELDON HARRIS, *Blues Who's Who* (Da Capo, 1983).
TONY HEILBUT, *The Gospel Sound* (Simon & Schuster, 1971).
LEROI JONES (IMAMU A. BARAKA), *Blues People,* (Morrow, 1963).
CHARLES KEIL, *Urban Blues* (Univ. of Chicago Press, 1970).
LAWRENCE W. LEVINE, *Black Culture and Consciousness* (Oxford Univ. Press, 1977).
MIKE LEADBITTER, *Nothing but the Blues* (Oak Publications, 1971).
MIKE LEADBITTER and **NEIL SLAVEN,** *Blues Records, 1943-1970,* 2nd edition, Vols. 1&2 (London: Record Information Services, 1987).
LIVING BLUES, Nos. 1-79 (Center for the Study of Southern Culture, Univ. of Mississippi, 1970-1988).
GILES OAKLEY, *The Devil's Music* (Harcourt, Brace Jovanovich, 1976).
PAUL OLIVER, *Songsters and Saints* (Cambridge Univ. Press, 1984), *Blues Off the Record* (Hippocrene Books, 1984).
ROBERT PALMER, *Deep Blues* (Viking Press, 1981).
BARRY LEE PEARSON, *Sounds So Good To Me* (Univ. of Pennsylvania Press, 1984).
ROSS RUSSELL, *Jazz Style in Kansas City and the Southwest* (Univ. of California Press, 1971).
ARNOLD SHAW, *Honkers and Shouters* (Collier Books, 1978), *Black Popular Music in America* (Schirmer Books, 1986).
MICHAEL TAFT, *Blues Lyric Poetry: A Concordance* (Garland Publishing, 1984).
JEFF TODD TITON, *Early Downhome Blues* (Univ. of Illinois Press, 1979), *Downhome Blues Lyrics* (Twayne Publishers, 1981).

ACKNOWLEDGEMENTS

In making this book I have been helped by many people. Foremost, I am grateful to the blues artists who inspired this work. This book is dedicated to these musicians and to the memory of those I heard but never met.

I am also thankful to the researchers and collectors who made their work available to me: John Wheat of the Barker Texas History Center; Bill Ferris of the Center for the Study of Southern Culture at the University of Mississippi; Jim O'Neal and Peter Lee of *Living Blues* magazine; Dick Shurman in Chicago; Chuck Nevitt and Tim Schuller in Dallas; Sumter Bruton in Fort Worth; Tary Owens, Susan Antone, Paul and Diana Ray, and L.E. McCullough in Austin; Lorenzo Thomas, Tracy Hart, Benny Joseph, and Lanny Steele in Houston; Tom Mazzolini, Pat Monaco, and Chris Strachwitz in the San Francisco Bay area; Esther Crayton and Tina Mayfield in Los Angeles; Michael Smith in New Orleans; Valerie Wilmer, Roger Armstrong, Ray Topping, and Bruce Bastin in London; Hans Ekestang, Erik Lindahl, and Tommy Löfgren in Sweden; and Jan Donkers, Hans Kramer, and Marcel Vos in Holland.

My documentation of Texas blues was assisted in part by the Dallas Museum of Art in 1984 and by grants from the National Endowment for the Arts and the Texas Commission on the Arts in 1983 and 1988.

The concept of this book coalesced during the summer of 1987 when I toured the major European blues and jazz festivals writing travel articles. Transportation was provided by Delta, KLM Airlines, FinnAir, and Eurail to Denmark, Finland, Sweden, Holland, France, Switzerland, and England. Although many of the people I met during these weeks of travel do not figure directly in this book, their fascination with the subject helped me to clarify my point of view and to understand the cross-cultural appeal of blues. I extend my appreciation to these individuals and to the organizers of the Copenhagen Jazz Festival, the Pori Jazz Festival, the North Sea Jazz Festival, the Grande Parade du Jazz, and the Montreux Jazz Festival, who offered me generous hospitality and thoughtful dialogue.

INDEX

Page numbers in **bold face** indicate photograph.